THE BOND FILES

By Andy Lane:

The Babylon File

THE BOND FILES

THE ONLY COMPLETE GUIDE TO JAMES BOND IN BOOKS, FILMS, TV AND COMICS

Andy Lane & Paul Simpson

First published in Great Britain in 1998 by
Virgin Publishing Ltd
Thames Wharf Studios
Rainville
London W6 9HT

The right of Andy Lane and Paul Simpson to be
identified as the Authors of this Work has been
asserted by them in accordance with the
Copyright, Designs and Patents Act 1988.

ISBN 0 7535 0218 6

Typeset by Galleon Typesetting, Ipswich
Printed and bound in Great Britain by
Mackays of Chatham PLC

March 1999

'It is a very sad thing that nowadays there is so little useless information.'

Oscar Wilde

You can tell he never studied for any medicine exams!
Congratulations and Happy Birthday
Lots of love
Amy
xx

ACKNOWLEDGEMENTS

Dan Abnett, Alan Barnes, Harry Crabe, Paul Cairns, Ben and Fingers, Sean Forbes, Marcus Hearn, Lila Hoffman, Man Jolly, Simon Joslin, Andrew Skinner, Justin Richards and Gary Russell for provision of crucial research materials and for error-correction, the staff of the British Newspaper Library at Colindale, North London, for their patience and assistance; Lotta, the Swedish waitress at Dillon's in the Strand, for her translation skills, and the James Bond Fan Club for spotting the deliberate mistake on the back cover in time.

CONTENTS

Introduction

Of the 45 years since Ian Fleming's first novel was published in 1953, there have only been two in which an original James Bond adventure did not appear in Britain – and there's good evidence to suggest that original stories appeared abroad during those two years. The phrase 'original stories' includes not only the novels and short stories by Fleming himself and by any of his four authorised successors but also the newspaper comic strips, the comics, the role-playing games and the majority of the films.

Forty-five years. That means Bond has been an icon to at least three generations. Nothing survives that long or becomes that popular if it does not fulfil some deep-seated need.

However, no one can deny that society has changed over that time. A population with direct experience of being bombed is now a population who think war is something you watch on television. Values once held as sacred truths are now regarded as dangerously old-fashioned and jingoistic. A system of government regarded as wise and parental is now perceived as a corrupt, authoritarian regime whose interference in people's lives must be reduced as much as possible.

Yet Bond goes on: ageless, incorruptible, indefatigable. He cannot be fulfilling the same need that he fulfilled in 1953. He cannot represent the same ideals that he represented then: the society in which he operates, the society he serves, has changed too much. So the question remains: what exactly is Bond an icon of?

In order to answer that question, numerous books have been written about James Bond. However, despite the wealth of original Bond stories, the vast majority of those books have concentrated on the films. That's because far more people want to buy a book about films than about comic strips, especially if the book is large, glossy and full of pictures. If the rest of the material was mentioned at all then, it was shoved away in a chapter at the back, with Ian Fleming's novels getting the lion's share of the attention and the rest of Bond's non-cinematic adventures being dismissed in a few lines.

That is why we have written *this* book.

Bond deserves more. Bond deserves a book that gives equal weight to all his adventures, no matter in what form they appear, no matter whether they are good, indifferent or so bad it's difficult to accept they're Bond at all. This book is, as far as we can tell, the first one to cover Bond in all his different incarnations: the first to list the comics, the first to cover all the non-Ian Fleming books, the first even to mention the role-playing game and the first to go into any detail at all on what is perhaps the only true continuation of Ian Fleming's legacy – the newspaper comic strips. It's a lot chattier than other Bond books, because that's the Virgin style, but, paradoxically, it's a lot less cluttered with extraneous information. It's unique. It's definitive. It's also not authorised, either by Glidrose – the company to whom Ian Fleming sold the literary copyright in his creation – or by Eon Productions, to whom Fleming sold the film rights. That means we don't have to be nice.

There is a problem with treating Bond's adventures in this level of detail, and it's that they are incompatible. Unlike *Star Trek* or *Babylon 5*, where everything happens within the same all-encompassing universe, the Bond of the books cannot be the Bond of the films. How, for instance, can the same events happen to Bond in the book of *Live and Let Die* and the film of *For Your Eyes Only*? How can Felix Leiter get his leg eaten by a shark in the book of *Live and Let Die* and the film of *Licence to Kill*? The role-playing game is incompatible with both the books and the films, given that it replaces SPECTRE with an almost identical organisation called TAROT. Even within the books or the films, there are discontinuities: John Gardner's book *No Deals, Mr Bond* is almost identical in theme and approach to his *Death is Forever*, while the films *You Only Live Twice*, *The Spy Who Loved Me* and *Tomorrow Never Dies* can all be reduced to the same basic plot. And even if they could all be rationalised – even if the books, films, comics and everything else could be brought under one all-encompassing umbrella of continuity – it ignores the fact that James Bond should be 74 years old this year, based on the date of birth given in one of the books.

No, Bond will always be in his late thirties or early forties, just as Bond will always be a hero: a man who will stop at nothing, who will do whatever it takes, to get the job done. The world needs heroes just as much now as it did in 1953.

And it needs books about them even more.

A Bond Timeline

Year	Books	Films/Television/Radio	Comics/Comic Strips
1953	Casino Royale		
1954	Live and Let Die	Casino Royale (TV)	
1955	Moonraker		
1956	Diamonds Are Forever	Moonraker (radio)	
1957	From Russia With Love		
1958	Doctor No		Casino Royale Live and Let Die
1959	Goldfinger		Moonraker Diamonds Are Forever
1960	For Your Eyes Only 'From a View to a Kill' 'For Your Eyes Only' 'Quantum of Solace' 'Risico' 'The Hildebrand Rarity'		From Russia With Love Doctor No Goldfinger
1961	Thunderball		Risico From a View to a Kill For Your Eyes Only Thunderball
1962	The Spy Who Loved Me 'The Living Daylights'	Dr No	
1963	On Her Majesty's Secret Service 'The Property of a Lady'	From Russia With Love	Dr No (film adaptation)
1964	You Only Live Twice	Goldfinger	OHMSS
1965	The Man With the Golden Gun	Thunderball	You Only Live Twice
1966	Octopussy 'Octopussy'		The Man With the Golden Gun The Living Daylights Octopussy
1967	The Adventures of James Bond Junior 003½	You Only Live Twice Casino Royale (film)	The Hildebrand Rarity The Spy Who Loved Me
1968	Colonel Sun		The Harpies
1969		OHMSS	River of Death Colonel Sun
1970			The Golden Ghost

4

1971		Diamonds Are Forever	Fear Face
			Double Jeopardy
			Star Fire
			Trouble Spot
1972			Isle of Condors
			The League of Vampires
1973	James Bond: The Authorised Biography	Live and Let Die	Die With My Boots On
			The Girl Machine
			Beware of Butterflies
1974		The Man With the Golden Gun	The Nevsky Nude
			The Phoenix Project
1975			The Black Ruby Caper
			Till Death Us Do Part
			The Torch-Time Affair
1976			Hot Shot
			Nightbird
			Ape of Diamonds
1977	James Bond, the Spy Who Loved Me	The Spy Who Loved Me	When the Wizard Wakes
1978			↑
1979	James Bond and Moonraker	Moonraker	*See Note 3*
1980			↓
1981	Licence Renewed	For Your Eyes Only	Doomcrack
			The Paradise Plot
			For Your Eyes Only (film)
1982	For Special Services		Deathmask
1983	Icebreaker	Octopussy	Flittermouse
		Never Say Never Again	Octopussy (film)
1984	Role of Honour		Polestar
1985		A View to a Kill	↑
1986	Nobody Lives For Ever		*See Note 4*
1987	No Deals, Mr Bond	The Living Daylights	↓
1988	Scorpius		
1989	Licence to Kill Win, Lose or Die	Licence to Kill	Permission to Die
			Licence to Kill (film)
1990	Brokenclaw	You Only Live Twice (radio)	
1991	The Man From Barbarossa	James Bond Jnr (TV)	James Bond Jnr (TV + original)
1992	Death Is Forever		Serpent's Tooth
1993	Never Send Flowers		A Silent Armageddon
			Light of My Death
1994	SeaFire		Shattered Helix

5

			Minute of Midnight
1995	GoldenEye	GoldenEye	The Quasimodo Gambit
1996	Cold		GoldenEye (film)
1997	'Blast From the Past'	Tomorrow Never Dies	
	Zero Minus Ten		
1998	The Facts of Death		

Note 1: The short-story collection *For Your Eyes Only* in 1960 contained the stories 'From a View to a Kill', 'For Your Eyes Only', 'Quantum of Solace', 'Risico' and 'The Hildebrand Rarity' in their first appearance. The short-story collection *Octopussy* in 1966 contained reprints of the short stories 'Octopussy' and 'The Property of a Lady'. When the book was published in paperback it contained a reprint of the additional short story 'The Living Daylights'.

Note 2: The comic-strip adaptation of *Thunderball* was abruptly curtailed.

Note 3: The following syndicated comic strips were published abroad but not in Britain.

Sea Dragon	The Scent of Danger
Death Wing	Snake Goddess
The Xanadu Connection	Double Eagle
Shark Bait	

Note 4: The following comic strips were published in Scandinavia but not in Britain.

Codename: Nemesis	Deadly Desert
Operation: Little	Terror Time
The Mad Emperor	The Vanishing Judges
Operation: UFO	Flights From Vietnam
Operation: Blucher	The Undead
Codename: Romeo	Istanbul Intrigue
Data Terror	With Death In Sight
Experiment Z	Danse Macabre
Spy Traps	Operation Uboki
Deadly Double	The Living Dead
Greek Idol	Codename: Mr Blue
Cuba Commandos	Goodbye, Mr Bond
The Amazons	Operation Yakuza
Lethal Dose	

File 001:
The Novels
and Short Stories

CASINO ROYALE (1953)

Starring: The hero – James Bond
The villain – Le Chiffre, agent of SMERSH
The love interest – Vesper Lynd

Written By: Ian Fleming

Plot: The Head of Station S of the British Secret Service has devised a plan to dispose of a high-profile Russian agent, Le Chiffre, who operates in France. Le Chiffre has embezzled money from his Soviet masters, and is desperately trying to win it back at the gambling tables at Royale-les-Eaux. Agent 007, James Bond, is sent to discredit him. Bond is assisted by René Mathis of the Deuxième Bureau, Felix Leiter on attachment from the Joint Chiefs of Staff of NATO, and another British agent, Vesper Lynd. Bond's presence in Royale-les-Eaux is known almost immediately, and an attempt is made on his life by two Bulgars, who blow themselves up instead. Bond plays an extended game of baccarat against Le Chiffre, and when he loses on a hand at 16 million (old) francs it seems as if the opportunity is lost, until Felix Leiter bales him out with a further 32 million francs. Bond wins that hand, and humiliates Le Chiffre by cleaning him out of his remaining 8 million francs.

Bond goes out to celebrate with Vesper, but she is kidnapped. Bond pursues the culprits – Le Chiffre and his men – but when Le Chiffre drops a rack of spikes into the road, causing Bond's tyres to explode, the agent crashes and is captured. Le Chiffre interrogates Bond sadistically, and, just as Bond believes he can take no more, an agent of the Russian Secret Service, SMERSH, kills Le Chiffre, and, because he has no orders to do so, does not kill Bond, although he cuts a distinguishing mark on the back of Bond's right hand.

Bond awakes in hospital, unsure if he wishes to continue in the Secret Service. He recuperates and finds he is falling in love with Vesper. However, she unexpectedly kills herself. A suicide note explains that she was a Russian agent who had betrayed Bond at the start of the mission, but now was afraid that SMERSH would come for her as well. Bond, who had been on the verge of asking her to marry him, masks his own feelings as he reports that 'the bitch is dead'.

Observations: James Bond, agent 007, is the finest gambler in the British Secret Service. He smokes about seventy cigarettes a day, and knows his wine. At the end of *Casino Royale*, he is scarred by an unidentified SMERSH agent with an upside-down M, the Cyrillic letter SM. He has created his own vodka Martini, which must be shaken and which he originally intends to call a Vesper.

Bond does not report directly to the head of Service – he goes via the head of his section, Clements. 00 numbers are awarded to those agents who have had to kill someone in cold blood in the line of duty.

The Secret Service operates from a gloomy building overlooking Regent's Park. Its overall head is known only as M, whose existence is not known to the outside world. M has a Chief of Staff, Bill Tanner, who was a young sapper on the secretariat to the Chiefs of Staff committee, having been wounded during a sabotage operation in 1944. M's secretary is Miss Moneypenny, known affectionately as 'Penny'.

The quartermaster's section is appropriately run by Q. 'The Broker' deals with financial matters with the Treasury. Agents phoning in from abroad contact a liaison officer called 'The Link'.

Station S covers the Soviet Union; F covers France. The Head of Station S has only one arm (an armless agent – isn't that a contradiction in terms?), and his Personal Assistant at the start of *Casino Royale* is agent 3030, Vesper Lynd.

Felix Leiter is a Texan aged around 35 who works with the Joint Intelligence Staff of NATO at Fontainebleau, Paris, and is deputed to work with Bond on this assignment. He was named for Ian Fleming's friend John Leiter. René Mathis is the liaison from the French Secret Service, the Deuxième Bureau.

Amherst Villiers, who apparently made the supercharger on Bond's car, was a friend of Ian Fleming.

Locations: Royale-les-Eaux, north of Dieppe, France, June–July 1952 (?). (*Goldfinger* dates this to 1951, which is unlikely.)

My Name Is . . . James Bond, of Port Maria, Jamaica.

Bond's Past Life: James Bond bought a 4½-litre Bentley with a supercharger by Amherst Villiers, nearly new, in 1933. He worked with René Mathis before World War Two on a case in Monte Carlo, watching two Romanians. He gained his 00 number for killing a Japanese cypher expert in New York, and a Norwegian double-agent in Stockholm, both during the war. He was stationed in Hong Kong at the end of the war, where he discovered pyjama-coats. He has operated in unspecified operations against the Russians since the end of the war, as well as in Jamaica.

Patronising Lines: Bond's whole attitude to Vesper throughout the mission is extremely patronising. 'What the hell do they want to send me a woman for?' he asked bitterly. 'Do they think this is a bloody picnic?'; 'Women were for recreation'; 'As a woman, he wanted to sleep with her, but only when the job had been done'; and the whole section after Vesper has been 'kidnapped': 'These blithering women who thought they could do a man's work . . .'

Fleming's not overkeen on the French, either, dismissing their health with, 'Since all French people suffer from liver complaints.'

Villainous Foibles: Le Chiffre has a large sexual appetite, and is a compulsive gambler. He also inhales benzedrine when he is nervous.

Sadism: When he is captured by Le Chiffre, a naked Bond is placed on a cane chair, from which the seat has been cut out. Le Chiffre then uses a carpet-beater to thrash his unprotected genitals. It's possibly the nastiest piece that Fleming ever wrote.

Lines to Flick Past: '. . . the conquest of her body, because of the central privacy in her, would each time have the sweet tang of rape'; 'Bond awoke in his own room at dawn and for a time he lay and stroked his memories.'

LIVE AND LET DIE (1954)

Starring: The hero – James Bond
      The villain – Mr Big
      The love interest – Simone Latrelle,
          a.k.a. Solitaire

Written By: Ian Fleming

Plot: Gold coins, from what appears to be the seventeenth-century pirate Bloody Morgan's treasure, are turning up in America and are being sold to finance the Soviet espionage network there. The operation is being masterminded by a black man known as Mr Big. M sends Bond to New York to investigate, where he teams up with Felix Leiter, who is now acting as a CIA/FBI liaison. Mr Big has a stranglehold on the black underworld, with people working for him and reporting to him from everywhere. When Bond and Felix go into Harlem, their progress is monitored, and when they visit the Yeah Man club they are put on Table Z, which descends into the floor, bringing them face to face with Mr Big and his henchman Tee-Hee.

The two agents are separated, and Mr Big brings in Solitaire, a white fortune-teller, to check if Bond is telling the truth. For her own reasons, she backs up Bond's lies. After getting Tee-Hee to break Bond's little finger, Mr Big decides to let him go.

Undeterred, Bond decides to continue the investigation in St Petersburg, USA, where Big's yacht, the *Secatur*, often puts in, but before he can leave for the train south Solitaire rings, desperate to join him. Although suspicious, Bond agrees.

Bond and Felix visit the Ouroborous Worm and Bait shop,

but are warned off. At the same time, Solitaire is kidnapped. That night, unbeknown to Bond, Felix returns to Ouroborous, and the next morning he is delivered to Bond's room, mangled from a fight with a shark, with a note pinned to him: 'He disagreed with something that ate him'. Angry, Bond goes back to Ouroborous, and finds gold coins hidden in the poison fish tanks. Mr Big's henchman, the Robber, nearly captures Bond, but 007 turns the tables on him, and kicks him into the shark tank.

Bond then flies down to Jamaica, where the local agent, Strangways, tells him about Big's island, Shark Island. With the aid of Cayman Islander Quarrel, Bond prepares himself for the swim out. When the *Secatur* arrives, with Big and Solitaire on board, Bond and Strangways realise that they are making their final collection of bullion, so Bond must go that night. However, he is caught, and tied up along with Solitaire, but not before he has placed a bomb on the hull of the *Secatur*.

Bond and Solitaire are tied to the back of the yacht, and Big intends to keelhaul them, dragging them over a coral reef, to attract the sharks and barracuda. Luckily, he decides to leave at the time for which Bond has set the bomb, and the device explodes just seconds before they would be pulled over the coral. Big survives the blast – but falls foul of the same death he wished on Bond and the girl. M grants Bond 'passionate' leave . . .

Observations: James Bond holds diplomatic passport no. 0094567 and has the option whether to take an assignment or not. He claims to have read most of the books on voodoo. He takes benzedrine tablets for increased strength and stamina. The scar left by the SMERSH agent in *Casino Royale* has been covered with a skin graft from his upper arm (which M thinks might make the hairs grow differently).

It comes as a surprise to us that he gets turned on by a stripper.

Station A covers the United States; C, the Caribbean. The head of A is called Damon, while Strangways, a one-eyed,

13

35-year-old former RNVR Commander, is the chief Secret Service agent for the Caribbean. The Secret Service uses the fake company 'Universal Export' as a cover. The quartermaster's section is called Q Branch.

M, who smokes a pipe, Bill Tanner and Moneypenny all make a return, as does Felix Leiter, who is now a liaison between the CIA and the FBI, apparently reporting to superiors in both organisations. He pays a heavy price for his help to Bond.

Fleming's original title for this was *The Undertaker's Wind*.

Although Mr Big features in the film of *Live and Let Die*, the attack on Leiter appears in *Licence to Kill*, and the keelhauling sequence is transferred to the film *For Your Eyes Only*.

Locations: London; New York; down by train to St Petersburg, USA; then Jamaica; January–February 1954.

My Name Is . . . John Bryce (a nod towards Ian Fleming's friend Ivar Bryce) when he knows that Mr Big is after Bond. May, Bond's housekeeper, was named for Bryce's housekeeper, May Maxwell.

James Bond, Fashion Victim: 007 with a military haircut?

Bond's Past Life: Bond has not been to America since the end of World War Two. He was on a long assignment in Jamaica when the Communist Headquarters in Cuba tried to infiltrate the Jamaican unions. He hasn't cried since he was a child.

Patronising Lines: Although at the time Ian Fleming was extremely proud of the way that black people talk in *Live and Let Die*, a lot of Bond's (i.e. Fleming's) observations are patronising in the extreme. There are numerous expressions of amazement that a black man is capable of such villainy, or that a black woman can get a job such as chauffeuse. Fleming is also condescending about American cooking, singling out anything that is vaguely edible as a surprise.

Goodbye, Mr Bond: A prototype from Mr Big: 'A short, but very good night to you both.'

Villainous Foibles: Mr Big has chronic heart disease, which has left him with grey skin. He has a 'great football' of a head, which is hairless except for short tufts over the ears – he even has no eyebrows or eyelashes.

Sadism: Felix Leiter is smashed into a wall by Big's goons. Mr Big backhands Solitaire, before ordering Tee-Hee to break Bond's little finger. Bond kicks the Robber into the shark tank in revenge for Felix's attempted murder. Mr Big intends to kill Bond and Solitaire by dragging them behind his yacht, over a coral reef, so that the sharks and barracuda will eat them. He's hoist by his own petard.

Mistakes Can Be Fatal: Bond was controlled through Jamaica in *Casino Royale* because of his familiarity with that area, yet here he has no knowledge of Station C.

Bond is told not to wear pyjamas – yet *Casino Royale* told us he'd switched to a pyjama-coat from being naked anyway. He has apparently travelled 'two thousand miles' and five deaths to reach the end of the trail. Presumably, therefore, although it's described in great detail, Fleming is discounting Bond's 3,500 miles to get to New York in the first place!

In *Casino Royale*, a blue light indicated that M was not to be disturbed. Here, it's become green.

MOONRAKER (1955)

Starring: The hero – James Bond
                The villain – Hugo von der Drache,
                   alias Sir Hugo Drax
                The love interest – Gala Brand

Written By: Ian Fleming

Plot: A rather embarrassed M asks Bond (an inveterate gambler) to cast his professional eye over Sir Hugo Drax, a national hero and a member of M's club. Drax has put his not inconsiderable fortune behind building a nuclear rocket deterrent for Britain, but M suspects he cheats at cards. The two do not seem to go together, and it has M worried. Bond determines pretty quickly that Drax *is* cheating, and turns the tables, obtaining a considerable amount of money from a not-best-pleased millionaire.

Shortly afterwards, the security liaison working for Drax on behalf of the British Government is murdered, and Bond is sent in to replace him. Bond makes contact with Gala Brand – an undercover policewoman working as Drax's secretary – and together they investigate Drax's rather bizarre rocket-construction arrangements. An attempt is made on their lives, and spurred on by this they discover evidence that Drax plans to aim the first test-firing at the heart of London rather than out into the Channel, with a real nuclear warhead rather than a dummy. The security liaison had discovered some of this, and had to be silenced.

Drax kidnaps both Bond and Brand, and tells them that he is a Nazi who has been masquerading as a British subject since the end of the war, and that he is currently in the employ of the Soviet Union. Bond and Brand escape and reprogramme the rocket's guidance system. Through luck rather than design, it hits the submarine that Drax was escaping in, killing him.

Observations: Bond is the best shot in the Service, even if no one is going to tell him so. He earns £1,500 a year, and has £1,000 tax free from private income, but on his assignments he can spend freely. He is not allowed to operate within the United Kingdom, but because of the pressing nature of this assignment, and a requirement that the agent speak fluent German, special permission is given. He is aged 37, and must retire from active duty at 45. He holds the CMG (Companion of the Order of St Michael and St George). He has never particularly liked moustaches, even on men. He does not know the names of wild flowers.

Bond is given only two or three assignments a year that

merit his special talents. M (with a green light guarding the inner sanctum), Bill Tanner (who is the same age as Bond) and Miss Moneypenny reappear. Ronnie Vallance at Scotland Yard and Bond's secretary Loelia Ponsonby, who acts for the whole of the three-man 00 section, appear for the first time. Loelia, or Lil, was named for Ian Fleming's friend of the same name who became Loelia, Duchess of Westminster.

Bond is senior to 008 (Bill), who is rescued from Berlin during *Moonraker*, and 0011, who has been 'lost' in Singapore. Station D is in Germany (Deutschland).

M's real name is Admiral Sir Miles M— (i.e. Fleming didn't want to specify anything more than the initial). He rarely uses Bond's first name in his office. He is a member of Blades Club, where Bond often dines with him.

The Prime Minister wants to award Bond the George Cross at the end of *Moonraker*, but it is not Service policy to allow officers to accept.

The disposal of the gold located at the end of *Live and Let Die* is briefly discussed between Bond and M, and we learn more about Bond's mission in Monte Carlo before the war.

Had Fleming run out of names already? 'Tanner' reappears as the waiter at Blades.

Ian Fleming considered various titles for this book before settling on *Moonraker*. These included *The Moonraker Secret*, *The Moonraker Plot*, *The Infernal Machine*, *Wide of the Mark* and *The Inhuman Element*. We always thought it was a gift, coming up with brilliant Bond titles, but apparently not.

A radio adaptation of *Moonraker*, starring future *Blockbusters* host Bob Holness as 007, was broadcast on South African radio, and later transmitted by the BBC.

Locations: London and Kent, Monday to Friday at the end of May 1954.

Bond's Past Life: Bond has been in Paris and frequented *'maisons tolerées'* (i.e. brothels). He has also been attached to the Embassy in Moscow, where he developed a liking for a specific way of drinking vodka. He was in Germany the year before *Moonraker*. He was taught card-sharping skills by a man named Steffi Esposito before the war, and used his talents to expose some Romanian cheats in Monte Carlo. He also used to dabble on the fringes of the racing world.

Patronising Lines: '[Gala] might be a policewoman and an expert at jujitsu, but she also had a mole on her right breast. With that comforting thought . . .'
   'Scratch a German and you find precision, thought Bond.'

Villainous Foibles: Hugo Drax has been through major plastic surgery, and one side of his face is permanently scarred. This plus his red hair and wild moustache give him a rather bizarre appearance which Ian Fleming likens to a circus ringmaster.

Sadism: Bond brutally interrogates Krebbs with the aid of a bottle. Drax smacks Gala across the face, and flails wildly at Bond when he is tied up. He intends that Bond and Gala be burnt by the rocket exhaust of the Moonraker, and then authorises steam to be used to attempt to flush them out of hiding when they escape. He also authorises their torture with a blowtorch.

Mistakes Can Be Fatal . . . Or at least unfortunate. The sinking of the Goodwin Lightship in November 1954 means that this has to be set during 1954, thereby throwing out the timescale Fleming has created between Drax's letter to the Queen offering the services of his rocket, the arguments about that, and its construction.

   It seems odd to us that Sir Hugo Drax received his knighthood *before* the country saw the benefits of his great rocket. Pardon us for being unduly cynical, but wouldn't the award normally *follow* the act?

   Bond kisses Loelia Ponsonby only at Christmas, on her birthday and before he does dangerous things . . . but he has tried it on with her. Not a very fast worker, obviously!

DIAMONDS ARE FOREVER (1956)

Starring: The hero – James Bond
The villains – The Spang Brothers
The love interest – Tiffany Case

Written By: Ian Fleming

Plot: James Bond is assigned to bring to a halt a diamond-smuggling operation out of Africa. The courier for the line, Peter Franks, has been arrested, and Bond is to take his place. Bond joins the Gem Squad on a visit to the House of Diamonds, run by Rufus B. Saye, since they are certain that Saye is the London part of the pipeline. Bond goes to Franks's assigned rendezvous with the mysterious Tiffany Case, who tells him that he is to take the diamonds to Michael 'Shady' Tree in New York. After he departs, she then reports to 'ABC' that Bond will be the courier.

Just before Bond leaves for America, M tells him that Saye is really Jack Spang, one of the Spangled Mob from Las Vegas. If Bond makes 'dangerous contact' with the Mob, he is to break off and leave it to the FBI.

Bond delivers the diamonds to Shady Tree, who pays him $1,000 and tells him to bet on Shy Smile at Saratoga Races the following Sunday. The race is fixed so Bond will receive his full $5,000. Felix Leiter, now working for Pinkerton's Detective Agency, is investigating a scam on the horse, and the two old friends combine forces. Bond and Felix travel to Saratoga, where Leiter persuades Shy Smile's jockey to throw the race so they can follow the criminal chain a little further. Although the jockey comes through, his act doesn't fool the Spangled Mob, who send a hooded hitman to cover him in boiling mud as a punishment.

Bond complains that he has not been paid, and is ordered to play blackjack at Las Vegas. He receives his payment at a crooked table in one of the casinos – with Tiffany as croupier – but gets greedy, and gambles the $5,000 up to $20,000 at the roulette wheel. The following day, Bond is captured by Spang's men. Bond is taken to Spectreville, Spang's reconstruction of a Wild West town, and brought before the second Spang brother – Serrafimo Spang – in the Cannonball, a beautiful 1870 locomotive that acts as Spang's headquarters.

Tiffany helps him to escape down the tracks in a smaller locomotive. Spang pursues, but Bond sends the Cannonball down a branch line and shoots Spang as he passes.

Their passage back to Britain on the *Queen Elizabeth* is marred by the presence of Spang's henchmen, Wint and Kidd, who have been ordered by him to kill Tiffany and capture Bond. Bond receives a cable from London warning him of this, and he goes to Tiffany's rescue, shooting both hitmen. In the epilogue, Spang is closing down the pipeline in Sierra Leone, killing all the smugglers. However, Bond has flown out, and blows Spang's helicopter out of the sky, shutting the line permanently.

Observations: Bond is still aged under forty at the time of this assignment. It takes place two weeks after he comes back from leave in France (which might be the holiday he was planning on taking with Gala Brand at the end of *Moonraker*). He wants children, but knows that he would have to leave the Service if he did so.

Felix Leiter has left the CIA as a result of his injuries in *Live and Let Die*, and is now working for the detective agency Pinkerton's, carrying out a parallel investigation to Bond while he's on American soil. M, Bill Tanner, Loelia Ponsonby and Miss Moneypenny all play a brief supporting role at the Regent's Park headquarters. Ronnie Vallance, Bond's Scotland Yard liaison in *Moonraker*, is now an Assistant Commissioner.

Bond has to deal with the Inspectoscope (about which he was reading a report in *Moonraker*). When he is hallucinating, he believes he is reliving his swim to Shark Island in *Live and Let Die*.

Diamonds Are Forever contains one of Fleming's most descriptive travelogue passages, as Bond flies from London to

New York. Otherwise there is an air of languor about the book, as though Fleming, like Bond, doesn't quite rate these gangsters on a par with his previous 'supervillains'.

Locations: French Guinea, London, New York, Saratoga, the *Queen Elizabeth* and Sierra Leone, July–August 1956 (4 August is a Saturday).

My Name Is . . . Sergeant James, investigating diamond smuggling at the offices of Mr Rufus B. Saye; Peter Franks, a diamond smuggler working for Mr Rufus B. Saye.

Bond's Past Life: When Bond joined the Secret Service, some of his earliest jobs were as a courier – through Strasbourg into Germany, through Niegoreloye into Russia, over the Simplon, across the Pyrenees.

Toys for the Boys: Bond's briefcase hides his silencer and thirty rounds of ·25 ammunition for the Beretta.

Villainous Foibles: All of the Spangled Gang are archetypal American hoods, except for the hitmen, Wint and Kidd. Wint sucks a wart on his thumb, and is petrified of flying – he has a tag with his blood group on his luggage. The two are gay. In the first edition of the book, Kidd was given the nickname 'Boofy' as a reference to a friend of Ian Fleming – 'Boofy' Gore – who later became Lord Arran. Gore was reportedly very unhappy that his nickname had been purloined, and Fleming had it changed in later editions to 'Boofuls' Kidd.

Sadism: The sequence in the mudbaths, with the black attendant hit with a pistol, Tingaling Bell being hit while he's in the stall, and the boiling-hot mud being poured over him is, ironically, quite chilling. Bond is given a Brooklyn stomping (only 80 per cent, mind you) by Wint and Kidd – luckily between chapters.

Single Entendres: 'Don't push it in; screw it in.' Even Fleming seems to feel this is too risqué coming from M.

FROM RUSSIA WITH LOVE (1957)

Starring: The hero – James Bond
The villain – SMERSH via Red Grant and
    Rosa Klebb
The love interest – Tatiana Romanova

Written By: Ian Fleming

Plot: In a long opening sequence, the assembled heads of
the various Soviet intelligence agencies plot to embarrass
their Western opposites by killing a Western secret agent in
a particularly disgraceful way. The agent chosen is James
Bond. He is to be lured to Turkey on the basis that a female
Soviet cipher clerk wishes to defect with a top-secret code
machine, and while he and the woman are travelling back to
England on the Orient Express they are to be killed. Evidence
will be planted to make it look like Bond killed the woman
as part of some sordid sexual tangle and then committed
suicide.

The trap is baited, and Bond does indeed travel to Istanbul.
He is suspicious, as is Darko Kerim – the SIS Station Head in
Turkey – but the lure of the cipher machine is too great to
resist. Bond makes contact with the woman, whose name is
Tatiana Romanova, and they begin their journey back across
Europe.

Bond becomes aware of Soviet agents on the train, and
manages to get rid of most of them by having them questioned and removed by border police, but the remaining one
kills – and is killed by – Kerim. Bond is, however, unaware
that SMERSH's chief killer, Red Grant, is also travelling on
the train. Grant makes contact with Bond, posing as an SIS
agent, and subdues both him and Tatiana. Grant attempts to
kill Bond but his bullet is deflected by a handily placed
cigarette case and book. During the ensuing fight, Bond
shoots Grant.

In Paris, Bond attempts to apprehend SMERSH operative
Rosa Klebb at a meeting she was to have with Grant. Klebb is

too cunning, and manages to stab Bond with a poison-coated blade. Bond slowly topples to the floor as the poison spreads through his system . . .

Observations: Via the SMERSH file on Bond, we learn a lot about him. He is 183 cm tall, weighs 76 kilos, and speaks French and German fluently. He has gone back to sleeping naked; he distrusts men who tie Windsor knots. We meet May, his Scottish housekeeper, who refers to him as '-s', and learn of his fastidious routine when he is in London. He reads only *The Times* (although he is aware of the contents of other newspapers).

Tiffany Case, Bond's American lover, left Britain in July, after moving out some months earlier. She has gone to marry an American serviceman.

Bond doesn't actually make an appearance until well into the book. The entire first third is devoted to SMERSH's plotting.

It's been three years since the events of *Moonraker* and several months since *Diamonds Are Forever*.

Chief of Staff, Loelia Ponsonby and Miss Moneypenny make fleeting appearances. M, who rather prematurely closed his own files on the Burgess and Maclean affair in 1951, is forced to lay aside his Victorian morality and encourage Bond effectively to prostitute himself for his country.

René Mathis is now head of the Deuxième Bureau while our Secret Service doesn't notice when people disappear at the start of each year. This strikes us as a touch odd.

SMERSH are back, and they pick over the bones of their previous encounters with Bond in *Casino Royale*, *Live and Let Die* and *Moonraker*. They also are aware of his operations in America during *Diamonds Are Forever*.

At the end of *From Russia With Love*, Bond crashes to the floor, filled with poison by Rosa Klebb. This could have marked the end for the series.

Locations: Russia, London, Istanbul, across Europe on the Orient Express to Paris, June–September 195? (see **Mistakes Can Be Fatal**).

My Name Is ... David Somerset, travelling with his wife Caroline.

Bond's Past Life: In his teens, Bond climbed the Aguilles Rouges in Switzerland with two companions from the University of Geneva. He began working for the Secret Service in 1938. He certainly held his 00 number in 1950. In 1951, Bond was in a French-speaking country. Bond was awarded the CMG in 1953.

Toys for the Boys: Bond's briefcase contains ammunition, flat throwing knives, a cyanide pill (which Bond disposes of immediately), a silencer inside a tube of Palmolive, and fifty gold sovereigns. Red Grant has an electrically operated gun hidden in a book. Darko Kerim has a periscope which rises into the corner of the KGB planning room in Istanbul from a hidden tunnel beneath. He also has a rather large bomb there, to be exploded if he dies.

Patronising Lines: 'I thought we were all agreed that homosexuals were about the worst security risk there is,' says Captain Troop, to which Bond replies, 'All intellectuals aren't homosexual.' Nice of him to think that.

Villainous Foibles: Grant is a narcissistic, asexual psychopath who gets murderous impulses around the time of the full moon; Rosa Klebb displays distinctly lesbian tendencies towards Tatiana. Kronsteen, the SMERSH planner, thinks of people only as chess pieces.

Sadism: The cat fight between the two gypsy girls is described in loving detail!

Mistakes Can Be Fatal: The year of *From Russia With Love* is a major problem. It is set from June in the year after *Diamonds Are Forever*, and three years after *Moonraker*. This would indicate it's 1957. Yet the description of the SMERSH meeting dates it at 1955, and it's also ten years since Grant's defection in 1946. Bond's comments about the Burgess and Maclean affair unfortunately also date it prior to the revelation of Philby's deception. John Pearson dates it to 1955 or

24

1956 in *James Bond: The Authorised Biography*. Despite all this, we tend to go for 1957 as the best option.

During the fight in the gypsy encampment, Bond notes that he has six bullets left. He fires four – but tells Kerim that he has only one remaining.

Possibly the worst mistake in the entire canon occurs after Kerim has killed Krilencu. 'Bond had never killed in cold blood,' says Fleming. This blatantly contradicts everything about Bond so far, starting with his own line to Mathis in *Casino Royale:* 'A double 0 number in our Service means you've had to kill a chap in cold blood in the course of some job.' It's just incredibly sloppy.

M's light has turned red for 'no entry' (it's been blue and green previously – perhaps the bulb keeps blowing).

DOCTOR NO (1958)

Starring: The hero – James Bond
The villain – Doctor Julius No
The love interest – Honeychile Ryder

Written By: Ian Fleming

Plot: Bond is sent by M on a supposedly cushy assignment to investigate the disappearance of Strangways, the SIS Head of Station in Jamaica. It is assumed that he ran off with his secretary, but Bond isn't convinced. The delivery of poisoned fruit and a poisonous centipede to his hotel room only serves to confirm his suspicions. The obvious suspect is the mysterious Dr Julius No, a local bird-dung merchant who guards the privacy of his island sanctuary to such an extent that two ornithologists camping on his island have died and an aircraft carrying an investigating team has crashed while landing. Bond and his friend Quarrel sail unnoticed to the island, but the rather more obvious arrival of the beautiful Honeychile Ryder looking for rare seashells triggers a full-scale manhunt.

Taking Honeychile along with them, they penetrate deeper into the heart of the island, but Quarrel is killed and both Bond and Honeychile are taken prisoner by Dr No. He explains that he is being employed by the Soviet Union to cause havoc to American military missile tests in the vicinity. So far he has merely caused the missiles to fail, resulting in the abandonment of numerous promising lines of US military research, but he soon hopes to capture some of the missiles and sell them to the Soviets. Should suspicion fall upon him, he can divert missiles on to local towns and islands and escape in the chaos.

As part of a sadistic desire to test the limits of human pain he has Honeychile tied up in the path of a giant crab migration and causes Bond to go through an obstacle course of electric shocks, scalding heat, poisonous spiders and a giant squid. Bond unexpectedly survives, suffocates Dr No under a heap of bird dung and rescues Honeychile.

Observations: Bond now travels on a passport describing him as an Import and Export Merchant. During this book, he is made acting Head of Station in Jamaica (replacing the unfortunate Strangways). Bond, whose left hand is narrower than his right, doesn't seem at all embarrassed about the idea of paying for sex – it is 'quite a long time since I had' a call girl. His financial resources are enough that he can afford to pay for Honey to have the operation she requires.

Strangways and Quarrel return from *Live and Let Die*; Moneypenny and Tanner pop in. M has an ex-Leading Stoker as his driver, and was in the PQ convoys, presumably travelling to Murmansk, during the war. He seems rather to have it in for Bond by sending him on what appears to be a 'cushy' assignment in Jamaica.

Maybe as a result of Red Grant's revelation to Bond in *From Russia With Love* that SMERSH captures a Secret Service agent annually, and their actions have never been noticed, the Service is much hotter about following up missing agents. The Caribbean now falls under Section III, rather than Station C as previously. Sir James Molony, the famous neurologist, works for the Secret Service when he is not at St Mary's Hospital. He is named for J.A. Molony, a dental specialist consulted by Ian Fleming during the writing of the book. Agent 258 is based in Washington.

The Service Armourer is Major Boothroyd, named after the real Geoffrey Boothroyd, who wrote to Fleming pointing out the inadequacies of the Beretta for Bond's work. Both real and fictional Boothroyds recommend the Walther PPK, the gun that is most associated with 007.

Doctor No is based round Bond's 'convalescence' after Rosa Klebb's poison at the end of *From Russia With Love*. Klebb 'died'. Honey Ryder lives in the Great House at Beau Desert – the same estate that Bond and Quarrel used as a base in *Live and Let Die*, which is stated as being five years earlier.

Ian Fleming admitted that Dr No was his attempt to emulate Sax Rohmer's character Fu Manchu. The plot is taken wholesale from Fleming's 1956 plot for a *Commander Jamaica* television series for the American network NBC, which he co-wrote with the producer and millionaire Henry Morgenthau III.

Given that this is one of the most sadistic of Fleming's novels, we find it virtually unbelievable that a special 'Junior' edition of this book was published in the early 1970s, with the violence carefully tuned down and the sexual content removed entirely.

Locations: Jamaica and London, in February/March (but see **Mistakes Can Be Fatal**).

My Name Is . . . John Bryce, an ornithologist working with the Audobon Society of New York. Dr No isn't fooled for a moment. Bond also rents a house as Mr James.

Bond's Past Life: Bond has used the Beretta for fifteen years, prompting the question: what gun did he use in his early years in the Service?

Toys for the Boys: Bond's attaché case this time comes with thick steel wire as an accessory.

Villainous Foibles: Dr No is extremely tall and has a bald skull, with no lines on his face, or eyelashes. He wears contact lenses, and has mechanical claws instead of hands. His heart is on the right-hand side of his body, and he seems to glide around the room.

Sadism: 'Slowly, lovingly,' the Chigro kills Strangways' secretary. Quarrel deliberately hurts Annabel Chung's 'Mound of Love' (it's the fleshy part of the thumb). Quarrel dies an agonising death – and Dr No has prepared a torture run for 007 to evaluate the human body's resistance to pain.

Lines to Flick Past: '. . . with the anger balling up inside him like cat's fur . . .'; 'He broke off. His eyes were alight with cruelty. He looked past Bond at the girl. The eyes became mouths that licked their lips.' Huh?

Mistakes Can Be Fatal: The timescale of this story seems wrong again. It has taken three months to identify the toxin that was injected into Bond – yet that was in September, and we are now in March.

When Dr No relays his life story, he says clearly that he came to Crab Key in 1942, fourteen years before. If *From Russia With Love* is set three years after *Moonraker*, which has to be in 1954, we must be in 1958 by now!

GOLDFINGER (1959)

Starring: The hero – James Bond
                  The villain – Auric Goldfinger
                  The love interests – the Masterson sisters,
                      and briefly Pussy Galore

Written By: Ian Fleming

Plot: On his way back from a mission in Mexico, Bond is recognised by Junius du Pont, whom he met at Royale-les-Eaux. Du Pont plays canasta each day against Auric Goldfinger, a millionaire agoraphobic, and is being cheated, but doesn't know how. Bond discovers that Goldfinger has a young woman, Jill Masterson, telling him what du Pont's cards are. He takes over the transmitter, makes Goldfinger confess, and heads for New York with Masterson in tow. He is surprised a week later when he is summoned to M, who tells him he is going to investigate a gold-smuggling case. The Bank of England believe Goldfinger is responsible for a great deal of gold going off the market, and M thinks that Goldfinger could be acting as SMERSH's banker.

Knowing that Goldfinger plays golf at the Royal St Mark's course near Sandwich, Bond arranges to be there 'accidentally' at the same time. The two men engage in a duel of golf, with Goldfinger cheating at least three times, until, at the seventeenth hole, Bond makes Goldfinger lose by using the wrong ball. Bond takes up Goldfinger's invitation to dinner, but the millionaire leaves Bond alone on a pretext. Snooping around, 007 sees the bodywork on Goldfinger's Silver Ghost being replaced. The next day Goldfinger leaves for the Continent.

Bond follows Goldfinger using a homing device planted in the Rolls-Royce, and encounters Tilly Soames, who also seems to be on Goldfinger's trail. Scouting out Goldfinger's factory, Bond realises that the gold is being smuggled in the sheets of bodywork that make up the frame of the car. He also stumbles on Tilly, who wants to kill Goldfinger – she is really Jill's sister. Jill was killed by being painted gold all over, so dying of suffocation. However, Goldfinger's Korean servant Oddjob discovers Bond and Tilly, and takes them to Goldfinger, who proceeds to torture Bond . . .

Bond awakes to find he is entering the United States. Goldfinger has decided that Bond and the woman can be of use to him in Operation Grand Slam, his plan to steal the gold from Fort Knox. Goldfinger has assembled five major gang leaders, including representatives of the Spangled Mob and the Mafia, as well as Pussy Galore, who is a lesbian. All bar one of the gang come on board – the other is killed. Goldfinger plans to kill the population of Fort Knox with a deadly toxin, and then take the gold off to Russia. Bond manages to secrete a message on the reconnaissance plane used, but, as the plan goes ahead seemingly without problems, he isn't sure if it got through. Suddenly, the 'dead' arise and, led by Felix Leiter, the plot is foiled, although Tilly is killed. Goldfinger escapes, along with Oddjob and Pussy, and they kidnap Bond at the airport. For her own reasons, Pussy changes side and helps Bond kill both Oddjob and Goldfinger, before Bond crash-lands the plane in which they are flying into the Atlantic.

Observations: Bond is familiar with Charles Laughton's portrayal of Henry VIII. He is a nine handicap at golf, and often plays at Huntercombe. He used to play at Royal St Mark's at Sandwich, and was trained there by Alfred Blacking. He hates drinking tea. During his shift as Duty Officer, he is contemplating writing a self-defence manual entitled *Stay Alive!*

Bill Tanner, Miss Moneypenny and Felix Leiter are all present and correct while M turns down the American President's request for Bond to receive the American Order of Merit. The Secret Service operates a White Cross Fund for families of Secret Service agents killed on assignment. Station H covers Hongkong (sic).

Karate is little known in Britain at this time.

Bond's interest in Goldfinger is piqued by Junius du Pont, who was present in 1951 at Bond's card battle with Le Chiffre in *Casino Royale*. He travels on the Silver Meteor, as he did in *Live and Let Die*. He remembers the *Moonraker* affair as he is operating in a similar part of the United Kingdom; Goldfinger, like Drax, is a member of Blades. Jack Strap has inherited the Spangled Mob from the late Spang brothers (*Diamonds Are Forever*). Bond thinks that 008, introduced in *Moonraker*, will be sent to replace him, although oddly he says that M would give 008 a licence to kill Goldfinger if Bond is killed. Up until now, it has seemed that the licence to kill is open.

SMERSH, Bond's adversaries for so long, are being bankrolled by Goldfinger's operation (presumably making up for the loss suffered when Mr Big's network collapsed after *Live and Let Die*).

Trypanosomiaisis is actually not just convincing medical technobabble – it's a real medical term covering a collection of diseases, including sleeping sickness, caused by a single-celled organism.

The Royal St Mark's course is based on the Royal St George's golf course, with the description of the holes corresponding nearly exactly.

Locations: Mexico (in flashback), Miami, Kent, France, Switzerland, New York, Fort Knox, Kentucky, 1959 (Colonel Smithers has been pursuing Goldfinger for five years since 1954).

My Name Is . . . James Bond, an import/export merchant dealing with arms sales to friendly foreign powers.

Bond's Past Life: In his teens, Bond used to play two rounds of golf a day at St Mark's.

Toys for the Boys: The Walter PPK is hidden inside 'The Bible Designed to be Read as Literature'. Bond's customised Aston Martin DBIII has switches to alter the lights, re-inforced steel bumpers, extra-capacity hiding places and a homing device.

Patronising Lines: A waiter is described as a 'pansified Italian'. Bond's and Tilly's 'eyes met and exchanged a flurry of masculine/feminine master/slave signals'. Bond's thought processes on the subject of why people are homosexual reveal a lot about 1950s opinion.

Villainous Foibles: Well, Goldfinger cheats at cards, and, as with Hugo Drax, this is Bond's first indication of villainy. He is a grotesque, short man, with a huge round head, carrot hair and a thick, ugly body. He likes pornography, carries a million dollars' worth of gold with him (does he check the markets each morning, and take a little piece out if the price has gone up?), and signs each bar of 'his' gold with a tiny Z in the corner – which is the telltale giveaway. He also gets his kicks from painting women in gold, normally leaving a small area on the backbone to allow their skin to breathe. In the case of Jill Masterson, he gets his revenge by painting her all over.

Oddjob, his Korean henchman, has a cleft palate, and he understands English clearly. He has fingers all the same length, and his hands are solid muscle down either side. He dresses as a civil servant – but his bowler hat is steel-rimmed, and can be used as a murder weapon. Oh, and he eats cats.

Sadism: Goldfinger's torture of Bond with the saw coming up towards 007's groin.

Mistakes Can Be Fatal: Bond has apparently been in the 00 section for only six years – yet here *Casino Royale* is dated as 1951, eight years earlier.

When Goldfinger decides to bring Bond on to his team, so to speak, why doesn't he check him out with SMERSH? Why *does* he need Bond and Tilly? He has been planning Operation Grand Slam for a considerable time, yet we have to believe that he will suddenly accept a passing nuisance into his entourage. Why does he need Pussy Galore at the end? It certainly can't be for sexual reasons – and we can't see her putting up with being painted gold for his amusement. There's no reason for him not to shoot her along with the other four gangsters.

And why, oh why, does Pussy change sides? Did Fleming realise that he'd painted himself into a corner? Bond wasn't going to get any of the girls – he'd got Jill Masterson killed, Tilly had some lesbian tendencies, and was dead, so in order to have Bond reassert himself as the great lover Pussy has to go against every instinct she's shown so far. The Bond that Fleming portrays certainly doesn't seem to have such a magnetism that a woman would go against her nature!

'FROM A VIEW TO A KILL' (1960)

Starring: The hero – James Bond
The villains – a group of unnamed Soviet
agents
The love interest – Mary Ann Russell

Written By: Ian Fleming

Plot: A motorcycle dispatch rider carrying secret documents from SHAPE (the Supreme Headquarters, Allied Powers, Europe) to the Secret Intelligence Service station at St Germain is shot and killed while on the road, and his documents are stolen. Bond is sent to investigate. He discovers that a detachment of Soviet spies have installed themselves in an underground base in the nearby forest, and are making forays to intercept the dispatch riders. Bond dresses as a dispatch rider to lure one of them out, kills him, takes his place and then exposes the rest of them.

Observations: Bond rather hypocritically gets annoyed at Mary for claiming he is playing at Red Indians, when this was the force of his argument with Mathis in *Casino Royale*.

There's something oddly disturbing about a Bond who seriously considers buying sexual favours from a high-class tart.

This short story, published in the short-story collection *For Your Eyes Only*, was adapted by Ian Fleming from one of the plots he wrote for a planned, but never made, *James Bond* American TV series. Only the amended title made it as far as the 1985 film.

Locations: France – the St Germain region.

Bond's Past Life: Bond lost his virginity on his first visit to Paris when he was sixteen (but see the entry on *Brokenclaw*).

'FOR YOUR EYES ONLY' (1960)

Starring: The hero – James Bond
                  The villain – von Hammerstein
                  The love interest – Judy Havelock

Written By: Ian Fleming

Plot: After escaping from Germany at the end of the war, Nazi war criminal von Hammerstein had set himself up as Head of Counter Security under Batista's regime in Cuba. Now, with Castro gaining influence, von Hammerstein is looking for a bolt hole. Finding a nice house in Jamaica he likes the look of, he sends his accomplice – Major Gonzales – either to buy it from the owners (Colonel and Mrs Havelock) or kill them and buy it from their next of kin. They refuse to sell, so Gonzales kills them. Unfortunately for Gonzales and von Hammerstein, the Havelocks were good friends of M, who indicates that he would like Bond to exact revenge for him.

Bond travels to Vermont, where von Hammerstein is temporarily staying, and is just about to shoot him from a distance when he is interrupted by Judy Havelock – daughter of the murdered couple. She too wants revenge on von Hammerstein, and kills him with a bow and arrow before Bond can stop her. Bond kills Major Gonzales, and the couple escape.

Observations: The story can definitely be dated to before *OHMSS*, as Bond, who is aged under forty in this story, reflects that he has never suffered the tragedy of a personal loss (presumably he's ignoring the death of his parents when he was a child).

Sir Miles Messervy, who appears here in an uncharacteristically unsettled mood, could have been the 5th Sea Lord, had he not taken up the post as M. Perhaps unsurprisingly, he knows J. Edgar Hoover (head of the FBI).

This formed the title piece of Fleming's short-story collection, and was adapted by Ian Fleming from one of the plots he wrote for a planned, but never made, *James Bond* American TV series.

Locations: Jamaica, London, Ottawa (Canada), Vermont (USA).

My Name Is . . . Mr James (well that's original).

Patronising Lines: To Judy Havelock – 'Don't be a silly bitch, this is man's work.'

Villainous Foibles: Von Hammerstein machine-guns innocent woodpeckers.

Mistakes Can Be Fatal: Bond is surprised at M's use of the word 'bloody', but he's used it before to describe Sir Hugo Drax in *Moonraker*.

'QUANTUM OF SOLACE' (1960)

Starring: The hero – James Bond
                   The villain – none
                   The love interest – none

Written By: Ian Fleming

Plot: Following a rather distasteful mission stopping arms from reaching Cuban rebels, Bond is dining with the Governor of Bermuda. He is bored with the other dinner guests until the Governor tells him a story about a young man who once worked for him and who fell in love with an air stewardess. They married, but she soon started having a blatant affair and made him the laughing stock of the British community on Bermuda. Turning the tables, he managed to ruin her financially and socially before divorcing her and leaving the island. The relevance of the story is made clear when the Governor reveals that the woman then married a Canadian millionaire and was one of the 'boring' dinner guests. Bond realises that surfaces can be deceptive, and there can sometimes be more drama in the 'real' world than in the world he inhabits.

Observations: This also appeared in the short-story collection *For Your Eyes Only*. It remains one of the few Fleming plots not to have been adapted in some form for the cinema, probably because of Fleming's deliberate attempt to copy the style of the short-story writer W. Somerset Maugham.

Locations: Nassau in Bermuda.

'RISICO' (1960)

Starring: The hero – James Bond
The villain – Kristatos, a drug smuggler
  funded by the Soviet Union
The love interest – Lisl Baum

Written By: Ian Fleming

Plot: Bond is sent to Rome to stop a major drugs smuggler. When he gets there his contact, a man named Kristatos, who is working with the US authorities, tells Bond that the local 'Mr Big' is Enrico Colombo, and asks Bond to kill him. Bond gets to know Colombo's mistress and follows her to Venice, where Colombo captures him. Colombo tells Bond that Kristatos is the real 'Mr Big', and that he is being paid by the Soviet Union to smuggle large quantities of drugs into the West to undermine democracy. Bond and Colombo join forces to raid a warehouse belonging to Kristatos. During the course of the raid, Bond kills Kristatos.

Observations: Scotland Yard Assistant Commissioner Ronnie Vallance has applied pressure to get the Secret Service involved with the drugs trade. Bond has been pulled off his usual work and put on to the narcotics desk, much to M's displeasure. M, who is on his usual crusty form, knows Allan Dulles, a real-life Director of the CIA. Dulles resigned in 1961, so we can date the story to before then.

This short story, which also appears in *For Your Eyes Only*, was adapted by Ian Fleming from one of the plots he wrote for a planned, but never made, *James Bond* American TV series. It forms the second main strand for the 1981 movie *For Your Eyes Only*, with the action transferred to Greece. Whole chunks of Fleming's dialogue and situations were used verbatim.

Locations: Rome, Venice.

'THE HILDEBRAND RARITY' (1960)

Starring: The hero – James Bond
                  The villain – Milton Krest
                  The love interest – Liz Krest

Written By: Ian Fleming

Plot: On holiday in the Seychelles having completed an intelligence-gathering mission, Bond falls in with boorish millionaire Milton Krest, who is on an expedition to find a rare fish known as the Hildebrand Rarity as part of a tax dodge. Krest mistreats his wife, Liz, and poisons several thousand other fish in order to get one specimen of the Hildebrand Rarity. Neither action endears him to Bond. One night, on his ship *Wavekrest*, the millionaire is found dead – choked by the Hildebrand Rarity, which had been stuffed down his throat as he slept. Who killed him – his wife Liz or Bond's friend Fidele Barbey, who had been insulted by Krest? One thing is for certain – for once, Bond is innocent of murder.

Locations: The Seychelles, Milton Krest's boat *Wavekrest* and the waters around the small Chagrin Island.

Bond's Past Life: According to a letter from Ian Fleming to Lord Ridley (dated 18 June 1958), James Bond had been in the Seychelles foiling an attempt by Greek commandos to rescue Archbishop Makarios III from his exile there when the events of 'The Hildebrand Rarity' took place. This material is not mentioned in the short story, but dates the story to either 1957 or 1958.

This first appeared in the magazine *Today* in 1960, and then in the short-story collection *For Your Eyes Only* the same year. The character of Milton Krest, and the *Wavekrest*, appear in *Licence to Kill*, although his use of the stingray is transferred to the main villain of that film, Franz Sanchez.

Villainous Foibles: Krest uses the tail of a stingray as a particularly vicious weapon with which to beat his wife.

THUNDERBALL (1961)

Starring: The hero – James Bond
The villain – SPECTRE,
    especially Emilio Largo
The love interest – Domino Vitali

Written By: Ian Fleming, based on a screen treatment by
Kevin McClory, Jack Whittingham and
Ian Fleming (but see **Observations** below)

Plot: Bond is sent to Shrublands, a health farm, after a medical report deems him unfit. There he encounters Count Lippe, who bears a small tattoo. Bond's idle curiosity about it leads Lippe to try to kill Bond on a traction machine from which he is lucky to be rescued. In revenge, he traps Lippe in a Turkish bath, and thinks no more of it.

However, this has upset the plans of SPECTRE, a global criminal organisation based in Paris, run by Ernst Stavro Blofeld, a villain of Polish descent. Following various successful operations, they are now beginning 'the Big Affair' – the theft of two atomic bombs from NATO. A bomb carrier is hijacked by Giuseppe Petacchi, based at an Air Force base in Sussex, and flown to the Bahamas, where Petacchi is killed, and the bombs hidden – all masterminded by SPECTRE's No. 1, Emilio Largo. A ransom demand is sent simultaneously to the Prime Minister and the American President, giving one week for payment of $100,000,000 or a 'major piece of property' will be destroyed, followed two days later by a major city.

M plays a hunch and sends 007 to the Bahamas. Before Bond can leave, Count Lippe tries to kill him – but is himself murdered by SPECTRE. In Nassau, Bond engineers a meeting with Domino Vitali, Largo's 'niece', when he learns of Largo's cover in the West Indies: a treasure hunt. His CIA contact turns out to be Felix Leiter, who has been drafted back because of the international emergency, bringing with him a disguised Geiger counter, which will show excess radiation levels.

Bond and Felix are given a guided tour of Largo's hydrofoil, the *Disco Volante*, but there is no sign of radiation – unsurprisingly, since Largo has stashed the bombs already. Bond and Largo clash in the casino that evening, with Bond needling the Italian about a 'spectre' at his shoulder. In conversation with James afterwards, Domino casually reveals that her brother is Giuseppe Petacchi.

Bond investigates the hull of the *Disco Volante*, but is ambushed by a SPECTRE diver, who he kills, and is then attacked with grenades. Meanwhile, Felix has spotted an apparently dead physicist in the Casino, and they decide it is time to call in the *Manta*, the top-of-the-range American nuclear submarine. While they wait, they make an aerial survey of the area, and locate the plane. Bond dives down and collects Petacchi's identity tags. Bond tells Domino of her brother's death and to get her revenge on Largo, Domino agrees to take the Geiger counter on to the *Disco Volante*, so she will know when Largo has collected the bombs. She will then signal Bond.

Bond and Felix have overflown the Grand Bahamas rocket base in their survey, and believe that it is Target 1. When the *Manta* arrives, it's with bad news – because of the draught of the submarine compared with that of the *Disco Volante*, it can't follow the hydrofoil. They decide to gamble, and wait for Largo near the rocket base. Largo has discovered Domino's treachery and tortures her to find out for whom she is working. The *Disco Volante*, with one bomb on board, sets sail. Bond, Leiter and a group of Navy submariners lie in ambush. In a fierce underwater battle, SPECTRE is defeated, and Largo is killed by Domino, who has escaped from the yacht and joined the fray. The second bomb is found, but Blofeld escapes before the CIA can catch up with him.

Observations: Bond has invested in a different car: a Mark II Continental Bentley with a Rolls Mark IV engine. M breaks the rules to bring him up to speed about the threat facing the free world; Moneypenny, Loelia Ponsonby, May, Chief of Staff and Mathis are all viewed in passing.

This is the first time in the books that the Secret Service is referred to as the SIS. Agent 009 is next in command of the 00 section after Bond – the first time he is mentioned. SMERSH was disbanded in 1958. (Obviously nobody told Goldfinger!) The Detroit Purple Gang, whose leader was killed by Goldfinger, is mentioned in passing, as is Bond's previous experience with rocketry in *Moonraker*.

Thunderball introduces Fleming's answer to the disbanding of SMERSH: SPECTRE, the Special Executive for Counterintelligence, Terrorism, Revenge and Extortion, run by Ernst Stavro Blofeld from headquarters in Paris under cover of La Fraternité Internationale de la Resistance Contre l'Oppression (The International Brotherhood of Resistance Against Oppression). SPECTRE is formed of 21 main members, who are given numbers from 1 to 21, with the Chairman currently being number 2 (see **Mistakes Can Be Fatal**, below). Like airline pilots, their language of communication is English.

SPECTRE has been in operation since 1956, and has been responsible for recovering Himmler's jewels from the Modsee; a sale of Russian secrets from East Berlin to the CIA; a sale of heroin to a Los Angeles gang; selling Czech germ-warfare phials to the British Secret Service; blackmailing a former SS Gruppenführer; the assassination of a defector to the

Russians; and the kidnapping of a Detroit Purple Gang contact's daughter.

Felix Leiter has been drafted back into the CIA from Pinkerton's.

Rather oddly, the landlord of Largo's hideout, Palmyra, is a Mr Bryce – Bond's nom de guerre in the previous books.

The genesis of *Thunderball* is complicated, and this can, of necessity, only be a brief summary. It can be traced back at least as far as a short story written by Fleming's friend Ernest Cureo in May 1959. Ian Fleming and he were part of a film partnership, Xanadu, with Ivar Bryce and a film maker Fleming admired, Kevin McClory. A plot involving the Russians and culminating in an underwater battle was mixed in with Bond caught up with a group of actors. After discussion between the partners, Fleming rewrote the story with the Mafia as the central villains, telling of 'Henrico' Largo's plan to steal an atomic bomb.

At this stage, McClory suggested bringing in another writer, and Jack Whittingham joined the team. His expansion of the story added the element of Largo's girl being related to the thief of the bomb. Fleming and Whittingham both made further passes at the story, before Whittingham worked on a full screenplay over the New Year of 1960, while Fleming went to his house, Goldeneye, to work on 'the book of the film'. When the book was published, McClory filed a suit against Fleming, claiming that the work was based on the various scripts that he and McClory had worked on. As the whole of this agreement is currently the subject of legal proceedings, we cannot comment further, but after a drawn-out legal battle McClory was awarded the rights to make *Thunderball* as a film (which he did in conjunction with Harry Saltzman and Albert R. Broccoli in 1965), and the book was republished with the ascription as above. Of course, as well as the 1965 film, *Thunderball* is the basis for Sean Connery's return to Bondage, *Never Say Never Again*, in 1983.

Locations: London, Sussex, Paris, the Bahamas, May–June 1959.

Bond's Past Life: Bond had to jump from the Arlberg Express around the time of the Hungarian Uprising in 1956. He has been on a submarine only once before, when he was in RNVR Special Branch.

Toys for the Boys: Felix and later Domino use what appears to be an ordinary camera, but is in fact a Geiger counter.

Patronising Lines: Shortly before he dies, Giuseppe Petacchi muses that 'He would only drive the car really fast when he wanted to get a girl. They melted in a fast car.'

'Women are often meticulous and safe drivers, but they are very seldom first-class . . .' is the opening of a wonderful tirade against female drivers. Not that we would agree with such sentiments, of course.

Villainous Foibles: Blofeld is a very big man, with a massive belly, as a result of his muscles going to waste. He neither drinks nor smokes, and is believed to be asexual. Before committing any unpleasant act, he sweetens his breath.

Emilio Largo has a vast sexual appetite, extremely large hands – twice the size they should be proportionately – and makes a fetish of keeping calm in a crisis.

Sadism: The duel between Count Lippe and 007 becomes sadistic, with a traction machine and a Turkish bath as the weapons of choice. Blofeld electrocutes a rapist SPECTRE member, while another employee gets eaten by barracuda. Emilio Largo has a wonderful way using the application of a burning cigar and an ice cube, which is left mostly to the imagination . . .

Mistakes Can Be Fatal: At the first SPECTRE meeting we eavesdrop on, there are twenty members present, plus Blofeld – but No. 1 (Largo) is in the Bahamas. There should therefore be one empty chair.

Fleming seems to have forgotten that Felix Leiter lost a leg as well as an arm in *Live and Let Die*. If Felix has just been drafted into the CIA after at least five years with Pinkerton's (allowing *Live and Let Die* to be set in 1954), he has had one hell of a crash course in the latest technology, since he is able to give Bond chapter and verse on the capabilities of the *Manta*.

THE SPY WHO LOVED ME (1962)

Starring: The hero – Vivienne Michel
               The villains – Sol Horror and Sluggsy Morant
               The love interest – James Bond

Written By: 'Ian Fleming with Vivienne Michel' (see **Observations** below)

Plot: Vivienne Michel, a 23-year-old French Canadian, is looking after a motel in the Adirondacks, waiting for the owner to arrive. We learn of her early life.

There is a dreadful storm, and she accidentally puts the VACANCY sign on. Two hoodlums arrive – Sol 'Horror' Horowitz and Sluggsy Morant. Sluggsy tries it on and Vivienne hits him, but they restrain her and demand food. She tries to escape, they recapture her and, when she slashes at Horror with an icepick, they beat her up. Cowed, she makes them their food, but Sluggsy tries it on again, and she goes for him with a knife. That is too much, and he starts to rape her . . .

Another visitor arrives, an Englishman called James Bond. He takes Vivienne's desperate hints, and comes in. The hoods try to persuade Bond that she is the one at fault, but he doesn't believe them and, to keep her mind occupied, explains that he works for the British Government, and has just been on an assignment in Toronto, where SPECTRE had taken on the job of assassinating a defector for the Russians. Bond had taken the place of the target and captured the SPECTRE agent. He then was motoring down to Washington, but got a puncture and had to stop.

Sluggsy goes out to check the security while Bond rags Sol about the possibility of setting fire to the motel. He then checks Vivienne's room is safe, and gives her a spare gun. She goes to sleep, but wakes and in her wardrobe finds Sluggsy, who knocks her out. The next thing she knows is she's outside, and the motel is ablaze. Bond has rescued her from being the scapegoat in an insurance scam. The hoods believe they have killed Bond. Although at one point Bond has the upper hand, he loses it, and there is a gun battle between the four parties, culminating in Bond shooting Horror at the wheel of his car, which goes into the lake.

Bond and Vivienne make love, but afterwards Sluggsy attacks, and Bond disposes of him. When Vivienne awakes the next morning, Bond has left a note for the police, and Vivienne is counselled by a police officer to forget Bond – although she knows she will never forget 'the spy who loved me'.

Observations: *The Spy Who Loved Me* is a total anomaly within the Bond canon. It does not fit into the established continuity, is allegedly a true story, and is told in the first person.

In fact, Ian Fleming was getting tired of the criticisms of the Bond novels, and this was his attempt at something different, more like Mickey Spillane. All it turns out to be is a massive waste of time. Fleming realised that it was a mistake, and stated that he did not want a paperback edition to appear.

'I tried to break away from my normal formula,' Fleming said later, 'but the readers were so furious that James Bond didn't appear until about three-quarters of the way through, and that it was written ostensibly by a girl . . . that I must confess it wasn't a success and it took quite a beating from the critics.' For a time Fleming even played to the press by claiming that he 'found the manuscript' sitting on his desk in Goldeneye.

Pan Books did not therefore acquire the paperback rights to this until 1967, when it appeared at the same time as the posthumous collection of short stories, *Octopussy*, after it was proved that Fleming did not mean what he had said.

Thunderball apparently happened less than a year before.

Since this book is categorically set in October, after Jack Kennedy was President (which he became in November 1960), and *Thunderball* occurred in June 1959 (as per SPECTRE's ransom demand), we are clearly in an alternate dimension.

Bond again says he has never been able to kill in cold blood. This contradicts everything we know about him. For what it's worth, he gives his address as c/o Ministry of Defence, Storey's Gate, London SW1.

The 1977 film, although bearing the same title, has no elements of the book in it, a specific requirement of Fleming when he sold the rights to Eon.

Locations: Quebec, London, Windsor, the Adirondacks, October 1961 (probably), with flashbacks.

Bond's Past Life: He has been on a mission in Canada. Don't believe a word of it.

Toys for the Boys: Bond's attaché case has spare ammunition in it.

Patronising Lines: The whole book qualifies, but especially 'Now, don't hang on my gun arm, there's a good girl', and 'All women love semi-rape'.

Villainous Foibles: Sol Horror (a.k.a. Sol Horowitz, a.k.a. Mr Thompson) has steel-capped teeth and bloodshot eyes; Sluggsy Morant (a.k.a. Mr Jones) is an albino with alopecia. Makes us wonder if Fleming found two medical complaints neighbouring in the medical dictionary!

Sadism: Vivienne is beaten up by Horror, and nearly raped by Sluggsy.

Lines to Flick Past: 'Nothing makes one really grateful for life except the black wings of danger' – really?

Mistakes Can Be Fatal: Why does Vivienne buy a Vespa in London and have it shipped over to Canada? Why doesn't she just buy one out there?

'THE LIVING DAYLIGHTS' (1962)

Starring: The hero – James Bond
The villain – the Soviet assassin known as Trigger
The love interest – the Soviet assassin known as Trigger

Written By: Ian Fleming

Plot: A double agent is coming over to the West through Berlin. Both East and West know what stretch of the Berlin Wall he's coming through, and roughly when, but there's no way of warning him off or getting him to change his plans. Hearing that the Soviets are sending their top assassin to kill the double agent as he makes the journey across no-man's-land, M sends Bond out to kill the assassin. Ensconced in a safe house facing over the area where the agent will cross, Bond waits with his rifle trained on the window from which he knows the assassin will fire. He wiles away the time by watching the comings and goings in the building, including what appears to be an entirely female orchestra.

When the double agent finally tries to cross, the assassin shows herself – it's the cellist from the all-woman orchestra. Bond fires to scare her rather than kill her – he knows he may lose his 00 licence for this blatant disregard for orders, but he has fallen for the cellist and cannot kill her.

Observations: While hanging around Berlin, Bond seriously considers visiting a brothel. Surely he doesn't have to *pay* for sex? Not James Bond? Not any more, anyway?

Bond half remembers the name of a well-known cellist – 'Amaryllis somebody'. In fact, Amaryllis Fleming was Ian Fleming's half-sister, and she did play the cello.

M and Bill Tanner (M's Chief of Staff) both make an appearance. Station WB is in West Berlin.

The original working title of the story was 'Trigger Finger'. It appeared in 1962 in the first issue of the *Sunday Times* colour magazine, and then in book form in 1966, in the short-story collection *Octopussy and the Living Daylights*.

Locations: Berlin, England.

ON HER MAJESTY'S SECRET SERVICE (1963)

Starring: The hero – James Bond
                    The villain – Ernst Stavro Blofeld
                    The love interest – Contessa Teresa di Vicenzo
                      (Tracy)

Written By: Ian Fleming

Plot: Bond is on holiday on the Continent, and is thinking of submitting his resignation to M. He is sick and tired of trying to find Blofeld, and wants out. He meets Contessa Teresa (Tracy) Vicenzo, races against her, saves her honour at the Casino Royale in Monte Carlo when she cannot pay her bills, sleeps with her, falls in love with her, prevents her from committing suicide and is taken captive, along with her, by her father. Her father turns out to be Marc-Ange Draco, head of the Union Corse (a French/Corsican organisation similar to the Mafia). Draco is worried about his daughter, and offers Bond a million pounds if he will marry her. Bond refuses, but accepts a bargain – he will continue to see Tracy if her father will locate Blofeld for him.

Back in London, Bond discovers that the Royal College of Arms has been contacted by Blofeld. The master criminal wants to establish a familial connection to the de Bleuville titles and fortunes, and proposes (through an intermediary) to fund the Royal College of Arms' research into the subject. Knowing that the British Government were seeking Blofeld, the College decided to raise the alert.

Disguised as Sir Hilary Bray of the Royal College of Arms, Bond travels to the Swiss mountain stronghold where Blofeld is ensconced under the title Monsieur le Comte Balthazar de

Bleuville, meeting along the way Blofeld's companion and factotum Irma Bunt. Blofeld appears to be running some kind of sanatorium, treating women suffering from allergies by a process involving diet and hypnosis.

Bond's investigations are interrupted by the forced arrival of another British Secret Service agent – Shaun Campbell of Station Z (Zurich). Campbell has been investigating around Blofeld's mountain-top retreat, and has been taken captive by Blofeld's guards. Knowing that Blofeld is already suspicious of him, and will torture Campbell in order to investigate his bona fides, Bond determines to escape.

Bond skis down the mountain away from Blofeld's base, but is pursued. His pursuers catch up with him in the local town, but he is rescued by Tracy di Vicenzo, who had been told by her father where Bond was likely to be. Before returning to London, Bond asks her to marry him.

During a briefing at M's house, it becomes clear (based on things Bond saw at Blofeld's retreat and on what has happened since some of Blofeld's 'patients' have returned to England) that Blofeld is planning a biological warfare attack on the country, probably funded by Russia. The female 'patients' at his sanatorium are being hypnotised to release containers of biological material – fowl pest, swine fever, anthrax – when they return to England. The country will be devastated.

M authorises an attack on Blofeld's headquarters, and Bond goes to Marc-Ange Draco to obtain the manpower and the helicopters necessary. The attack goes well: Blofeld's biological warfare laboratory is taken and the women who have returned to England are intercepted before they can release their various deadly cargoes, but Blofeld escapes on a bobsleigh.

Bond and Tracy marry, but as they start off on their honeymoon Blofeld and Irma Bunt make an attempt on their lives. Tracy is killed, but Bond survives.

Observations: James Bond returns to Vesper Lynd's grave at Royale-les-Eaux each year (*Casino Royale*). His promise of 'we have all the time in the world' is actually first made to Solitaire in *Live and Let Die*. He gets married on 1 January 1963 at 10.30 a.m.

Agent 006, an ex-Royal Marine Commando, makes his first off-stage appearance. Station Z is Zurich. Station M is Munich (no longer Station D for Deutschland). Universal Export, the SIS's longstanding cover, is all but known worldwide now (so why hasn't it been changed?).

It's just over a year since the events of *Thunderball* (but see **Mistakes Can Be Fatal**), and there has been no trace of Blofeld. Bedlam is alternately the code name for the clean-up operation of SPECTRE, and for Blofeld himself. Blofeld's history, and the fact that there were three Union Corse members of the original SPECTRE, are recounted accurately from *Thunderball*. SMERSH gets a name check, and it's Mary Goodnight's turn to complain about Bond playing at Red Indians (*Casino Royale*/'*From a View to a Kill*').

Loelia Ponsonby has been married off to be replaced as Bond's secretary by Mary Goodnight; Bill Tanner and May make brief appearances; Sir James Molony gets a mention, and M liaises with Sir Ronald Vallance of the CID.

M was awarded the KCMG some years before. He lives at Quarterdeck, near Windsor, where he is looked after by Mr and Mrs Hammond, his Chief Petty Officer from his last ship, the *Repulse*, and his wife. He is not married, and enjoys painting in watercolours. He earns £5,000 per annum as head of the Secret Service, and a pension as a Vice-Admiral on the retired list.

It's an early hint of the lethargy that was creeping over him as for the first time Fleming assumes that his readers are aware of the rules of *chemin de fer*.

Once again, Fleming's characters voice the idea that women want to be raped (*Casino Royale*/*The Spy Who Loved Me*).

The real first edition of this book consists of a limited edition of 250 copies signed by Ian Fleming and with a frontispiece portrait of Fleming by his friend Amherst Villiers.

Locations: Royale-les-Eaux, September 1962; London (November); Switzerland; Marseilles, France (December).

My Name Is . . . Sir Hilary Bray, an emissary of the College of Arms in London, named for a friend of Ian Fleming.

Bond's Past Life: Bond's father was Scottish, his mother Swiss. He learnt to ski at the Hannes Schneider School at St Anton in Arlberg, winning the golden K. He has been down the Parsenn run. He has been to Singapore, and played bar games at a filthy dive.

Toys for the Boys: The Syncrophone (an early pager) summons Bond.

Patronising Lines: 'It was his experience that girls who drove competitively like that were always pretty – and exciting.'

'The idea of suddenly becoming a "lady" in their small community is so intoxicating that the way they bare their souls is positively obscene.'

Villainous Foibles: Blofeld is so desperate to be acknowledged as the Comte de Bleuville that he has plastic surgery to remove his earlobes (as well as disguising his corpulent figure from *Thunderball*).

Sadism: Surprisingly little. One of the ski instructors is sent down a bobsleigh run without benefit of vehicle, but that's off stage, as is the interrogation of SIS agent Campbell. Whether the sight of James Bond getting married counts as sadism towards his female fans is up to the reader.

Lines to Flick Past: SIS agent 501 'suddenly slapped his thigh'. He might be at M's on Christmas Day, but did he have to indulge in pantomime?

'He gave her another long and, he admitted to himself, extremely splendid kiss, to which she responded with an animalism that slightly salved his conscience.'

It's Only a Book: Bond has switched allegiance to the *Daily Express* – which must be interesting for him, as the exploits of James Bond were delighting that organ's readers. At Piz Gloria, Irma Bunt points out Ursula Andress to Bond – Andress had just played Honey Ryder in *Dr No*.

Mistakes Can Be Fatal: The events of *OHMSS* totally contradict *The Spy Who Loved Me,* in that SPECTRE has not been heard of since *Thunderball*. We can't say that we disapprove of Fleming's decision!

Once again, the year of this is a problem. *Thunderball* is set in 1959, yet this is definitely set in 1962 – and only a year has elapsed.

M has changed from not swearing to only rarely swearing at stupidity.

Bond thinks that the death of the ski instructor was a typical SPECTRE death. How does he know? He wasn't present at the board meetings in Paris!

Bond says he never expected to be proposing marriage – yet his mental anguish in *Casino Royale* over Vesper is precisely because of this.

Reference is made to the Government being involved in 'another' U2 scandal – but Gary Francis Powers was working for the Americans, not the British.

'THE PROPERTY OF A LADY' (1963)

Starring: The hero – James Bond
                  The villain – the Resident Director of the
                      KGB station in London
                  The love interest – none

Written By: Ian Fleming

Plot: There is a double agent working in the Secret Intelligence Service. She's a clerk in the Communications Department, and M has known about her from the start. In fact, he feeds her a continuous stream of false intelligence for her to send back to her masters in Moscow. The only thing that has worried M is how exactly she has been paid, as her bank balance reflects only her Civil Service salary. His answer comes when she puts up for sale an immensely valuable Fabergé egg – apparently left to her by a now deceased relative. M suspects that whatever she makes on the egg at auction will be her reward for years of spying. Bond points out that a senior KGB agent will also have to be present at the auction in order to bid for the egg and force its price up, otherwise it might sell for a smaller amount than their spy deserves. If Bond can identify the other bidder, they can identify the KGB head of station.

At the auction, Bond watches the bidders carefully, and eventually spots the Russian bidder. MI5 trail him back to the Russian Embassy for the final proof before expelling him from the country.

Observations: This first appeared in *The Ivory Hammer* (the yearbook of the auction house Sotheby's) in 1963, then (for the mass market) in the first paperback edition of *Octopussy* in 1967. Ian Fleming apparently accepted no payment from Sotheby's for writing it because he was dissatisfied with it. It is set between *OHMSS* and *You Only Live Twice*, when supposedly Bond was not involved with a successful mission.

M appears, as does Mary Goodnight. Chief of Staff and Sir Ronald Vallance of Scotland Yard are mentioned. Section 100 of the SIS deals with double agents.

Location: London, June 1963.

YOU ONLY LIVE TWICE (1964)

Starring: The hero – James Bond
         The villains – Ernst Stavro Blofeld and
            Irma Bunt
         The love interest – Kissy Suzuki

Written By: Ian Fleming

Plot: M does not know what to do with Bond following his decline after Tracy's death at the end of *OHMSS*. Sir James Molony suggests giving him a taxing assignment, and M masks Bond's sideways move as a promotion to the Diplomatic Section to re-establish good relations with the Japanese Secret Service. Bond is to offer the fruits of 'the Blue Route' through Macao in exchange for Magic 44 – the code name for the Japanese access to Soviet radio transmissions. In Japan, he is briefed by Australian Dikko Henderson, who introduces him to Tiger Tanaka, the head of the Japanese Service, a former kamikaze pilot, educated in England. Tanaka shows Bond a translation of an instruction by the USSR to try to blackmail nuclear weaponry out of England. He has gained it thanks to Magic 44. Bond relays this to Britain, and averts a major global confrontation.

However, the Blue Route has already been penetrated by the Japanese, so in exchange for Magic 44 Tanaka wants Bond personally to do his Service a favour. He tells Bond about Dr Guntrun Shatterhand, a Swiss botanist, who has created a Garden of Death in a ruined castle in the south of Japan. Loaded with deadly plants, animals and fish, it has become a Mecca for Japanese wishing to commit suicide. If Bond kills Shatterhand, Tanaka will share Magic 44. Bond agrees, and is disguised as a Japanese miner. Tanaka takes him to the ninja training school, where Bond is taught the techniques. However, Tanaka is being followed by one of Shatterhand's men, who dies before they can interrogate him.

Bond's method of entry to the castle is by sea, going from an Ama island nearby. When Tiger shows him a photo of Shatterhand and his wife, Bond is horrified to find that they are Blofeld and Irma Bunt. He does not tell Tanaka he knows them, but goes to Kuro Island and meets Kissy Suzuki, a fisherwoman who went as an actress to Hollywood. She helps him get fit for the swim, and falls in love with him.

She leads Bond through the straits to the castle, and Bond scales the wall, then hides his gear in an outhouse. On the way, he sees two suicides, and the next morning watches Blofeld and Irma Bunt inspect their garden. That night, he breaks into the castle, but falls into an oubliette. Irma Bunt thinks she recognises Bond, and Blofeld places him over a controlled geyser which will go off at 11.15. If Bond really is a deaf and dumb miner intent on suicide, he won't move – but at 11.14 he does, and nonchalantly ambles away. After a brief duel of words, Bond and Blofeld battle, wooden sword against staff. Eventually Bond manages to throttle Blofeld. He grabs the rope of a helium balloon to escape, as Irma Bunt raises the alarm. However, a bullet hits him and he crashes into the sea.

Kissy finds Bond, who is suffering from amnesia. She gets the other islanders to conspire to hide him, and 007 is presumed dead, with his obituary appearing in *The Times*. Some months later, though, he finds the word Vladivostock on a piece of paper – which triggers his memory. Still not knowing he is an SIS agent, Bond sets off for Russia . . .

Observations: Bond is apparently still under forty (with his new date of birth as 1924), and born in a Year of the Rat. He is promoted to 7777, the Diplomatic Section. The aftermath of Tracy's death at the end of *OHMSS* affects Bond throughout the story. His battle in *Doctor No* is mentioned in passing.

Blofeld's schemes in *Thunderball* and *OHMSS* are discussed. Bond is unaware of what a 'poofter' is; he doesn't like beef; and weighs 182 pounds (13 stone). In coded conversation, Bond refers to M as 'Mother' – interestingly, the code name given in the Linda Thorson years to *The Avengers*' John Steed's boss. Mary Goodnight has worked for Bond for three years at the time of his supposed death in November 1963. This ties in with her replacing Loelia Ponsonby after *Thunderball*.

Bond's colleagues, Mary Goodnight, M and Sir James Molony, are all concerned about him; Moneypenny can barely conceal her annoyance initially, or her delight after Bond's promotion; and Colonel Bill Tanner (the first time his rank has been mentioned) carefully pushes the party line about Bond's promotion. M dines with Sir James at Blades, which closes throughout September.

The SIS is still using Universal Export as its cover, even

though Bond knows it was blown during *OHMSS*. The SIS has not had a station in Japan since 1950, although Colonel Hamilton still runs Station J from Britain.

Blofeld is also now suffering from 'accidie' (as did Mr Big in *Live and Let Die*). The book's obsession with death reflects Fleming's state of health at the time of writing – he had had one heart attack, and was very aware of his own mortality.

A faithful radio adaptation by Michael Bakewell, starring Michael Jayston as 007, was broadcast on 21 December 1990 on BBC Radio 4.

Locations: Tokyo and southern Japan, 31 August 1963–May 1964.

My Name Is . . . Taro Todoroki, a deaf and dumb coalminer from Fukoka.

James Bond, Fashion Victim: The Japonified Bond must have been a sight for sore eyes!

Bond's Past Life: Bond was given a month's leave after Tracy's death, part of which he took in Jamaica. He then bungled two assignments between *OHMSS* and now. He has been under Sir James Molony around twelve times in his career.

He has never been East of Hongkong (sic), and had a grounding of Latin and Greek at school.

More details about his early life are given in his obituary.

Patronising Lines: 'The Japanese are a separate human species'; 'This is man's work.'

Villainous Foibles: Blofeld has built a Garden of Death, through which he parades in seventeenth-century armour. He has gone insane, ranting and raving like a lunatic.

Sadism: Tanaka's agent keeps on hitting Blofeld's spy even after he's dead.

Blofeld's, or, rather, Dr Shatterhand's, garden is a sadist's pleasure dome in which we witness two suicides and a murder.

Bond is beaten up before being placed over a hole through which a geyser will erupt precisely every fifteen minutes.

Lines to Flick Past: 'No self-respecting man could get through the day without his battery of four-letter words to cope with the roughage of life and let off steam.' Each to their own.

It's Only a Book: Ian Fleming's books exist in Bond's fictional world, with M making a mention of them in Bond's obituary.

Kissy Suzuki says that only one man has ever been kind to her – the actor David Niven. Niven was Fleming's original choice to play Bond, and finally achieved that dubious distinction in the spoof film *Casino Royale*.

Mistakes Can Be Fatal: Bond makes reference to the '64-dollar question' – it was *The $64,000 Question*, an American quiz show, brought to Britain as *The 64,000 Question*.

Bond's obituary gave Fleming a chance to take a few years off Bond's age, but unfortunately other mistakes then creep in. Bond's birth is set as 1924: so, nine-year-olds buying Bentleys?

Bond was awarded the CMG in 1954? In *From Russia With Love*, SMERSH's files date it to 1953.

M must have been annoyed that Bond didn't invite him to his wedding, as he gets the year wrong – it was 1963, not 1962.

Bond doesn't like beef, eh? Odd, because in *OHMSS* we are told that he practically lives on grilled sole, eggs coquotte and cold roast beef.

THE MAN WITH THE GOLDEN GUN (1965)

Starring: The hero – James Bond
                  The villain – Francisco Scaramanga
                  The love interest – Mary Goodnight

Written By: Ian Fleming

Plot: James Bond returns to London, brainwashed by the KGB into attempting to kill M. The attempt is foiled, and Bond is restored to something approaching normality by electroshock therapy. M, concerned over Bond's mental health, sends him on a mission to assassinate a professional killer named Francisco Scaramanga. Scaramanga works for Fidel Castro, and is responsible for the deaths of at least six SIS agents.

Bond arrives in Jamaica on the trail of Scaramanga and manages to arrange an 'accidental' meeting. Scaramanga, impressed with Bond's coolness under pressure, offers him a job – he is holding an important conference at a half-built hotel out in the marshlands of Jamaica, and needs someone to act as a security consultant. Bond accepts, goes along to the conference, and discovers that Scaramanga is brokering deals between the Mafia and the KGB, the aim of which is to increase Mob profits and destabilise the Western economy by holding up the sugar harvest.

Scaramanga becomes increasingly suspicious of Bond, and the KGB representative realises that Bond is an SIS agent. Scaramanga and Bond confront each other on a private train heading across the undeveloped areas of Jamaica and, after Bond has killed the KGB agent and Scaramanga has badly wounded Felix Leiter, they hold a duel in the marshes. Bond wins, but is shot with a poisoned bullet and spends several weeks recuperating.

Observations: Bond saves the world's sugar. It's a bit of a comedown for England's top agent, isn't it?

It's been three or four years since Bond and Leiter last met. Oddly, his obituary was reprinted in 'the Trib', presumably the *New York Tribune*. Why?

Bond and Leiter are awarded the Jamaican Police Medal (well that's something to tell the kids about); 007 is offered a knighthood at the end for services rendered but turns it down (see also **Mistakes Can Be Fatal**).

M's full name, Admiral Sir Miles Messervy, is revealed for the first time. His office, which still shows a red light to indicate he's busy, has a transparent shield in the ceiling which can drop down between M and a potential assassin. This was installed after M's predecessor was killed at his desk by one of his agents (irritated at the constant carping of his boss, one presumes).

We have references to SIS agents 098, 267, 742, 768 and 943 (implying that the SIS has at least a thousand or so agents). The SIS has two initial interrogators: the Hard Man (Mr Fred Robson), and the soft (Major Townsend). Bill Tanner has been second in command of the Service for ten years or more.

Stations B and W are both in West Germany. Head of Berlin Station is a friend of Bond's; the Head of Station C is Alec Hill. Bond was brainwashed by the KGB at an Institute near Leningrad, and is treated by Sir James Molony at the Park, a Service hospital and convalescent home in Kent.

The Spangled Mob (*Diamonds Are Forever*), and the Detroit Purple Gang (*Goldfinger*) are represented at Scaramanga's congress of gangsters.

Miss Moneypenny becomes involved with Bond's return from the dead; Porterfield, a waiter at Blades, reappears; Felix Leiter, drafted back into the CIA, goes undercover as Mr Travis to help Bond.

Bond's former secretary Mary Goodnight is now stationed in Jamaica; she uses the car of the former Jamaican resident Strangways. Bond reflects on both Doctor No and Honeychile Ryder (now married). Bond calls her Honeychile Wilder here – we'll be charitable and assume this is her married name, rather than a mistake.

Q Branch design the clothing for overseas agents (so they're the ones responsible for Bond's terrible safari suits in the later Roger Moore films, then).

The SIS has finally got round to creating a new cover: Transworld Consortium, based, oddly, in Kensington.

It's been a year since the events of *You Only Live Twice*.

According to a theory going around at the time, a homosexual man can't whistle . . .!

Ian Fleming goes overboard on the cultural references,

talking familiarly about 'ganja' and also going into some detail on the beliefs of the Rastafarians. Nice to see that old Fleming touch with the research hadn't deserted him.

The Man With the Golden Gun was published posthumously. Fleming had died in August 1964.

Locations: London, November 1964; Jamaica some two to three months later.

My Name Is . . . Frank Westmacott (a cover provided by the KGB); Mark Hazard of Transworld Consortium.

Patronising Lines: 'Of all the doom-fraught graffiti a woman can write on the wall . . .' This is good coming from Bond, who got married only a year or two earlier!

Villainous Foibles: Scaramanga has a third nipple. He is an indiscriminate womaniser who makes love before a kill to improve his eye. He enjoys killing. And, like von Hammerstein in 'For Your Eyes Only', he kills innocent birds.

Sadism: There's less than usual, although Scaramanga's death is long and drawn out.

Mistakes Can Be Fatal: Bond was promoted to 7777 in *You Only Live Twice*. Nobody refers to him as anything but 007 in this book.

The Russian double agent in Section 100 is mentioned again, but unfortunately she is called Maria Freudenstadt, rather than Freudenstein ('Property of a Lady').

Felix Leiter has lost only an arm, not an arm and a leg. Fleming claims that Leiter and Bond have never shaken hands, yet, when the two agents meet in New York at the start of *Live and Let Die*, 'Bond grasped the hard hand and shook it warmly'.

Up until now, M has always turned down awards for members of the Service, but he approves Bond's potential knighthood.

At the beginning of the book, the service M is in charge of

is referred to as the SS (the Security Service, or MI5). By the end of the book, it's back to being the SIS (the Secret Intelligence Service, or MI6).

When Bond first arrives in Jamaica we learn that he is 'barely familiar' with the town. Within a page, we learn that he has undertaken 'many assignments' there. Either that's a mistake, or he's remarkably unobservant for a secret agent.

Two questions: why doesn't Bond take any of the many opportunities he gets to kill Scaramanga, and why on earth does Scaramanga offer a complete stranger a job as security consultant for a conference with the Mafia and the KGB?

'OCTOPUSSY' (1966)

Starring: The hero – James Bond
                The villain – Major Dexter Smythe, OBE
                The love interest – none

Written By: Ian Fleming

Plot: Following the discovery of a murder victim frozen in an Austrian glacier for twenty years, Bond is sent to Jamaica to get some details from Major Dexter Smythe, the last man to see the victim – Hannes Oberhauser – alive. Bond makes it clear that he believes Smythe is responsible for the death of Oberhauser and, faced with his certainty, Smythe confesses. He had been with an intelligence team operating in Germany and Austria shortly after the end of the war, and had discovered that a cache of German gold had been hidden high in the Austrian mountains. He had hired Oberhauser to take him up to the location, then shot him and got the gold down the mountain by himself. Bond leaves Smythe to do the decent thing, after revealing that Oberhauser had taught him how to ski when he was a child. Rather than kill himself, Smythe goes out swimming with his pet 'Octopussy' and decides to brazen it out at the inescapable court martial. He is, however, killed by the hand of fate masquerading as a poisonous scorpion fish.

Observations: This was published posthumously in the short-story collection *Octopussy*. The events happened to the eponymous Octopussy's father in the 1983 film.

Major Smythe suffers from 'accidie' (laziness or boredom), as did Mr Big and Blofeld. And, of course, Fleming.

Locations: Jamaica, with flashbacks to Austria.

Bond's Past Life: Bond was taught to ski as a teenager in Austria by Hannes Oberhauser after his parents died.

THE ADVENTURES OF JAMES BOND JUNIOR 003½ (1967)

Starring: The hero – James Bond Jnr
        The villain – Merck
        The love interest – Sheelagh

Written By: R.D. Mascott

Plot: Agent 007's nephew, James Bond Jnr, left with a housekeeper when his parents go on holiday, wants to get back items he left at Hazeley Hall, as the place is now in new hands. Unfortunately, it is now surrounded by barbed wire. James sees an attractive girl there, but can't get in. He persuades the postman to smuggle him in, and gets a view of the new owner, Merck. James then encounters the girl, Sheelagh, and agrees to meet her the next morning.

He meets with his former gang, the Pride, who have been waging guerrilla warfare against Merck since he moved in. They try to annoy the guard dogs, but the dogs won't respond, and later James sees a camouflaged truck and a police car, driven by Merck, leaving the Hall.

James meets Sheelagh next morning and they retrieve his key for his trove in the Hall. James gives her some of his treasure – pencils and drawing pads – and returns home to find a newspaper detailing a bullion hijack. He tries to tell his suspicions to a local bigwig, Commander Conningtower, whom he saw the previous evening with a woman who wasn't his wife, but gets told not to be a silly little boy.

James sees the lorry coming back and is caught by Sheelagh. They are then questioned by Merck, but claim that James is just Sheelagh's friend. Sheelagh shows him her paintings, which include the woman with the Commander, whom she says is Merck's girlfriend. One of James's gang recognises her as an actress.

James steals out that night and investigates the ammunition dump near where he saw the lorry that day, which is now guarded by a Doberman. The dog gets caught in a mantrap, and James runs. Merck kills the dog and his men chase after James, who escapes. He tells the housekeeper what he thinks he knows, and, as he falls asleep, she calls the Commander. It turns out that the Commander was already suspicious and the police were about to raid. The 'girlfriend' was a dog-breeder as well as an actress and together somehow they foiled the plot. James finds Sheelagh and helps her to be reunited with her mother.

Observations: James Bond Jnr is the son of Captain David Bond, 007's brother. His grandfather (presumably 007's father) had died three years earlier and left them a house on the Kent–Sussex border. Everyone knows that James Bond senior is agent 007 – even the boy's housemaster makes a joke of it. Since *You Only Live Twice* established that Bond didn't have any living relatives, let alone any who know his operational number and habits, we can take this as totally apocryphal.

The Adventures of James Bond Junior was licensed by Fleming's copyright holders, Glidrose, and first appeared in 1967, gaining a reprint in 1974. Frankly, we'd rather have the animated series (to which this has no connection save the title) – and that is saying a lot!

Villainous Foibles: Merck has African features, but isn't black – he's ginger, with close-cut ginger curls and a beard without a moustache. He speaks in a cod-German accent. He keeps guard dogs (Alsatians and Doberman pinschers).

Mistakes Can Be Fatal: The book is set in 1967 and indicates that 007's father died in 1964. Ian Fleming's chronology indicates he died in the 1930s. John Pearson, in his later *James Bond: The Authorised Biography*, plumps for 1933.

COLONEL SUN (1968)

Starring: The hero – James Bond
The villain – Colonel Sun Liang-Tan
The love interest – Ariadne Alexandrou

Written By: Robert Markham (alias Kingsley Amis)

Plot: M is kidnapped from his home. A piece of paper is planted at the scene, with Greek names and numbers on it, and Bond is sent on the trail. M is taken to a Chinese agent, Colonel Sun Liang-Tan, on the Greek Island of Vrakonisi, who needs both M and Bond for his own ends.

In Athens, Bond deliberately walks into a trap set by Ariadne Alexandrou, a Greek working for the Soviets. After a third party attacks them both, the two agents team up, with the Soviets' blessing. An important 'event' is taking place, and there is clearly a threat to its security. The British Head of Station, Stuart Thomas, disappears, and Bond and Ariadne decide to head for the location of the 'event', for which they will need a boat. Ariadne enlists Niko Litsas, a member of the resistance during the war, who bears a major grudge against von Richter, a German officer who killed his family and is involved with their adversary.

They set sail for Vrakonisi, and Bond deduces that their foe must be Chinese. A Russian-hosted peace conference is taking place and Bond guesses that the Chinese plan is to destroy it, and to leave his and M's bodies there as 'proof' that the British were responsible. Arriving at

Vrakonisi, Ariadne tries to convince General Arenski, the Russian in charge of conference security, of the plot, but he doesn't believe her.

Bond sees Sun and von Richter choosing the spot from where they will launch a mortar attack on the conference. Ariadne and Litsas plan their assault on Sun's base, but when they make their move Arenski's men get in the way. Bond swims for shore, but is captured. Sun plans to torture Bond to death – and dump what remains of his body with M's at the conference site. Bond survives the torture, which involves the specific stimulation of pain centres with the aid of a doctor. After one of Sun's assistants secretly cuts him free Bond knifes Sun. He frees the others, killing Sun's henchmen, while Litsas takes von Richter for a sailing trip from which only he returns.

However, Bond discovers that Sun has survived and has killed the woman who helped Bond. Sun tries to hold Bond off with a grenade, but loses control, and Bond knifes him through the heart.

Observations: Bond knows a bit of Greek but can't speak Russian, and is offered the Order of the Red Banner by Comrade Kosygin.

M is ill at the start of this book, and is referred to as Sir Miles throughout, rather than by his code name. Bill Tanner plays a much more important role than normal; M's servants, the Hammonds, are killed when M is kidnapped; Assistant Commissioner Sir Ronald Vallance's office is used for the planning meeting.

Sir Ranald Rideout is the Minister concerned with the Secret Service. Stuart Thomas, Head of Station G (Greece), was agent 005 before retiring from field duty.

Scaramanga (*The Man With the Golden Gun*) and Bond's problems before and during *You Only Live Twice* are mentioned as starting a couple of years before. M's house, Quarterdeck, is the location for the earlier scenes.

Colonel Sun was the first official continuation of the Bond saga, published around the same time as the *Daily Express* began printing original comic strips. At one stage it was suggested that the book be published under the pseudonym George Glidrose, and the copyright-holders Glidrose had planned to use that pseudonym – and the one finally chosen – to cover writers after Kingsley Amis (including Geoffrey Jenkins – for which see File 007).

The Dr Allison who treats Bond after he has been drugged and escapes from Quarterdeck is named for Amis's own doctor – who, incidentally, came up with the terrible torture inflicted on Bond by Colonel Sun.

Amis had written *The James Bond Dossier* (thereby depriving the authors of this book of the title) in 1965, and had critiqued the manuscript of *The Man With the Golden Gun* for Glidrose. In our opinion, this is equal to a lot of the Fleming canon, particularly the sixties novels, and far superior to a lot of what has appeared subsequently. Amis continues some of Fleming's obsessions (Bond being a St George figure against the dragon – Vrakonisi means Dragon Island) and is more explicit than him about sex.

Just a thought about that plot again: something important to Britain is kidnapped, and Bond goes on the trail via a piece of paper with information on it. He arrives in a Mediterranean major town where he first is attacked by and then teams up with a Soviet agent to deal with a third force which is threatening both parties. This could be either *Colonel Sun* or the film of *The Spy Who Loved Me*!

Locations: Windsor and London (UK), Athens and Vrakonisi (Greece), September onwards 196(5?).

Bond's Past Life: In the period since *The Man With the Golden Gun*, Bond has taken a trip to America, and had a 'miserable visit' to Hong Kong in June. John Buchan's novel *The 39 Steps* has haunted Bond since his childhood, a lot of the summer holidays of which he spent in a converted Brixham trawler.

Toys for the Boys: Bond has a midget transmitter in his shoe, along with a picklock, as well as hacksaw blades in his suit. He doesn't use them – and Amis/Markham obviously despises them.

Patronising Lines: 'The Albanians, as a race, are not noted for their beauty.'

Villainous Foibles: Colonel Sun Liang-Tan is a tall man with heavy eye-folds. He is an expert interrogator, loves torture and is unmoved by women. When he speaks English, it's with a weird mixture of dialects.

Von Richter has a muzzle burn on his face (gun, rather than dog, we assume).

Sadism: Bond and Ariadne dispense with two thugs who are following them at the Parthenon in Athens, and there is a great battle between Bond's crew and the boat following them. M has been tortured on his chest, before Bond arrives, and of course, since Colonel Sun believes he is a true sadist, there's a lovely scene for Bond involving his skull being skewered.

Lines to Flick Past: 'That mouth was made to give her brutal kisses, not to become distorted in a grimace of agony; those hands existed to caress her body, not to be stamped on by the torturer's boot.' Well, that settles that, then.

Mistakes Can Be Fatal: Bond talks about his mission against Scaramanga being the previous summer. It wasn't – it was set in the spring.

Reference is made to two assassinations in Japan – but only Blofeld was killed. We only find out what happened to Irma Bunt in 'Blast From the Past' nineteen years after this was written.

Markham tries to place *Colonel Sun* not too far after the Fleming stories – but, as ever, time has marched on and, while all other internal evidence points to this taking place in 1965, Ariadne talks about Oleg Penkovski being shot in 1965, clearly some time in the past. (We suppose this could almost count as a continuity point, given Fleming's notorious weaknesses in this department.)

Why would Bond refer to fuel as 'gas'?

JAMES BOND:
THE AUTHORISED BIOGRAPHY OF 007
(1973)

Starring: The hero – James Bond
                  The villains – various
                  The love interests – various

Written By: John Pearson

Plot: The book is a biography of James Bond from his birth to just after the events of *Colonel Sun*. The premise is that Bond exists, and that M was persuaded to let Ian Fleming write books about him and his exploits to convince SMERSH that he was an invention of the SIS. They did this because SMERSH were out to kill Bond after the events of *Casino Royale*, and the only way to put them off the scent was to persuade them that Bond had been invented as propaganda. By the time they realised he *did* exist, they were too embarrassed to say anything. The events of the book weave in and around those described by Fleming, with the addition of a large amount of extra detail about Bond's early life and what happened to him in between. It ends with Bond being sent by M to confront Irma Bunt (Blofeld's quondam mistress) in Australia, where she is breeding mutant killer desert rats.

Observations: Bond does not speak Arabic.

The 00 section was formed by M in 1950. The holders of the 008 and 0011 codes both died in 1951. Agent 002 was rescued by Bond from Portuguese police HQ in Macao in 1954. Agent 003 was badly injured. The holder of 009 died in 1955 in Hungary. SIS Station P is in Paris. Station N is Cyprus (Nicosia), Station K is in Kingston, Jamaica. Stations H and F are in Finland, Station A is Austria.

There was, perhaps unsurprisingly, an 007 before Bond ('The 007 number has been vacant for some time,' says M). Hey – maybe it's David Niven!

James Bond has a son, also named James, by Kissy Suzuki.

May, who looks after Bond's flat, has the surname McGrath.

There are mentions of too many people to count from past adventures.

My Name Is . . . Haynes (his code name during training); Pieter Zwart (his cover name during one of his first operations).

Bond's Past Life: Bond was born in Germany on 11 November 1920 (making him 77 as of the publication of this book). His mother was Swiss; his father Scottish. He has (or had) a brother named Henry.

Bond's first lover was Marthe de Brandt, a notorious brothel-keeper and occasional spy (neatly explaining both of the predilections Bond was to display in Ian Fleming's books). Bond killed her, having been (mis)informed that she had betrayed both him and Britain. He got the scar on his cheek in the car crash that he arranged for her.

Bond was engaged in 1941 but broke it off. He joined the SIS in 1937 but left in 1946 and spent four years working as a troubleshooter for a group of French bankers before being lured back.

I've Seen That Character Before: Mentions of too many people to count.

Mistakes Can Be Fatal: If Pearson's description of Bond's meteoric rise through Civil Service grades is to be believed, he outranked Bill Tanner by the mid-1950s.

Bond's brother's name is Henry here, but David in the 'juvenile' book *The Adventures of James Bond Junior 003½*.

JOHN STEED –
AN AUTHORISED BIOGRAPHY
VOLUME ONE – JEALOUS IN HONOUR
(1977)

Observations: It's almost, but not quite, pointless mentioning this item, but Bond does appear briefly in it. The book purports to be the authorised biography of British secret agent John Steed (he of *The Avengers* fame), and serves much the same function as John Pearson's *James Bond: The Authorised Biography*. According to Heald, Steed and Bond cross paths at Eton in 1934; there is a statement to the effect that they did not get on, and that they met a number of times in later life.

There was, by the way, no Volume Two.

LICENCE RENEWED (1981)

Starring: The hero – James Bond
The villain – Anton Murik, Laird of Mulcady
The love interest – Lavender 'Dilly' Peacock

Written By: John Gardner

Plot: The SIS have become aware of meetings between Franco Oliviero Queoscriado, an international terrorist, and Anton Murik, a nuclear physicist who left the International Atomic Energy Commission under a cloud. M assigns Bond to investigate.

Bond is checking over Murik's Scottish castle when he is captured by Caber, Murik's very large chief henchman. Murik seems to be taken in by Bond's cover that he is an ex-Army officer looking for mercenary work. Bond bugs Murik's quarters and hears Murik and Franco discussing a plan involving the takeover of 'stations'.

As Laird of Mulcady, Murik hosts Highland Games and persuades Bond to fight Caber. Using knockout gas concealed in his lighter, Bond defeats the giant, and Murik takes him into his confidence. He wants Bond to kill Franco, after Franco has carried out one last task.

Murik's ward, Lavender Peacock, helps Bond to escape but, after a car chase, 007 is recaptured. Despite torture, he maintains his cover story and he is taken with Murik and his party to Perpignan in the South of France, where he manages to escape again. Having realised that Murik intends to take over nuclear power stations, he tries to get a message to M, but is nearly recaptured. Bond realises that the target Murik has given Franco is his ward Lavender Peacock (he wants her dead because she is the true heir to the Mulcady title) and distracts Franco at the critical moment. Bond shoots Franco, but Caber captures him.

Murik tells Bond his full plan: six nuclear power stations are being taken over, and he is demanding $50 billion in diamonds as a ransom. Bond and Lavender are taken aboard a Starlifter aircraft which is serving as Murik's airborne command centre. The reactors are captured according to plan, and Murik delivers his message. Incredibly, the Western world immediately capitulates – but all will be well, as Bond manages to get himself free, and sends the 'mission successful' code which he has deduced. Caber and Bond fight it out in the open cargo bay of the Starlifter – until Lavender stabs Caber, saving the day. Murik, however, escapes.

Bond gets 48 hours to try to capture Murik his own way. With Bill Tanner's assistance, Bond lays a trap at Mulcady Castle for Murik, who has gone back for the papers that show Lavender's inheritance. Despite being speared with a bolt from a crossbow, Murik tries to flee, and Bond disposes of him with an old Gyrojet pistol. Lavender's inheritance is safe . . .

Observations: Bond mentions that his father was a Highlander. He has acquired a cottage near Haslemere, Surrey; although his previous cars are mentioned, he is now driving a Saab 900 Turbo, with modifications (all of which, Gardner is at pains to point out, are real). He has become a connoisseur of high fashion. He has taken to doing karate exercises in the morning. He has stopped using the Walther PPK because of the kidnapping attempt made on Princess Anne in the Mall in 1974. Reference is made to the scar inflicted by the SMERSH agent in *Casino Royale* (see **Mistakes Can Be Fatal**). His cigarette case saved his life from Red Grant's bullet in *From Russia With Love*.

Bond's relationship with the other regular characters is

portrayed quite differently in Gardner's books than in Fleming/Markham. Gardner's M is more avuncular, and there's often by-play between M and Bond at other people's expense. Bond has become a 'blunt instrument' following the disbanding of the 00 section two years before *Licence Renewed* opens, and is an executive officer to M. The friendship between Tanner and Bond picks up from *Colonel Sun* neatly, but, where Fleming would have Bond wondering what M or Tanner's reaction to his actions would be, Gardner shows it to us, occasionally somehow ruining the suspense (we can't imagine the end of *Goldfinger* being nearly so effective if we had known that Felix had received the message).

The sparring with Moneypenny is straight from the films, rather than the books. Bond no longer has a secretary, and, although Gardner correctly uses 'Penny' as Bond's pet name for Miss Moneypenny, this is clearly Lois Maxwell.

Either the SIS has taken on a new cover name (Transworld Export Ltd), or it's a mistake.

Gardner cleverly incorporates the real changes in SMERSH into Bond's fictional world, something that his books do across the board. Unlike Fleming's SIS, Gardner's functions within the 'real' intelligence community, with considerable liaison between the various branches. Sir Richard Duggan heads MI5, while Deputy Assistant Commissioner David Ross is i/c Special Branch. The Prime Minister (sex not given) is involved in final decisions of the COBRA committee (the Cabinet Office Intelligence Committee).

Although Q Branch is still run by Major Boothroyd, he has an assistant, Ann Reilly, known (unfortunately) as Q'ute, who plays a lovely trick on Bond (and us) with expectations of a sixties seduction scene.

Felix Leiter is mentioned obliquely in passing – M says Bond has an old friend in the CIA.

Gardner acknowledges H.R.F. Keating's assistance in the negotiations for him to take on Fleming's mantle.

The final battle between Necros and Bond in *The Living Daylights* (1987) takes place in the cargo bay of a cargo aircraft – as does Caber and Bond's here. The sequence with

Bond's BMW being driven by remote control in *Tomorrow Never Dies* (1997) is a relocation in part of Bond's remote-control driving of the Saab sixteen years earlier. Equally, the scene with the Highland Games between Caber and Bond bears some similarities to the 1967 film of *Casino Royale*.

Locations: London; Scotland; Perpignan, France (June 198? – we would argue for 1981, although there is no mention of the royal wedding).

My Name Is . . . Major James Bond, former Guards and SAS officer.

Bond's Past Life: Since the disbanding of the 00 Section, Bond has carried out four missions as '007', during one of which he 'took out' Achmed Yastaff, a terrorist. In the seventies and early eighties, he has cut back drastically on his alcohol intake, and changed his cigarettes to a low-tar mixture, although still with the three rings. He has just started showing minute flecks of grey hair.

Bond has been to Perpignan on many occasions, the last time three years before this.

He was a devotee of popular music in his school days (are we talking thirties, forties or fifties by now?).

Toys for the Boys: Q Branch supplies a briefcase with a bugging device and surveillance detector; a pen alarm transmitter; a flashlight; and a duplicate Dunhill lighter containing halothane gas. His belts have loads of nifty things like sharp knives and different currencies in them.

Goodbye, Mr Bond: Caber gets the Scots version: 'This is where we say fare ye well – for auld lang syne, Bond.'

Villainous Foibles: Anton Murik stands barely five feet tall, and walks in darting steps like a grounded bird. He collects old weapons and torture instruments and is desperate to be highly regarded as the Laird of Mulcady.

Sadism: Bond has been to the 'Sadist School' near Camberley (easy to get to from his new cottage . . .). The torture sequence seems positively tame compared with Fleming's or Markham's, as if Gardner's heart isn't quite in this bit.

Lines to Flick Past: 'To Bond it felt as though they had both escaped from time and trouble and were floating with increasing joy towards a whirlpool of earthly delights'. So, no orgasm then?

Mistakes Can Be Fatal: The SIS was known as Transworld Consortium in *The Man With the Golden Gun* and *Colonel Sun*. Here, without warning, it's become Transworld Export Ltd.

The letter that was carved on Bond's hand was the Cyrillic letter SM according to *Casino Royale* (not SH as here).

Lavender goes to Bond's room to warn him off. 'I just came as a kind of Cassandra, uttering warnings,' she says. Obviously she wants to be the kind of Cassandra whose warnings are listened to then, rather than the one from Greek mythology whose weren't!

Why does Murik trust Bond initially, just because he's defeated Caber at the Games? It seems oddly out of character. Then again, trust seems to be the watchword of this book. Franco knows he's dealing with someone called 'Warlock' (although he obviously doesn't go and look the word up, as Bond does) who is about to extort money from major governments – and he quite happily accepts that he's going to be paid later? Come on, this guy is supposed to be a highly respected international terrorist!

Bond has been to Perpignan before. He knows that's where they've landed. So why is he surprised to find that the time is an hour ahead of Britain?

There seems to be a surprising lack of concern in Europe at Murik's message being blasted on all radio and TV channels in different languages. It's a neat trick, when you think about it – there's almost an implication that everyone will hear it in their own language.

And why did Murik keep the incriminating papers about Lavender's inheritance? Why not just destroy them?

FOR SPECIAL SERVICES (1982)

Starring: The hero – James Bond
The villain – A new Blofeld and SPECTRE
The love interest – Cedar Leiter

Written By: John Gardner

Plot: Bond is summoned by M to meet Felix Leiter's daughter, Cedar, a CIA undercover agent. The CIA are investigating Markus Bismaquer, an ambitious millionaire who may have a connection with a revitalised SPECTRE operating under a relative of the dead Blofeld. Posing as Professor and Mrs Penbrunner – possessors of newly discovered Hogarth prints which Bismaquer will covet – Bond and Cedar travel to New York. Bismaquer is unlikely to resist the opportunity of purchasing the prints, allowing them a closer look at his operation. After they are attacked, Bond decides to accompany 'Mrs Penbrunner' under his own name, ostensibly as her bodyguard.

Bond and Cedar are welcomed to Bismaquer's ranch by Walter Luxor, Bismaquer's right-hand man, where they are introduced to Bismaquer and his wife, Nena. Bismaquer challenges Bond to a duel by car for the prints – Bond will race against Walter Luxor the next day. That night, Bond's cabin is filled with deadly harvester ants. Bond kills them by blowing it up.

Bond defeats Luxor in the race, despite the latter cheating. Somehow, during this, Cedar discovers that she and Bond have been identified. Bond still goes to a prearranged tryst with Nena; they make love, then Bond goes off to spy on a meeting held in Bismaquer's Conference Centre. It's a SPECTRE meeting, chaired by a relative of Blofeld, and Bond discovers that SPECTRE's target is the military satellite network controlled by the USA. Using an ice cream which makes the eater susceptible to orders, SPECTRE will take over the NORAD (North American Air Defence) base in Colorado.

Bond is captured by SPECTRE and hypnotised into

believing he is General James A. Banker. 'Banker' pulls a surprise inspection of NORAD – in reality, allowing SPECTRE's senior men to infiltrate the base. Bond suddenly switches sides – his hypnotic conditioning having been broken by Bismaquer, who finds him sexually attractive and doesn't want him to be killed – and orders the NORAD troops to resist Blofeld's attack. During the pitched battle, Nena swoops in to collect Bond and takes him to her house on the bayou. To his horror, Bond sees Nena kill Bismaquer for helping Bond break free of the hypnosis, and she reveals she is Blofeld's illegitimate daughter. After a fight, she tries to escape across the bayou, but is crushed by her own pet pythons. Felix arrives and gives her the *coup de grâce*. Bond and Cedar head off on what Bond is determined will be a platonic vacation . . .

Observations: Bond is carrying on playing musical guns – he now has a Heckler & Koch VP70. His cigarettes are now made for him by H. Simmons of Burlington Arcade, London.

Q'ute, Bill Tanner, M and Miss Moneypenny all make passing appearances, while Felix Leiter turns up at the end.

Obviously, there are a lot of references to SPECTRE, and its founder, Ernst Stavro Blofeld. We haven't seen any evidence of a family before (in fact, according to *Thunderball*, he was meant to be uninterested in sex). Because, until virtually the end of the book, we still do not know for sure who is going by the name of Blofeld, Gardner is careful not to use personal pronouns which would give the game away. However, the very lack of use of 'his' or 'her' draws attention to itself.

There's also a checklist of previous girlfriends of Bond, listed in a slightly odd order, culminating with Tracy di Vicenzo (with whom Gardner starts what seems to be an almost unhealthy obsession on Bond's part, given that Fleming and Markham had Bond moving on . . .).

The network of informers in America is reminiscent of Mr Big's outfit in *Live and Let Die*, to whom Gardner pays credit.

Bond's Saab has a secret compartment – as does his BMW in *Tomorrow Never Dies* – while the sequence between Bond and Cedar in the elevator is reminiscent of the sequence in *A View to a Kill* between Bond and Stacey.

Locations: London briefly, then Louisiana, New York and down through the United States to Texas.

My Name Is ... Professor Joseph Penbrunner, an expert in rare prints; John Bergin; General James A. Banker (under hypnosis).

Bond's Past Life: Bond's housemaster during his two halfs at Eton was so memorable he can still imitate him.

Toys for the Boys: Bond carries what becomes his standard kit for the Gardner books – a briefcase crammed with useful items from Q Branch. This includes a Smith and Wesson 'Highway Patrolman', steel picklocks and other burglarious tools, padded leather gloves, detonators, plastic explosive and a length of fuse, and 35 feet of nylon half-inch rope with a couple of miniaturised grappling hooks.

Villainous Foibles: This Blofeld is a sadist. Walter Luxor looks like one of the walking dead, after being rebuilt from top to bottom following a crash; Markus is bisexual; Nena has only one breast.

Sadism: The giant python and its wonderful way of killing people – as the wayward De Luntz discovers at the start of the book.

Lines to Flick Past: ' "Late to bed, early to rise," Q'ute giggled, her hand moving under the bedclothes to add point to her humour'; 'Later Bond felt that he must have looked like a ninny ...'

It's Only a Book: Gardner reacts through Bond to some of the criticisms levelled at *Licence Renewed*: 'On his last mission, he had been severely criticised for using an old, yet highly efficient Browning.'

Mistakes Can Be Fatal: We always thought that the CIA couldn't (or strictly, shouldn't) operate domestically in the United States – so how come Cedar is assigned, and other operatives have been working on the Bismaquer case? (Then again, Bond isn't supposed to operate in Britain, yet that rule's broken quite often.)

Cedar recalls her father's description of Bond as being like Hoagy Carmichael – but the conversation was between Mathis and Vesper in *Casino Royale*, not Mathis and Felix.

No American hotel would ever have a thirteenth floor.

Why does Bond/Gardner refer to the two guards as the Dracula brothers – they're seven foot tall and look as if they should have a bolt through the side of their necks? Wrong horror film!

Before the car race, Bond wants to wish Walter luck, but is prevented. Yet, just before the race, they wish each other luck.

When does Cedar overhear all the useful bits of information she passes to Bond?

ICEBREAKER (1983)

Starring: The hero – James Bond
The villains – Kolya Mosolov and Aarne
   Tudeer, a.k.a. Count Konrad von Gloda
The love interest – Paula Vacker

Written By: John Gardner

Plot: Bond is briefed about 'Icebreaker', a joint operation against the National Socialist Action Army (NSAA), which is making a name for itself by murdering people connected with the Communist Party. At the meeting session in Portugal, Bond discovers that he is working with Nicolai 'Kolya' Mosolov of the KGB, Brad Tirpitz of the CIA and Rivke Ingber of Mossad, and that the probable leader of the NSAA is one Count Konrad von Gloda. The NSAA is being supplied with weapons from Alakurtii, a Russian military station in the

Arctic Circle, and Mosolov wants Bond to accompany him across the border on to Soviet soil to get proof.

An attempt is made on Bond's life with snowploughs as he drives to the rendezvous in Helsinki, where he discovers that Rivke is really Anni Tudeer – daughter of ex-SS officer Arne Tudeer. Alliances are forged as both Rivke and Brad try to prove their good standing to Bond – and Rivke tells him that she thinks 'von Gloda' is her father. Before they can go further, Rivke is injured in an explosion on the ski slopes, but, when Bond tries to locate the hospital to which she was sent, there is no trace of her.

The remnants of Icebreaker agree to continue, as Bond grows increasingly suspicious of Mosolov's motives, particularly when the position of von Gloda's hideout does not tally with the map London has supplied him. They head towards the Finnish–Russian border on snow scooters, but Tirpitz is caught in another explosion. Mosolov leads Bond into an ambush – where a girlfriend of Bond's, Paula Vacker, is waiting to lead him to the new Führer, Count von Gloda. Tirpitz is alive, and is the Martin Bormann to von Gloda's Hitler. Mosolov has delivered Bond to von Gloda for interrogation because one of the NSAA has been captured by the SIS and von Gloda needs to know what he has said. Bond will then be handed over to the former SMERSH to be interrogated.

Everyone is now double- and triple-crossing everyone else: on Mosolov's orders, the Russians bomb von Gloda's headquarters but the Count escapes. Bond and Paula, really an undercover Finnish Intelligence officer, eventually get back to Helsinki, where Mosolov has another try at capturing Bond: SMERSH want to interrogate him, then use him as a swap for some of their people who have been caught at GCHQ. Bond kills Mosolov, then deals with von Gloda as he is about to leave the country. In one last twist, Tirpitz turns out to be a genuine CIA agent after all.

Observations: Bond is interested in sailing, jazz and the books of Eric Ambler (author of *Epitaph for a Spy*). He gets sent on at least one gruelling field exercise each year. He is friends with the driving experts Erik Carlsson and Simo Lampinen (real people). His gun has changed yet again: it's now a Heckler & Koch P7. He has learnt to speak Russian since *Colonel Sun*, and has an eclectic knowledge of poetry.

Gardner misquotes M's comments to 007 about the unofficial troubleshooting from *Licence Renewed*. Brad Tirpitz uses messages from both Felix and Cedar Leiter to prove his bona fides. Bond still has nightmares about Tracy's death (*OHMSS*). He recalls Sir Hugo Drax (*Moonraker*), Auric Goldfinger, Ernst Stavro Blofeld and 'his relative'; and dreams of Royale-les-Eaux, scene of *Casino Royale*, both as it had been when he was a child, and when he was a younger man.

M (whose disapproval of Bond's womanising comes to the fore again), Miss Moneypenny, Bill Tanner and May are all present and correct.

Locations: Libya, London, Helsinki, Funchal (Portugal), and near the Finnish–Russian border.

Bond's Past Life: Bond was in Rome three years ago, and then in New York and Dieppe. He was in the Falklands during the 1982 conflict, even appearing briefly on television. He performed a complicated surveillance and character assassination on a Romanian diplomat in Paris two years earlier alongside Cliff Dudley. He has driven through East Germany to West Berlin in the wintertime.

Toys for the Boys: Bond carries his standard Q Branch briefcase (as per *For Special Services*). He also has a Speedline towing pack with 275 metres of cable and a Ruger Redhawk ·44 Magnum added to the refinements on the Saab 900 Turbo.

Villainous Foibles: Von Gloda appears to be very charismatic, with glittering grey eyes that bore into the back of the head (not his own obviously). He believes himself to be the next Führer, when he's really only a former small-time SS officer.

Sadism: Bond is tortured by immersion into the freezing cold of the Arctic.

Lines to Flick Past: Paula has 'lips shaped for one purpose'. So she doesn't talk, then?

'The warnings were cauterised in the conflagration as their lips touched.'

It's Only a Book: Bond's Martini, 'because of certain publications, had become a standard with many people'.

Mistakes Can Be Fatal: 'M never used strong language' – we suppose it depends on your definition of strong, but by the standards of the fifties M was a proper swearer.

Why is Bond surprised that they might be working with Moscow Centre? He has done so on at least one occasion in the past (*Colonel Sun*).

Why does Bond waste time trying to contact the Service resident in Helsinki when he knows that von Gloda has disposed of him?

ROLE OF HONOUR (1984)

Starring: The hero – James Bond
The villains – Dr Jay Autem Holy and
   Tamil Rahani of SPECTRE
The love interest – Percy Proud

Written By: John Gardner

Plot: When Bond inherits a large legacy from his Uncle Bruce, it is used as an excuse for him to leave the Service, allowing him to operate undercover. M wants him to investigate the late Dr Jay Autem Holy, a computer whiz kid who apparently died in a plane crash alongside General Rolling Joe Zwingli, a hardline career soldier. Holy's 'widow', CIA agent Persephone 'Percy' Proud, is sure that Professor Jason St John-Finnes is really Holy and is responsible for a spate of computerised crimes.

Bond is briefed about computer programming, then inveigles an invitation to meet St John-Finnes, his wife, Dazzle, and two other programmers, Cindy Chalmers (another CIA agent) and Peter Amadeus, for lunch. Cindy gives Bond evidence proving that St John-Finnes is behind the crimes, and mentions the Balloon Game, a major operation that is coming up.

When Bond tries to return to London, his car is forced off the road, but not before he has time to post the computer disks with the evidence. He awakes in 'Erewhon', a Mediterranean training ground for terrorists, run by 'Simon'. Bond meets Tamil Rahani, an electronics tycoon whom he has previously spotted with the supposedly late General Zwingli near St John-Finnes's headquarters. After disposing of a group of 'redundant' terrorists sent against him in a test, he is trusted and returned to Britain.

St John-Finnes tells Bond that his principals, whom he later reveals are SPECTRE, needed money: hence the crimes. They require Bond to get them the radio frequency used by the American President to send critical messages during an emergency. According to Holy, SPECTRE already has the frequency by which it can control the Russian forces, but not the American ones – with both, it can disarm the world. Bond is allowed to go to London to collect the frequency and takes the opportunity to meet with M: together they realise that a summit conference is taking place in Geneva, and the Goodyear Europa airship is to fly a goodwill mission over-head. If the airship is above the hotel, and a radio signal is sent from that, it will seem to the satellites as if it has come from the leaders in the hotel. Bond is given the frequency, but is hijacked on the M4 and taken to Berne.

Bond is needed now to act as co-pilot of the hijacked Goodyear, with Holy, Zwingli, Simon and Rahani on board. Holy's plan is to use the radio frequency to send the 'Swords into Ploughshares' command, and destroy all nuclear weapons. The US command is sent, but Tamil Rahani chooses the propitious moment to reveal that he is the new head of SPECTRE, and he will not be sending the equivalent Soviet message. Devastated, General Zwingli attacks Rahani, but is shot, as is Holy. Rahani then parachutes out, believing he has succeeded, although in fact the frequencies have already been countermanded. Bond and Percy go on leave, but are tracked by SPECTRE and go their separate ways, realising they can't be together until Rahani and SPECTRE are stopped.

Observations: Bond inherits a fortune from his uncle in Australia (maybe he met him when chasing Irma Bunt . . .?), and buys a Bentley Mulsanne Turbo. His service number was CH 4539876. Yes, he's got yet another new gun: the ASP 9mm.

Bond's mind goes back to his wife Tracy yet again. Fort Knox (scene of *Goldfinger*) is mentioned in passing. SPECTRE's return prompts memories of former battles. Major Boothroyd, Q'ute, Moneypenny, M and Bill Tanner all appear.

A section now handles the Service's accounts. It's changed from *Casino Royale*, when the Quartermaster section handled it. We suppose they've got enough to do now, inventing gadgets. Century House, then the home of SIS, is referred to as 'the mystery building'.

SPECTRE have become pro-communist, whereas previously they were above such things.

Locations: London, Monte Carlo, Banbury Cross (Oxfordshire), 'Erewhon' in the Middle East, Berne, and above Lake Geneva (Switzerland).

My Name Is . . . Gamesman, and, for the first time, Predator, a code name Bond adopts from here on in Gardner's books.

Bond's Past Life: Bond has a previously unknown Uncle Bruce, his father's brother (see **Mistakes Can Be Fatal**). He first visited Lake Geneva aged sixteen, and stayed with friends in Montreux, having an affair with a waitress and developing a taste for Campari-soda. He worked with Tony Denton on a 'bring-'em-back-alive trip' from Helsinki.

Toys for the Boys: Bond has his briefcase, and a phone in the new car. Otherwise the toys are all 'state-of-the-art' computers.

Lines to Flick Past: Gardner seems to be continuing Fleming's antipathy towards gay characters: Peter Amadeus has 'a pedantic streak crossed with occasional glimpses of verbal viciousness that would have been the only hint of his sexual predilection, had he not, as it turned out, been so blatantly honest about it'.

'Rahani's laugh had all the genuine warmth of an angry cobra.' Does this actually tell us anything?

It's Only a Book: Rahani makes reference to the *Mastermind* catchphrase, 'I've started so I'll finish'.

Mistakes Can Be Fatal: So, Mr Bond, you have an uncle? According to *You Only Live Twice*, Bond left no family. This appears to have come about from John Pearson's *James Bond: The Authorised Biography*.

SPECTRE goes to all this trouble to take over the Goodyear field, and the airship – and then doesn't have a pilot available? Some very bad planning on Rahani's part here – he almost deserves to fail!

NOBODY LIVES FOR EVER (1986)

Starring: The hero – James Bond
             The villains – Tamil Rahani and SPECTRE
             The love interest – Principessa Sukie Tempesta

Written By: John Gardner

Plot: Bond is driving across Europe to collect May from her convalesence at Klinik Mozart, a nursing home in Austria, but violence seems to dog his path. He rescues the Principessa Sukie Tempesta from being mugged, and discovers the body of an underworld enforcer. Bond is contacted by Bill Tanner, who tells him to stay in Strasbourg and await the Service Resident from Rome, Steve Quinn. On his arrival,

Quinn tells Bond that a macabre head-hunt is going on for 007, the dying wish of the SPECTRE leader Tamil Rahani. Representatives from many criminal and political organisations are vying for the prize.

May and a visiting Moneypenny are taken hostage by one of the many sets of people attempting to kill Bond, in an attempt to flush him out into the open. Bond, with Sukie and a friend of hers, Nanette Norrich, reluctantly in tow, heads straight for the Klinik Mozart to search for clues.

Nannie Norrich turns out to be head of Norrich Universal Bodyguards: her assignment is to protect Sukie. Before they can reach Salzburg, they are attacked, and then arrested by a corrupt policeman, known as Der Haken, who wants to claim the prize for himself. However, someone else deals with Der Haken before Bond frees himself. The trail leads to Paris, but before he can leave Bond has to kill a vampire bat that someone (probably SPECTRE) has left in his room. In search of more clues, Bond goes out to the Klinik, where he finds May's doctor, Kirchtum, under threat from Steve Quinn, who is in fact a KGB agent on loan to SMERSH. Bond turns the tables, leaving Kirchtum guarding Quinn, and discovers that his real destination should be Florida. He collects the women, and sends another agent on with the Bentley to Paris to throw SPECTRE off the scent.

On his arrival in Miami, Bond finds Kirchtum and Quinn, very much allies, waiting for him. They take him out to Key West, but Nannie and Sukie rescue him. Bond prepares to swim to Shark Island, which he deduces is SPECTRE's headquarters. He evades the security around the island, and reaches Rahani's bedroom – but is stopped from killing the dying leader by Nannie, who has drugged Sukie and headed out. Thanks to tools secreted in his waistband, Bond is able to escape from the cell he's placed in, and rigs Rahani's bed so it will explode when the bedhead is raised so the supine leader can watch Bond being guillotined. All goes according to Bond's plan: Rahani is blown up, Nannie guillotined, May and Moneypenny rescued, and Sukie brings the cavalry. Bond stays on Key West for 'remedial treatment' . . .

Observations: Bond had a very Calvinistic upbringing. Royale-les-Eaux gets a name check, and M wonders if Bond will go to the Caribbean, one of his usual haunts. Bond's love of jazz is mentioned again. While M and Bill Tanner play their usual roles, May and Miss Moneypenny become central characters to the plot.

SMERSH join the head-hunt, as do the Union Corse, whose leader in *OHMSS*, Marc-Ange Draco (also Bond's father-in-law), is dead. This prompts yet another mention of Tracy.

Steve Quinn is the Service Resident in Rome, but has been working for SMERSH.

SPECTRE is masquerading as 'La Société pour la Promotion de l'Écologie et de la Civilisation' – bit of a giveaway, isn't it? They are based on Shark Island – which appeared in their plans in an alternative dimension (*Warhead*). Bond, of course, has been to a different Shark Island in *Live and Let Die*.

Inspector Heinrich Osten is known as Der Haken. We thought we'd make this clear here, just in case you miss one of the thousands of times this point is made in the text.

The title of this book in the original editions is *Nobody Lives For Ever* (four words). In later listings, it's become *Nobody Lives Forever*.

Locations: Belgium, France, Germany, Switzerland, Florida.

My Name Is . . . Predator; James Boldman, company director.

James Bond, Fashion Victim: Even Nannie acknowledges that Bond looks like a black Kermit the Frog in his diving costume.

Bond's Past Life: As a young man, he had lazed around the Lake Maggiore area. He was in Strasbourg at least three years earlier.

Toys for the Boys: Ann Reilly has come up with The Toolkit, with miniature screwdrivers, picklocks, a battery and connectors and miniature explosives, all of which fit inside a belt.

Makes the briefcase a tad unnecessary. Bond's suitcase has a section where he can transport his gun unnoticed. And the waistband of his slacks has secret pockets to hide picklocks etc.

Villainous Foibles: Tamil Rahani is dying as a result of cancer brought on by a jar to his back during the parachute jump at the end of *Role of Honour*. His dying wish is to have Bond's head.

Der Haken gained his nickname from his use of a butcher's hook as a torture weapon when he was a young Nazi.

Sadism: Der Haken's death is most appropriate, and very gruesome. May and Moneypenny are both tortured. Well, Gardner did have to make up for the lack of sadism in *Role of Honour*, didn't he? And the end proposed for Bond – a trip to La Guillotine – is described with a great deal of relish.

Lines to Flick Past: 'Bond always mistrusted people of short stature, knowing their tendency to overcompensate with ruthless pushiness . . .' We're glad that we're both over average height, then.

Mistakes Can Be Fatal: Even Gardner acknowledges that Der Haken should have taken Bond's belt – no policeman would leave him with it, even without knowing about its extra properties.

Can you tell from dial settings on a radio that its target is 'a long way away'?

Bond is to use his 'Universal Export Passport B'? Hmm – are they quite sure that a twenty-year-old passport will be any use? The Service stopped using Universal Export by 1963.

NO DEALS, MR BOND (1987)

Starring: The hero – James Bond
          The villain – General Konstantin (Kolya)
              Nikolaevich Chernov
          The love interest – Ebbie Heritage

Written By: John Gardner

Plot: Five years ago, James Bond was instrumental in recovering a team of undercover agents from East Germany after their cover was blown. Their mission had been to seduce five specific foreign agents and either extract secrets from them or persuade them to defect. Now, two of them have been found murdered and their bodies mutilated. Someone is taking revenge.

M asks Bond to track down the three remaining agents in their new lives, ensure their safety and stop the murders. For reasons we discover later (one of the agents is believed to be a traitor, and M is facing calls for his resignation over his mismanagement of the whole affair), Bond will have to operate unofficially and without help. He locates the first agent – now called Heather Dare – and foils an attempt on her life. Together they fly to Eire to locate the second agent – now called Ebbie Heritage – but are captured by Heather's 'target', Colonel Maxim Smolin of the GRU (Soviet military intelligence). Smolin has captured Ebbie as well, but tells Bond that he was 'turned' by Heather in East Germany, and is a double agent working for M now. The KGB have been tipped off, and are wiping out the five British agents before turning their attention to Smolin. General Konstantin Nikolaevich Chernov – Chief Investigating Officer of what used to be called SMERSH – arrives in Eire and captures them all. Bond and Ebbie escape and follow Chernov to Hong Kong, where the fifth agent – now called Jungle Baisley – and his East German lover Susanne Dietrich have fled. Chernov captures absolutely everyone and forces Bond to take part in a bizarre gladiatorial contest. Bond kills the 'gladiators' and takes Chernov captive, having exposed Heather Dare as a traitor.

Observations: M turns up (believing that 007 doesn't know much poetry), as does Ann Reilly, May and Miss Moneypenny. There are references to Blades Club, Sir Hugo Drax (*Moonraker*) and Bond's marriage (*OHMSS*). Chernov used to head SMERSH.

The book takes place before the break-up of the Soviet Union but after the agreement that Hong Kong would be handed back to China, placing it after 1982.

The first UK edition of the book is dedicated 'To my dear friend, Tony Adamus'. The first US edition of the book is dedicated 'To my good friend Tony Adamus, with thanks'. Another difference between the editions is listed under **Lines to Flick Past** below.

No Deals, Mr Bond is the last Bond novel to be published in Britain under the Jonathan Cape imprint (the first was *Casino Royale*). It's also the last Bond novel to appear in the small, indeed discreet, hardback size that had been used since *Casino Royale*. From the next book on, Hodder and Stoughton would be publishing them in a larger size with more vibrant covers.

Locations: The Baltic, London, Eire and Hong Kong.

My Name Is . . . Bond's code name on the East German retrieval operation was Seahawk. During the course of the book, he uses his 'James Boldman' identity yet again. You would think the intelligence services of the world would be getting wise to that one by now. His official code name when dealing with the Irish Special Branch is 'Jacko B' (how original).

Bond's Past Life: Five years ago, Bond helped five under-cover agents get out of East Germany by submarine after their cover was blown. A year later, Bond took part in an operation in Eire, near Crossmaglen. Two years later he was in Hong Kong, and also in Paris.

Toys for the Boys: Bond has a handy survival pack provided by Q Branch which contains a flare, a grenade, a garrotte and a knife, but it's hardly the cutting edge of research. Oh, he also has a pen which fires metal darts.

Sadism: Chernov is prepared to rip out the agents' tongues *'pour encourager les autres'*.

Lines to Flick Past: The first US edition of the book described the 'cold wetness of the Baltic'. As opposed to the warm dryness of the Adriatic, we presume. The line is changed to the 'cold of the Baltic' in the first UK edition.

It's Only a Book: The book contains a veiled reference to Chapman Pincher, a writer of books and newspaper articles on intelligence matters. Chernov also mentions to Bond that 'You too have been resurrected, against much criticism, I gather.'

Mistakes Can Be Fatal: Gardner claims that a poison called Racin is favoured by the Bulgarian secret service. In fact, it's ricin (the poison they used to murder Georgi Markov).

A Soviet thug towards the end of the book is called Semen. No doubt a fine old Russian name.

At the end of the book, Heather Dare indicates that she stayed so close to Bond throughout the book so she could expose Smolin as a traitor. But hang on – earlier in the book Smolin tells Bond that Heather persuaded him to become a traitor over five years before. If she already knew, why not just tell Chernov? Why go to all the effort of following Bond around?

SCORPIUS (1988)

Starring: The hero – James Bond
            The villain – Vladimir Scorpius
                (otherwise known as Father Valentine)
            The love interest – Harriet Horner

Written By: John Gardner

Plot: Arms dealer Vladimir Scorpius has reinvented himself as Father Valentine, head of the Society of Meek Ones – a religious cult based in England. In fact, Scorpius is using hallucinogenic drugs and his own hypnotic powers to turn Society members into a group of assassins who are motivated only by religious fervour – a religious fervour he controls. For reasons that remain maddeningly unclear, he plans to disrupt global politics by killing prominent politicians, culminating in the assassination of the Prime Minister and the President of the USA. Following this he will bring the Western stock markets crashing down.

Bond is brought into the plot when the daughter of an old friend is killed after apparently escaping from the Society of Meek Ones. Repeated attempts on Bond's life indicate a mole close to M, so Bond strikes out alone. Together with an American Internal Revenue Service agent, Harriet Horner, he gets close to Scorpius, but the villain captures Harriet and escapes to his base in a swamp in South Carolina, having set his assassination plan in motion. Bond follows him, and deliberately gets captured in order to rescue Harriet and discover Scorpius's plans.

During his daring escape attempt across the snake-infested swamp, Harriet is killed, and Bond discovers that the CIA were about to storm the place anyway. Bond kills Scorpius and, after discovering the identity of the assassin primed to kill the President and the Prime Minister, foils that plan too.

Observations: Bond actually gets married again, albeit under the rather dubious auspices of Father Valentine, to Harriet Horner, although he is widowed again shortly thereafter. We also get veiled references to Bond's mental problems in *The Man With the Golden Gun*, to his love of jazz and to Tracy. He was involved with the Tamil Rahani business (*Nobody Lives For Ever*) less than two years before.

M and Bill Tanner (M's Chief of Staff) turn up, as do Ann Reilly and Sir James Molony (the Secret Intelligence Service's medical expert). Bond's faithful housekeeper May reappears. Miss Moneypenny and her deputy Miss Boyd are also present and correct.

M's office has been redecorated some time earlier. There are now portraits of his predecessors on the walls.

The Secret Service's rest-and-recuperation home has been

moved from Kent to Surrey (although, in *Icebreaker*, they couldn't afford any other buildings).

Britain has a female Prime Minister in *Scorpius*, and a senior Tory politician (Lord Mills), who has twice been Prime Minister, is assassinated. This immediately takes us out of the 'real' world, as the only men to have twice been Prime Minister in living memory are the Conservatives' Winston Churchill and Labour's Harold Wilson.

The Prime Minister has called a general election for 11 June. Since elections are traditionally held on Thursdays, we can date this book to 1987.

Bond makes a disparaging reference to Peter Wright's exposé of the intelligence services, *Spycatcher*.

Locations: England, South Carolina and Washington, DC.

My Name Is . . . Bond uses his regular code name Predator, and also the operational code name Harvester One. He also uses the James Boldman identity.

James Bond, Fashion Victim: Bond is forced at one point to wear nylon socks – something he had promised himself he would never do.

Bond's Past Life: Bond's friendship with Bill Tanner stretches back to their days together as midshipmen in the Navy, which, while not directly contradicting Fleming, is at variance with what he implies.

Villainous Foibles: Scorpius has strong, if undisciplined, hypnotic powers, helped by his 'black-as-night' eyes.

Sadism: Acting against orders, Bond forces Scorpius to walk into a swamp containing poisonous snakes and watches as the man is repeatedly bitten.

It's Only a Book: Bond watches *The Untouchables* while flying to America. Sean Connery is one of his favourite actors.

Mistakes Can Be Fatal: Bond (i.e. Gardner) treats Sir James Molony as if he were a psychiatrist, but he is a neurologist. There is a difference.

Bill Tanner suggests that Wolkovsky, the CIA liaison in London, should be brought in. A few moments later, M announces this as totally his idea.

Bond thinks he might be lucky to get a few lines in the obit column in *The Times*. Did no one ever show him the full-page spread that M wrote in 1963?

WIN, LOSE OR DIE (1989)

Starring: The hero – James Bond
The villain – Bassam Baradj,
    formerly known as Robert Besavitsky
The love interest – Beatrice Maria da Ricci

Written By: John Gardner

Plot: A fortuitous communications intercept alerts M to a terrorist plot directed against a joint British–Soviet naval operation code-named Landsea '89. The terrorists are a new organisation called BAST (the Brotherhood for Anarchy and Secret Terror), and they appear to know that Landsea '89 is a cover for a high-level summit meeting between the leaders of Britain, America and the Soviet Union. Bond is transferred back to the Navy and assigned to bodyguard duties on the ship that is to host the meeting, but BAST know who he is and, regarding him as a threat, attempt to kill him.

M sends Bond to Italy to bring BAST out into the open, but the plot backfires and a British agent (and Bond's lover), Beatrice da Ricci, is apparently killed. Another agent – Clover Pennington – tells Bond that da Ricci was a member of BAST, but Pennington is the real BAST agent. Bond and Pennington return to the ship, where the summit starts, but the terrorists infiltrate it and take the world leaders hostage. BAST's leader – Bassam Baradj – demands six hundred billion pounds for the safe return of Thatcher, Bush and Gorbachev. Baradj is actually Robert Besavitsky, a con artist who has set up a fake terrorist organisation in order to make money, but his scheme backfires when the British, American and Soviet governments refuse to pay. Bond and Beatrice, who faked her death to allow Cat, a BAST leader, to get near Bond, track Besavitsky to Gibraltar and kill him.

Observations: Bond is promoted from commander to captain in this book. He's gone off turkey as well as beef now.

M, who has somehow acquired a daughter and some grandchildren, Bill Tanner and M's faithful servants Mr and Mrs Davison turn up for the first (but not the last) time. Wonder if anyone told them what happened to their predecessors (*Colonel Sun*)?

Internal evidence sets the book firmly in the last months of 1988 and the first few months of 1989.

Margaret Thatcher, George Bush and Mikhail Gorbachev all appear. Thatcher refers to the events of *Scorpius*, while Bush, who was once Director of the CIA, mentions Bond's old friend Felix Leiter (too many books to mention). Bond also thinks about his marriage (*OHMSS*).

The book contains scenes with a Harrier jump jet and scenes on Gibraltar – just like the 1987 film *The Living Daylights*.

Locations: Somerset, Gibraltar, the Mediterranean, Naples and minor scenes in Portugal.

My Name Is . . . Predator.

James Bond, Fashion Victim: Well, he's back in uniform again.

Bond's Past Life: Bond's last Christmas with his parents was spent on Lago Lugano. Gardner implies that his parents died shortly after Christmas.

Bond qualified as a Naval pilot before joining the Secret Intelligence Service, and kept up his proficiency on jets and helicopters during his time with them. Gardner strongly indicates that Bond took an active role in the Falklands campaign, probably as a Naval pilot. During the course of *Win, Lose or Die* he goes through a conversion course for the Sea Harrier jump jet. He's been to Ischia on R and R before.

Patronising Lines: 'I have to be honest with you, Clover, I've always had great reservations about young women with either loud voices, or runaway tongues.'

'. . . I personally think of it as bad luck – women on a Naval vessel.'

Villainous Foibles: The four leaders of BAST are known as the Man, the Cat, the Viper and the Snake, but they are a remarkably boring lot.

Mistakes Can Be Fatal: Gardner states that Bond's work in the Falklands conflict has never been acknowledged, yet in *Icebreaker* we learnt that he was even spotted on television!

According to *OHMSS*, M is not married and hates all the trappings of Christmas.

BROKENCLAW (1990)

Starring: The hero – James Bond
The villain – Lee Fu-Chu
The love interest – Sue Chi-Ho
(known as Chi-Chi)

Written By: John Gardner

Plot: Lee Fu-Chu, the leading Chinese intelligence agent in the USA, has obtained details of a system for tracking military submarines (code-named LORDS) and a similar system for protecting submarines from the system (code-named LORDS DAY). He intends passing the information on to the Chinese Government for a large sum of money, and Bond is sent to infiltrate his organisation disguised as the Chinese agent sent to verify the information.

While in Lee's domain, Bond discovers that Operation Jericho, a Chinese plot to destabilise the US stock market by hacking into the stock-exchange computers, is about to be launched. He leads M and the CIA in, but Lee escapes.

Later, Lee kidnaps Bond's lover – CIA agent Sue Chi-Ho – and Bond has to travel to an Indian reservation and face Lee in mortal combat to win her back.

Observations: Bond learnt to lip-read thanks to Ebbie Heritage after the events of *No Deals, Mr Bond*. He is superstitious about the quote 'Eat, drink and be merry, for tomorrow we die', and anything from Shakespeare's Scottish play. The events of *Thunderball* and *Live and Let Die* are briefly referred to.

M uses the cypher Mandarin (it's an improvement on Mother). Bill Tanner and Ann Reilly also turn up. We meet Bill Orr, one of the Service doctors (has Sir James retired?), Brian Cogger, known as the Scrivener, who provides cover documentation, and Mr Franks, one of the Service's interrogators.

Brokenclaw takes place about a year after *Win, Lose or Die*, placing it in late 1989 or early 1990.

A similar submarine tracking system was used in the film version of *The Spy Who Loved Me*. The plot to destabilise the US economy was also used by Gardner in *Scorpius*, although it was the British stock market at risk in that book.

Locations: British Columbia, the area around San Francisco and Washington State.

My Name Is . . . Bond's code name for the operation is Custodian. He also takes on the identity of Chinese agent Peter Argentbright, otherwise known by the code names Peter Piper and Peter Abelard.

James Bond, Fashion Victim: Well, that depends whether being stripped naked and having your private parts smeared with rancid animal fat counts as a fashion statement.

Bond's Past Life: Bond lost his virginity when he was fourteen. Well, he would, wouldn't he? He's been to San Francisco before.

Villainous Foibles: The thumb of Lee Fu-Chu's left hand is on the wrong side of his palm (hence he is known as Brokenclaw Lee). Essentially, he has two right hands. He keeps a pack of wolves to which he throws people who betray him.

Sadism: Both Wanda and Chi-Chi are tortured, although we see only the results. Bond and Lee go through an agonisingly painful and protracted American Indian initiation ceremony which involves heavy stones being attached by thongs to the skin of their backs and thighs.

Mistakes Can Be Fatal: According to this book, Bond lost his virginity when he was fourteen, but according to Ian Fleming's short story 'From a View to a Kill', he lost it when he was sixteen.

THE MAN FROM BARBAROSSA (1991)

Starring: The hero – James Bond
                   The villain – General Yevgeny Yuskovitch
                   The love interest – Nina Bibikova

Written By: John Gardner

Plot: A new terrorist organisation calling themselves 'the Scales of Justice' kidnap an elderly man from New Jersey. They issue an ultimatum, stating that the man is in reality a Nazi war criminal who committed atrocities against Soviet Jews, and that if the Soviet authorities do not agree to place him on trial then the Scales of Justice will kill a series of high-ranking Soviet officials.

James Bond and Mossad agent Pete Natkowitz are sent to Moscow to cooperate with KGB agent Boris Stepakov. Stepakov has discovered that two British members of the Scales of Justice are flying to Moscow, and has requested help in substituting doubles. Bond and Natkowitz, together with Stepakov's own agent Nina Bibikova, are flown by the Scales of Justice to a strange hotel near the border with Finland. There, the Scales of Justice are putting the supposed war criminal on trial themselves after the Soviet authorities claim that they have kidnapped the wrong man.

Bond and Natkowitz discover that the Scales of Justice are a fake organisation created by hardline Soviet General Yevgeny Yuskovitch. The trial has been designed to embarrass the Soviet government – for reasons that remain maddeningly unexplained – while Yuskovitch continues with his real plan. He will explode a series of nuclear weapons in the Middle East, just as the Coalition forces are squaring up to meet Saddam Hussein in battle. With Western armies in disarray, he also intends exploding a nuclear weapon (inside a British Airways jumbo jet) above Washington, DC. Somehow, in the confusion, he intends taking over the Soviet Union and returning it to hardline communism.

Bond, Natkowitz and Stepakov are betrayed by Nina Bibikova – now revealed to be Yuskovitch's lover – but they escape and manage to blow up Yuskovitch's bombs, along with Yuskovitch and Nina. Stepakov, alas, dies.

Observations: Bond has been out of action for almost a year, recuperating from the events of *Brokenclaw*. At the end of the book, Bond is given the Order of Lenin on the instructions of President Gorbachev.

M, Bill Tanner and Brian Coggins appear. The 00 section of the Secret Intelligence Service has become an antiterrorist unit. SIS has agents Fanny Farmer, Nigsy Meadows and Pansy Wright working in Tel Aviv and Moscow.

The events of the book take place from 26 December 1990 to 17 January 1991 – the latter being in the same week the Gulf War started in earnest.

In many ways, *The Man From Barbarossa* contradicts *Icebreaker*. Bond is surprised at working with Moscow Centre, and even more surprised at teaming up with them and the Israeli Mossad at the same time – which is exactly what he had to do in *Icebreaker*. In fact the plot is nigh on a rerun: agents from the three countries team up to investigate a paramilitary organisation responsible for a number of killings which turns out to be operating near the Finnish–Soviet border!

Locations: London, Moscow, and near the Finnish–Soviet border.

My Name Is . . . James Boldman (although M tells him not to use that in Russia, as it must be blown by now), James Betteridge and Sergei Batovrin. He is also referred to by the code name Block (Tackle would have been more appropriate) and masquerades as a freelance cameraman, Guy.

Bond's Past Life: Many years before, Bond had undertaken a mission in Switzerland to catch a Soviet agent who was laundering money with which the Soviets were supporting an espionage ring in the UK.

Also many years before, Bond had carried out an assassination in Los Angeles – forcing a double agent's car off the road.

Toys for the Boys: Bond is equipped with a miniature transmitter, a tape recorder, a miniature notebook computer, a homer, a make-up kit and a set of filled hypodermics containing ketamine, which kills quickly.

Sadism: Bond kills a Russian soldier in cold blood, and then mutilates the man's face so people will think it's Bond's body.

Lines to Flick Past: John Gardner has a habit of reusing phrases he likes, often within the same chapter. Here it's particularly embarrassing, as he's trying to find a euphemism for oral sex. At one point, Nina does for Bond 'things at which many wives would draw the line'. Later, Yuskovitch recalls that Nina 'had done all the things his wife had strictly barred from their bedroom'. We *assume* that Gardner means oral sex here, because otherwise the implication is that Bond is engaging in practices that, frankly, we don't even want to consider . . .

Mistakes Can Be Fatal: Gardner indicates that the paintings in M's office have been changed from naval battle scenes; yet in *Scorpius*, M is surrounded by portraits of his predecessors.

It is said at one point that Bond isn't a great one for poetry. Odd, then, that he quotes chunks of Dante in *Win, Lose or Die* and T.S. Eliot in *Death is Forever*. Equally, M apparently doesn't know much poetry, yet in *No Deals, Mr Bond* he was berating Bond for *his* perceived lack of knowledge.

Michael Brooks and Emerald Lacey, two SIS double agents, apparently betrayed Britain in the 1960s – before Bond's time, so we're told!

M interrogated Berzin in the underground rooms at the Regent's Park headquarters in the late 1960s; however, according to *Icebreaker* (1982), the Service had only just gained its guest wing as a result of the defence cuts.

DEATH IS FOREVER (1992)

Starring: The hero – James Bond
              The villain – Wolfgang (Wolfie) Weisen
              The love interests – Elizabeth Zara (Easy)
                St John and Praxi Simeon

Written By: John Gardner

Plot: The Cabal network of British agents in East Germany vanished two years ago, just as German unification happened. Now they are turning up – dead – all across Europe. More worrying, the two agents sent to find them have also been killed.

Bond is sent to Germany in the company of CIA agent Easy St John to re-establish contact with the surviving members of Cabal, but the first member he meets is killed shortly afterwards, and the second one is an impostor working for the former East German spymaster Wolfgang Weisen. Weisen has been killing off the Cabal agents in revenge for their previous actions, but he has another plot on the boil – one that will lead to the destabilisation of Europe and the possible revival of communism.

Bond and Easy track Weisen to Venice, along with the surviving Cabal agents, but they are all captured. In a daring escape, everyone is killed apart from Bond and Cabal leader Praxi Simeon. They realise that Weisen plans to blow up a special inaugural train going through the Channel Tunnel with all of the heads of the EC on board – John Major, Helmut Kohl, François Mitterand and the rest.

The train is indeed hijacked, and Bond leads a crack team of French soldiers into the tunnel, managing to electrocute Weisen before the man can blow up the train. So, Bond completely fails to accomplish his primary mission – returning in this case with one out of a possible forty Cabal agents – but accidentally manages to save the Western world.

Observations: Bond quotes T.S. Eliot – odd for a man who, we were told in *The Man From Barbarossa*, doesn't have much time for poetry. He remembers his marriage to Tracy (*OHMSS*), and the line he says to her: 'We have all the time in the world.' Bond is asked to become a Knight of the British Empire, but refuses. He is, however, awarded the French Croix de Guerre.

M, Ann Reilly and Bill Tanner are all present and correct.

British agents who had been part of an undercover spy ring in East Germany are being killed off years after the ring was broken up, and one of them turns out to be a traitor. This could be either *No Deals, Mr Bond* or *Death Is Forever*.

Locations: Frankfurt, Berlin, Paris, Venice, Calais, the Channel Tunnel and London during October 1992. Definitely the best-travelled book so far.

My Name Is . . . Bond takes over the code name Vanya when the previous Vanya is killed. At various times in the book he also answers to James Boldman, James Bates, Jim Goldfarb, Joe Bain and John Bunyan.

Bond's Past Life: Bond learnt the art of knife fighting from a small, wizened Spaniard. Once, in Paris, he was tailed by

SMERSH agents and followed into the Louvre, where they tried to kill him. He killed them all. He was in Venice in summer 1988 or 1989.

Toys for the Boys: A tear-gas pen, a pen that fires explosive bullets, and a stun grenade.

Patronising Lines: 'Bond liked weeping women as much as he liked having his teeth drilled. His nerves were as strong as the next man's, but a weeping woman made him cringe.'

'When they had set out on this venture, he really had not imagined Easy would match up to her name.'

Goodbye, Mr Bond: 'Go and good riddance to you,' from Weisen.

Villainous Foibles: Weisen was a child protégé of Stalin, and is obviously rather squeamish. He also likes sadomasochistic sex.

Sadism: Wolfgang Weisen has eggs from the poisonous fiddleback spider hidden in sandwiches that Bond has ordered from room service. Well, the Government told us that eating eggs was dangerous.

It's Only a Book: There are mentions of Sean Connery and Mel Gibson – one played Bond, of course, and one was asked to play Bond. The Bond in this book also recalls that someone once likened him to Hoagy Carmichael with a cruel mouth – that someone was René Mathis in *Casino Royale*.

Mistakes Can Be Fatal: Gardner has Bond think about a 'slough of despair'. In fact, according to John Bunyan (one of Bond's identities in this book) 'the name of the slough was Despond'.

The death of one of the Cabal agents by 'flyswatting' (being hit by a car) is said to be an outmoded method – yet this is what Henri Rampert tried on Bond in *The Man From Barbarossa*.

Bond tells Easy that Big Hans and Very Big Hans can't be cops because of their clothing – yet a few pages later seems to realise suddenly that they aren't cops.

NEVER SEND FLOWERS (1993)

Starring: The hero – James Bond
                  The villain – David Dragonpol
                  The love interest – Fredericka (Flicka)
                    von Grüsse

Written By: John Gardner

Plot: Four unconnected assassinations around the world are somehow linked to the death of Laura March, an MI5 agent holidaying in Switzerland. Bond is assigned to investigate, alongside his Swiss counterpart, Fredericka von Grüsse, with whom he quickly falls in lust, then love.

A mysterious man carrying a distinctive walking stick has been spotted before most of the deaths, and a hybrid rose sent to each funeral. Bond and Flicka, as Bond dubs her, discover that Laura's brother was a serial killer who died five years previously; and she had just broken off her engagement to David Dragonpol, a world-famous stage actor who has become a recluse at the castle in Germany where he lives with his sister and is preparing a staged history of theatre. The sister, Maeve, is responsible for creating the hybrid rose.

Visiting the castle, Bond and Flicka discover that Dragonpol is the assassin and find a list of targets in Milan, Athens and Paris. Trying to catch Dragonpol in Milan, they discover that there is a second sibling – an identical twin, whom David claims is the assassin. David shoots his brother, ostensibly to save Bond's life, but it really is David who is the psychopath. His next targets are Princess Diana and the two young Princes when they visit EuroDisney. Bond lays in wait at Euro Disney and kills Dragonpol, while Flicka prevents the sister from finishing the job.

Observations: Bond has reverted to driving a Saab: no mention made of the Bentley's fate. He thinks obliquely of Harriet Horner (*Scorpius*) and Easy St John (*Death Is Forever*). He recognises Aristophanes' *The Frogs* from his

102

school days, and categorically states that he was an only child. Bye-bye James Bond Jnr!

M (whose light is red for no entry), Moneypenny, Bill Tanner and Ann Reilly all appear. M offers Flicka a job with the Secret Service when she is fired by her Swiss bosses, and later suggests that she might like a trip to Shrublands (cf. *Thunderball*). May is not particularly welcoming to Flicka when she moves in.

The Service doesn't have a Station in Switzerland any more; it has to operate through the Embassy. It does, however, own a company jet – an ageing Hawker Siddeley 125 Series 700, with the Transworld Consortium logo on it.

What is the root of the obsession John Gardner has with Andrew Lloyd Webber's show *Cats*? The show's slogan 'Now and Forever' turns up nearly every time he is describing a London scene!

Locations: Switzerland, London, Germany, Milan (Italy), EuroDisney near Paris – as well as brief scenes showing the assassinations elsewhere, between August and October 1992 (which causes a problem – see **Mistakes Can Be Fatal**).

My Name Is ... Mr Van Warren (Flicka is his wife), Predator, and White Knight (his code name in *Tomorrow Never Dies* four years later).

Bond's Past Life: He's been to Disney World, and greatly enjoyed it. We are seriously beginning to worry about Bond at this stage!

Toys for the Boys: His briefcase now basically contains a laptop and fax. Q'ute arms him with the ASP, a Gerber fighting knife and flares.

Patronising Lines: 'Under an astringent exterior, Ms Chantry was probably all woman, and then some', thinks Bond. She turns out to be bisexual.

Villainous Foibles: David Dragonpol is a psychopath who loves using his theatrical gifts for murders. (How much of his past life is true is open to debate, since, as M points out, it all sounds like it came from a Victorian novel.)

Mistakes Can Be Fatal: Finally, we get confirmation of a mistake back in *Licence Renewed* (or it's a mistake here). In Gardner's first novel, the Service cover was Transworld Export.

Gardner states that Flicka was the first woman to sleep in Bond's apartment. So where was Tiffany Case sleeping? It's stated in *From Russia With Love* that she's left Bond and moved out to a hotel.

When he discovers Dragonpol's note, Bond says it refers to 'PD; H; W'. Later, he recounts it more logically as 'PD; W; H' (Princess Diana; William; Harry).

Both *Death Is Forever* and *Never Send Flowers* have internal evidence showing them to be set at the same time! *Never Send Flowers* must be later, since it makes reference to Bond having worked previously with Colonel Veron of the French GIGN.

SEAFIRE (1994)

Starring: The hero – James Bond
The villain – Sir Maxwell Tarn
The love interest – Fredericka (Flicka)
von Grüsse

Written By: John Gardner

Plot: On holiday with Flicka after a year of intensive retraining for his new role as head of the Two Zeros section, Bond helps foil a hijack of a cruise liner, which is later sunk mysteriously. It is owned by Sir Maxwell Tarn, an emigré millionaire with interests in haulage, publishing and shipping, who is to be the Two Zeros' first target, as he is also (according to a mole within his organisation) an arms supplier. Bond tries to persuade Tarn that he is a disaffected former spy (again) and that he is about to be raided, at which point Tarn fakes his own death and disappears.

The mole within Tarn's organisation contacts M, arranging a rendezvous in Madrid, which Bond attends. The mole is killed, but Bond gets documents from him which include a note that sends Bond and Flicka out to Jerusalem to see Tarn's wife, a former model who hates him. She tells them that Tarn believes he is the new Führer, but she, and two bodyguards, Cathy and Anna (who are masquerading as males, Cuthbert and Archie), disappear before Bond can help her escape. Tarn then reappears and leads an obvious trail to a house in Essex where Bond finds Tarn's wife's body and a phone number for a hotel in Germany.

Bond realises that Tarn is one step ahead all the time, and he must have a spy in the operational committee running British intelligence, MicroGlobe. When he goes to Germany and investigates Tarn's lawyer's office he finds a tape identifying the spy. He also sees a neo-Nazi rally, and fakes his own death. Returning to Britain, he exposes the Junior Minister who was betraying them, and, when he is interrogated, the Minister talks about SeaFire, a project Tarn is working on. Bond ties this in with his knowledge of Tarn's base in Puerto Rico, and gets himself and Flicka assigned out there. Working with Felix Leiter, they discover that Tarn has got a group of marine biologists working on a project that will clear oil spills. Tarn intends to blow up an oil tanker, using a submarine he has bought, causing a massive oil slick, which he will then have cleaned up, thus showing what a great guy he is. Bond foils the plot, but not before Flicka and Felix are captured by Tarn's people and tortured . . .

Observations: Bond is back in love again, and asks Flicka to marry him, prompting him to remember Tracy, Vesper Lynd (*Casino Royale*), Honey Ryder (*Doctor No*), Domino Vitali (*Thunderball*) and Kissy Suzuki (*You Only Live Twice*). Oddly, he doesn't remember any of Gardner's own creations. He has a new secretary, Chastity Vain, and prefers Cambridge to Oxford. We are told that he has learnt to sleep easily – although one of the distinctive features of the Gardner books has been his odd dreams.

There have been major changes in the set-up of the Service. Bond now heads the Double–0 or Two Zeros section, which is not answerable to M, but to a Watch Committee dubbed MicroGlobe One, which includes representatives of all the main security services and is also answerable to the government. It is not expected that M is likely to stay as Chief of his Service much longer, and indeed he falls ill during *SeaFire*, meaning that there are numerous scenes at his home, Quarterdeck. However, he and Bill Tanner are still members of MicroGlobe. Ann Reilly is now head of Q Branch, and the Service's main interrogators are Burkenshaw and Hairman, inevitably known as Burke and Hare. We see Mr Natkowitz of the Mossad (from *The Man From Barbarossa*) again, except he's changed his forename from Pete to Steve!

Locations: London, Cambridge, Madrid (Spain), Germany, Puerto Rico.

My Name Is . . . James Busby, Brother James, James Boldman and Predator.

Toys for the Boys: Q'ute supplies Bond with explosives and fuses, and makes arrangements for him to use a Powerchute (a motorised hang-glider).

Mistakes Can Be Fatal: Flicka tells Bond that Tarn's supporters 'are not neo anything. They are Nazis plain and simple.' Four pages later, she refers to them as 'the neo-Nazi movement', and Bond corrects *her*. 'There's nothing neo about these fanatics.' OK, it's in different chapters . . .

According to *SeaFire*, Bond and Cedar Leiter working together gave Felix 'much concern'. In *For Special Services*, he was virtually forcing her on Bond!

COLD (1996)

Starring: The hero – James Bond
The villains – COLD (Children of the Last
Days), led by General Brutus 'Brute' Clay;
and the Tempesta clan
The love interests – Toni Nicolleti and
Beatrice da Ricci

Written By: John Gardner

Plot: Bond is assigned to investigate an explosion which destroyed Bradbury Airlines flight 299, apparently with the loss of his old friend, Principessa Sukie Tempesta (*Nobody Lives Forever*). However, she is not dead, and warns Bond against 'COLD' before her remains are found in a burnt-out car. The FBI are using a penetration agent, Toni Nicolleti, to gain evidence against Sukie's sons-in-law, who are involved in major crime. They need to lure them to America, and want to use Bond's connection to Sukie as bait. The Tempestas have been linked with the Calvinistic Children of the Last Days, who want to take over America.

In Italy the Tempesta brothers try to persuade Bond that Brutus Clay, a retired American General who has his own militia, may have had Sukie killed for turning him down. However, they decide to kill Bond, but he and Toni escape and are brought to meet M. Bond heads to America to investigate Clay, while M is kidnapped. Working with Felicia Heard Skifflet (Fliss), an FBI agent, Bond discovers Clay has M. Bond rescues M, stealing a helicopter. During the escape he shoots down Clay's helicopter, but Fliss dies when Bond has to crash-land. M decides there is no threat from COLD to the UK, so Bond is taken off the case.

Four years later, we catch up with Bond immediately after the end of *SeaFire*. Freddie (Flicka as was) is dying, and is taken to the SIS clinic in Surrey. Bond spends the rest of the year tending to her. However, a message from Beatrice da Ricci (*Win, Lose or Die*) draws him to Geneva, and back into the FBI's plot to catch the Tempestas. The FBI want to use Bond again, to which, following Freddie's death, he agrees. He is about to infiltrate the Tempestas' lakeside villa, where COLD is about to hold a major briefing, when Sukie is spotted arriving. When Bond appears, he and Beatrice, who has replaced Toni as the FBI's agent-in-place, are captured by Sukie and Kauffberger, a retarded giant. Sukie was responsible for the destruction of the Bradbury Airlines plane because COLD was being blackmailed by someone on board. She now plans to marry Clay, who survived the helicopter crash, and she does so, only to be murdered by Clay that night. Bond and Beatrice see COLD's briefing, and try to escape as the Italian Marines storm the villa. Clay takes them as hostages, but he is shot in the arm, falls into the lake, and drowns.

On Bond's return to Britain, M has retired, and a female M has taken his place. Bond heads to his first meeting with her.

Observations: James Bond distrusts money men, almost as much as politicians – hardly surprising after the plots against the stock exchanges which Gardner has pitched him into in recent books. He can quote from the Bible (the Song of Solomon and the Book of Kings), has seen both *The Wizard of Oz* and *Peter Pan*, and is familiar with T.S. Eliot's *The Waste Land*.

Continuity is almost obsessive. There are references to *Licence to Kill* (Bond knows the problems that come from personal vendettas), *Nobody Lives For Ever*, *You Only Live Twice*, *Goldfinger*, *OHMSS*, *Win, Lose or Die* and *SeaFire*. Bond returns for what he believes is the last time to Quarterdeck, M's home, and M is referred to as Admiral Sir Miles Messervy.

There's a whole cavalcade of guest appearances. It's the Old M's farewell performance, and he gets a quick trip to Italy and another kidnapping as a gift. Miss Moneypenny makes a fleeting appearance crying over the death of a friend. Bill Tanner is meant to be flying in after M's kidnapping but doesn't make it. Sukie Tempesta is dead, then alive, then dead, then alive . . . then irrevocably dead. Beatrice da Ricci turns up to lighten Bond's grief, while Flicka (who throughout this book is referred to as Freddie), who seemed destined to be the next Mrs Bond, dies off stage. Even M's servants, the Davisons, are mentioned.

M recovers from his illness in *SeaFire* but retires in favour of a female M (to bring the books in line with the film series). MicroGlobe One is still in existence, although M acts unilaterally. The SIS retains its clinic in Surrey.

When published in the USA, the title of this book was *Cold Fall*.

The book is divided into two sections, one supposedly set from March 1990 (the internal evidence is contradictory), the other in late 1994 immediately after *SeaFire*. In the American editions, the contents page makes it clear that the sections are 1990 and 1994. This is unfortunately omitted in the British edition.

This is not Gardner's best novel. There is no reason for Bond to be involved in the plot at all – why should he be investigating a plane crash? At least in the film of *Moonraker* it was an RAF plane that crashed. From there on in, he's simply a pawn of the FBI. He doesn't even get to kill the villain: Clay drowns after being shot by Beatrice!

Locations: London, United States (Washington, Virginia and Iowa), Italy (Rome, Pisa and Tuscany) and Switzerland.

My Name Is . . . You guessed it, James Boldman. Or, at one stage, Jim. Using his own name, Bond tries to pass himself off as a lecturer at Georgetown University. He also has the code names Predator and Grey Fox.

James Bond, Fashion Victim: Somehow the idea of Bond in a short denim jacket doesn't feel quite right.

Bond's Past Life: Bond had to memorise Churchill's 'beginning of the end . . . end of the beginning' speech at school – interesting, if he was buying a Bentley in 1933 (*Casino Royale*)! He has visited Tuscany previously in August, when he killed a traitor on a deserted beach.

He apparently cannot remember his father, and has always looked up to M as such.

There are only four women Bond has truly loved (Freddie, Tracy and Beatrice are named – the fourth is presumably meant to be Vesper Lynd).

Toys for the Boys: In the first part, Bond uses an attaché case with a laptop which conceals his weaponry; in the second part he has a communicator in his pen and his belt, matching Beatrice's lipstick and belt radios.

Lines to Flick Past: When Toni rescues Bond from being 'raped' by Luigi Tempesta's wife, she looks at what is obviously Bond's still erect penis. 'Down boy,' she mutters.

It's Only a Book: Sukie's nickname for Bond when talking to the Tempestas was 'The Spy Who Loved Me'. Beatrice's note to Bond says she wants to win, not lose or die (so dying doesn't count as losing then?).

Mistakes Can Be Fatal: If the first part of the book is set in March 1990, how does Bond know about Margaret Thatcher's resignation as Prime Minister? How do the agents know to use 'Bill' and 'Hilary' (presumably after the Clintons)?

Bond introduces himself to the crash investigation team as Jim Boldman, yet allows the FBI agents to call him 'anything but Jim'.

Bond describes M as the father he couldn't remember; in *Win Lose or Die*, he talks about the last Christmas he spent with his parents.

M apparently cannot stand bad language of any sort, yet we've even heard him use a four-letter word in *Brokenclaw* (and it wasn't 'Bond!').

When he's drowning, 007 recalls seeing a girl covered in gold paint. The *film* Bond did; the book version was only told about it by Tilly.

The reason for looking for fibre-optic cables is given twice, once in each section of the book, in case we weren't concentrating the first time round.

The Tempestas hire a good class of bodyguard. Roberto,

knowing he's got a killer handcuffed to him, gets drunk, and allows Bond to take him for a walk, and then believes Bond when he says he collapsed from drink!

The Tempestas leave Bond's gun on the floor of Beatrice's cottage so 007 can conveniently find it later. Equally, Roberto's change of side is pretty unbelievable as well – surely he must have seen Clay in action before?

Bond watches Clay drown, but then says he saw him being picked up by a launch? No he didn't!

'BLAST FROM THE PAST' (1997)

Starring: The hero – James Bond
                 The villain(ess) – Irma Bunt
                 The love interest – Cheryl Haven

Written By: Raymond Benson

Plot: James Bond receives a FedEx'd message purporting to be from his son, James Suzuki, in New York, asking his father to come and help him immediately. Bond travels to New York only to discover his son dead, poisoned. It is obvious that his son was dead when the plea was written – someone is trying to get his attention.

Finding the key to a safe deposit box near his son's body, Bond and SIS agent Cheryl Haven travel to the bank where Bond's son worked and try the key out. It sticks, and a maintenance man attempts to help. A bomb in the box explodes, killing the maintenance man. Bond rushes out of the bank and sees a bag lady watching him – the same bag lady he remembers seeing outside his son's apartment. Bond and Cheryl give chase, finally trapping the bag lady in a warehouse. Bond enters while Cheryl goes for help, but he is knocked out. When he awakes, he finds he is being held prisoner by Irma Bunt, former aide to Ernst Stavro Blofeld. She had almost died when Bond blew up Blofeld's Japanese castle, but after many years of physical and mental recuperation she had come to take her revenge. She tortures Bond with Japanese fugu poison – the same poison she used to kill his son – but when Cheryl arrives Bond manages to shoot and kill Bunt.

Observations: Bond has a son – James Suzuki. His mother was Kissy Suzuki, the Japanese fisherwoman with whom Bond had a relationship in the Ian Fleming novel *You Only Live Twice*; she has since died of cancer. (Benson picked this up from John Pearson's book *James Bond: The Authorised Biography*.) He is using the Walther PPK 7·65mm again.

The events of *Thunderball*, *OHMSS* and *You Only Live Twice* get a mention, with special reference to Ernst Stavro Blofeld, Irma Bunt and Tracy di Vicenzo.

This short story was first published in the January 1997 issue of *Playboy*. Benson puts in a line referring to the events at the end of John Pearson's *James Bond: The Authorised Biography*, which claimed that Irma Bunt was in Australia, but suggests that the reports were false.

'I get at least fifty letters a year saying, why don't I do the *big* trick and use Kissy Suzuki's son,' John Gardner told Raymond Benson in 1993. 'I'm not allowed to do it! When Glidrose signed the contract for *James Bond Junior* there was a clause in the contract that included the rights to "any offspring of James Bond". I can use any of the characters I want, but I cannot use a bastard child.' This situation obviously changed, as the first thing Benson did as a Bond writer was to bring in Kissy Suzuki's son.

Locations: London and New York.

Mistakes Can Be Fatal: Benson refers to the Secret Service representative in New York. This betrays a fundamental ignorance of the British intelligence services: we have a Security Service (MI5) who operate purely in the UK, and a Secret Intelligence Service who operate primarily abroad. We do not have a Secret Service, just as we do not have a Security Intelligence Service.

ZERO MINUS TEN (1997)

Starring: The hero – James Bond
                    The villain – Guy Thackery
                    The love interest – Sunni Pei

Written By: Raymond Benson

Plot: A series of deaths connected with the company EurAsia Enterprises in Hong Kong attracts the attention of the Secret Intelligence Service. Tension is rising in Hong Kong as the moment approaches for the handover of the colony to the Chinese Government, and the new M suspects that someone behind the scenes is attempting to cause unrest. M sends Bond out to Hong Kong to investigate, but Bond would far prefer to investigate a recent and unexplained nuclear explosion in the Australian outback.

Bond begins by investigating the Chief Executive Officer of EurAsia Enterprises – Guy Thackery – but his investigations are stymied when Thackery's car blows up, apparently killing the man. Bond believes the Chinese Dragon Wing Tong to have been responsible, but during a secret reconnaissance of a Tong meeting house he is discovered and taken prisoner.

Li Xu Nan, the head of the Tong, tells Bond that they are not responsible, and offers him a deal. Li Xu Nan will let Bond live if Bond will take a trip into China and steal a document for him. He explains that EurAsia Enterprises was, for over a hundred years, involved in smuggling heroin from the East to the West, but, under the terms of an agreement between Guy Thackery's great-great-grandfather and Li Xu Nan's great-great-grandfather, EurAsia Enterprises would be transferred from the Thackery family to the Li family if Hong Kong was ever handed back to China by the British. Unfortunately, a Chinese general named Wong Tsu Kam had the only copy of the signed agreement, and Li wants Bond to get it back. Bond agrees – more to preserve the life of the prostitute Sunni Pei than for any other reason.

113

Bond enters China in the guise of a solicitor, James Pickard, but his identity is penetrated by General Wong. Wong denies killing Thackery – he has no reason – and has Bond tortured. Bond kills Wong and escapes with the document.

Back in Hong Kong he decides to go to Australia, having found a map of an Australian mine in a EurAsia warehouse. Investigating the mine, Bond and Sunni discover not only a nuclear bomb but also the very much alive Guy Thackery. Thackery had faked his own death, and intends destroying Hong Kong shortly after the handover ceremony as revenge for the shabby treatment of its inhabitants and also to ensure that his systematic theft of EurAsia assets will not be discovered. Thackery takes Sunni back to Hong Kong with the bomb and leaves Bond to be killed. Bond escapes and follows. During a chase in Hong Kong harbour shortly before the handover ceremony, Bond locates and disarms the bomb, saves Sunni and chokes Thackery.

Observations: Bond has a new assistant – Helena Marksbury. He refers to the events of *Moonraker* and *Thunderball*, and also thinks about his Aunt Charmian (*James Bond: The Authorised Biography*), Vesper Lynd (*Casino Royale*), Tracy di Vicenzo (*OHMSS*), Fredericka von Grüsse (assorted, ending with *Cold*), Harriet Horner (*Scorpius*), and Easy St John (*Death Is Forever*). There are passing references also to Oddjob and Goldfinger (*Goldfinger*), Felix Leiter (*Live and Let Die*), Darko Kerim (*From Russia With Love*) and Quarrel (*Doctor No*). Now *that* is continuity.

The old M has retired (although Bond still sees him socially). The new M is a woman – consistent with the new M in the films. The signal that M cannot be disturbed in her office is a green light above the door. 'Some things never changed,' Bond thinks. Well, he obviously hasn't read Ian Fleming's books then.

Moneypenny and Bill Tanner have both transferred allegiance to the new M. The SIS is now based in a building beside the Thames. Based on the Pierce Brosnan films, it's obviously meant to be the real SIS building in Vauxhall. SIS Station A covers Australia; Station H covers Hong Kong.

James Bond has been demoted from captain to commander, for which no explanation is given.

Major Boothroyd is back in charge of Q Branch (Ann Reilly had taken over in *SeaFire*). In fact, Q'ute is conspicuous by her absence.

There is no reference to MicroGlobe One (the governing committee of the Secret Services set up in John Gardner's last two books) in *Zero Minus Ten*. The new M acts unilaterally once more.

The book takes place during June 1997.

The section where Bond is stranded in the Outback was inspired by the role-playing game module *You Only Live Twice II*, written by Benson, whose original title for this novel was *No Tears for Hong Kong*.

His three albino triplet Tong killers are reminiscent of the triplet henchmen in Tony Barwick's unused *Moonraker* plot: Tic, Tac and Toe.

Locations: Jamaica, London (briefly), Hong Kong, Macau, the Chinese mainland and Australia.

My Name Is . . . James Pickard, a London solicitor. Also John Hunter. The code name Predator makes a reappearance.

Bond's Past Life: Bond speaks Cantonese fluently, but his Mandarin is pretty rusty.

Toys for the Boys: Q Branch give Bond shoes with inflammable laces (let's hope he doesn't drop a match). They also have medical supplies, wire cutters and a plastic dagger in the heels.

Sadism: A naked Bond is beaten with a rattan cane.

Lines to Flick Past: '. . . one of the men struck 007 hard on the left arm with his chopper.' It's a good trick if you can do it.

It's Only a Book: Bond has apparently purchased Ian Fleming's Jamaican house after Fleming died. He has renamed it Shamelady (Fleming had called it Goldeneye, but it would have been too much for Bond to have a house named after one of his films).

THE FACTS OF DEATH (1998)

Starring: The hero – James Bond
                  The villains – The Decada
                  The love interest – Niki Mirakos

Written By: Raymond Benson

Plot: Mysterious deaths start occurring around the world, caused by an unknown plague. Bond is on the trail of the Number Killer, so called because a number is left at the scene of each crime. First death was MI6's Athens agent Whitten, who was investigating poisons being smuggled in frozen sperm. Then there have been two attacks on Army bases in Cyprus. All the deaths have been caused by poison. An attack is made on the Greek agent Niki Mirakos, but Bond foils it.

M's fiancé, Alfred Hutchinson, is the British Goodwill Ambassador to the World; he has information about the case but is murdered before he can tell. His assistant, Manville Duncan, takes over as Bond discovers that Alfred was victim 4. On the Greek island of Chios, the Decada, a group of ten high-ranking people who, unknown to their leader are divided in their aims, celebrates the successful completion of its first four sorties.

Bond goes on the trail of Hutchinson's son Charles, who is based in Austin, Texas. Teaming up with Felix Leiter and his lover, FBI field agent Manuela Montemayor, Bond finds that there is a link between the infertility clinic for which Charles works and the terrorist group known as the Suppliers, which provided the ricin that killed Alfred Hutchinson. Bond chats up Dr Ashley Anderson, head of the clinic, and, after learning that Charles is on his way to London, penetrates the clinic's security and finds a wealth of poisons in storage alongside the frozen semen. Anderson blows the clinic up, intending to leave Bond among the rubble, but 007 overpowers her. He then helps Felix capture one of the Suppliers' hideouts, where a metal briefcase is discovered.

As the death toll from the unknown plague, now called Williams' Disease, mounts, the Number Killer strikes target No. 5 – the Turkish barracks in Nicosia – using Sarin, then sprays a shiphold full of fruit and vegetables with anthrax. However, an anonymous phone call tips off the Cypriot authorities, and there are no victims. The call has come from Charles Hutchinson, distraught at the death of his father, who is then killed by the Decada.

Links between Alfred Hutchinson and one Konstantine Romanos start surfacing and both Bond and Manville Duncan fear that Hutchinson may have been involved with the enemy. Romanos owned a house in Texas to which Bond had followed Anderson, and is the head of Biolinks, the company that owned the infertility clinic. As news arrives that the metal briefcase found in Texas contains vials of Williams' Disease, M sends Bond to Athens, where he joins forces with Niki again. Greek intelligence had previously discounted a crank letter from the Decada threatening war between Greece and Turkey, but now they take it seriously.

Charles's body is found (victim 7), then Bond comes face to face with Romanos at a casino, where he is picked up by Hera Volopolous. She turns out to be second in command of the Decada, and leader of a splinter group of three women whose aims are much wider than just a war. Bond escapes from an execution party, where he would have been victim 8, and finds a clue. He passes this to Niki but is recaptured by Hera and brought before Romanos, who explains that he wants war but knows nothing about Williams' Disease and the Decada's link to it. Bond escapes and he and Niki realise that the target is the President of the Turkish Republic of Northern Cyprus and that Alfred Hutchinson was killed to allow Manville Duncan access to the President. Hutchinson was trying to warn M of the Decada's plans, although he was involved in a scam with Romanos. He left M a note saying that the other target is in Istanbul.

A rogue general, also a member of the Decada, has been able to steal a Pershing missile which is going to be fired from Chios. Bond goes to Chios but is captured. Romanos cannot resist leaving him a chance to escape, but at that point Hera and her two lesbian lovers make their play. She has a vaccine for Williams' Disease which she will hold to ransom. She leaves, not concerned if Bond prevents a war – which he does by solving the puzzle. He chases after Hera, and blows up the helicopter in which she is fleeing. She survives the crash and Bond drowns her, recovering a briefcase containing the vaccine.

Observations: James Bond is not fluent in Greek, although he can get by. The unnamed 004 is based in the UK at the start of the book.

Like Benson's first novel, *The Facts of Death* is a continuity-fest. We learn that the new M, Barbara Mawdsley, is divorced and engaged to Alfred Hutchinson. Unlike her predecessor, her identity is known to the public. The original M, his servants the Davisons, Miss Moneypenny, Helena Marksbury, Bill Tanner, Sir James Molony and May all appear to a greater or lesser extent, while Felix Leiter, whose service in the DEA (*Licence to Kill)* is alluded to, now uses a wheelchair. No reference is made to his wife Della or daughter Cedar, however, and although he might just be being tactful Felix surprisingly makes no comment about Flicka. On this occasion, though, there's no question that it's the film's Q, Major Boothroyd, who appears in the requisite Bond car briefing – he even says, 'Now pay attention, 007'!

There are countless references to previous adventures, notably, given the location, *Colonel Sun* (a novel to which interestingly John Gardner does not link back at any time). Stuart Thomas is stated as still being head of a cut-back Station G – which goes against the spirit, if not the letter, of

M's comment to Bond at the end of *Colonel Sun* that he is missing, presumed dead. Incidents or people from *Casino Royale*, *Moonraker*, *From Russia With Love*, 'Octopussy', and *For Special Services* get specific mention, while when Bond is being assessed as a sperm donor a catalogue of the scars and injuries he has received over the (45) years are recounted.

The original M is also given a larger family: he now has 'two daughters from the marriage that few people knew anything about'. This presumably includes Ian Fleming! One is now called Haley McElwain, divorced from an American, with children, nine-year-old Charles and six-year-old Lynne. This can't be the same daughter mentioned in *Win, Lose or Die*, set nine years previously.

This novel, set in October and November 1998, contains the most swearing of any Bond book. While neither of us is prudish, somehow four-letter words just don't fit in Bond's world (they are very few and far between in the movies).

Locations: Los Angeles, Tokyo, Cyprus, London, mainland Greece.

My Name Is . . . John Bryce, a writer about philosophy and religion.

Bond's Past Life: He's been to Greece on numerous occasions as well as for *Colonel Sun*.

Toys for the Boys: Bond uses a diving utility belt with flippers and aqualung. Q Branch equips him with the new Jaguar XK8 coupé, complete with impenetrable Chobham armour, self-healing metal, eletrically sensitive paints, interchangeable licence plate, GPS navigation, heat-seeking missiles, cruise missiles (!), deployable airbag, light- and heat-magnification systems for night driving, holographic projectors and a flying scout with camera and mine-dropping capability. Somewhere in there it also has an engine! Bond also gets an alarm-sensor nullifier, and the most up-to-date night-vision goggles.

Patronising Lines: This one is ascribed to Felix Leiter, but Bond agrees with it: 'Women are like stamps – the more you spit on them, the more they get attached to you.'

Villainous Foibles: Romanos is certain that the ancient Greek gods have spoken to him.

Lines to Flick Past: 'I do eat animals,' Bond says. 'I'm sure you do,' Ashley Anderson says suggestively.

'There was something appropriate about the act of copulation in full view of the Acropolis.'

Mistakes Can Be Fatal: The Number Killer is Hera Volopolous. OK, we can accept that. But then why does Benson use 'he' to describe her in scenes from her point of view?

Alfred Hutchinson has been Ambassador to the World for two years as of October 1998. There was a change of government in the UK in May 1997, with the commensurate change in ambassadorial personnel.

Bond refers to the old M as 'Miles' on occasion, rather than 'Sir Miles'.

As far as we are concerned, the resurrection of Stuart Thomas is contrary to the original book.

File 002:
The Films

DR NO (1962)

Starring: Sean Connery as the hero – James Bond
Joseph Wiseman as the villain – Dr No
Ursula Andress as the love interest –
Honey Ryder

Written By: Richard Maibaum, Johanna Harwood and
Berkely Mather (but see **Observations** below)

Directed By: Terence Young

Tag Lines: 'The first James Bond film!'
'Now . . . meet the most extraordinary gentleman spy in all
fiction . . . James Bond, Agent 007 . . .'
'That master of undercover operations is on his way!'

Relevance of Pre-Title Sequence? There isn't one.

Theme Song: 'The James Bond Theme', which segues into
the calypso version of 'Three Blind Mice' (opening). The
Bond Theme (closing).

Cringe-Worthy Title Sequence: Flickering lights forming
the words 'Ian Fleming's Dr NO' are followed by strips of
cinema film with '007' on them. These are pursued by
Pacman-like lights which lead into coloured silhouettes of
Martine Beswick dancing to 'Three Blind Mice'. Finally the
black assassins walk across the frame and into the opening of
the film.

Plot: When Strangways, the Secret Service resident in
Jamaica, disappears, MI7 agent James Bond is assigned to
discover what happened to him. The Americans are also
interested in that part of the world, as their rocket launches
from Cape Canaveral are being 'toppled'.

Bond is collected from Kingston Airport by a chauffeur
allegedly acting for Government House, but who in fact is
working for the enemy. The man kills himself rather than
answer Bond's questions. A photographer following Bond is

prepared to have her arm broken rather than talk. Helped by CIA Agent Felix Leiter, and a Cayman Islander, Quarrel, Bond follows Strangways' investigations onto the island of Crab Key, where he had found radioactive rocks. Bond and Quarrel go out to Crab Key, where they meet Honey Ryder, a young beachcomber. Quarrel is killed by security men who bring Bond and Honey to the headquarters of Dr No. Dr No is a scientific genius who is gaining revenge on the Americans for turning their back on him, and he reveals he is a member of SPECTRE. Bond survives a sadistic assault course when he escapes from his cell through the ventilation system, and forces No's reactor into overload. Bond and No grapple on the gantry over the nuclear reactor, and Bond forces Dr No into the reactor coolant, killing him. Bond and Honey escape, to be picked up by Leiter and the Navy.

Observations: James Bond is agent 007 of MI7 (not MI6, or the SIS, as it is called in Fleming's books), which operates undercover as Universal Exports. He carries a licence to kill, and is armed with a Walther PPK 7·65mm with a Brausch silencer by the Armourer, Major Boothroyd (Peter Burton). He has heard of, but not worked previously with, Felix Leiter. He obviously enjoys the high life: he prefers the 1953 Dom Perignon to the 1955 and is a member at Le Cercle, part of Les Ambassadeurs club in Mayfair. He carries his cigarettes in a gunmetal case and has a card printed with the address of his luxurious flat.

The head of service is known only as M (Bernard Lee). Since he took over, there has been a 40 per cent drop in 00 casualties. His secretary is Miss Moneypenny (Lois Maxwell), with whom Bond has a flirting relationship. When approaching M's office, Bond walks along a corridor and past a sign pointing to the offices of Universal Exports. When he enters M's office, the sign on the door also reads UNIVERSAL EXPORTS. This all indicates that MI7 don't have their own secure building – they just rent space in someone else's.

SPECTRE is introduced: the Special Executive for Counter-Intelligence, Terrorism, Revenge, Extortion (there's no 'and' –

that first makes its screen appearance in the trailer for *From Russia With Love*). It is headed by the greatest brains in the world, according to Dr No, and owes no allegiance to East or West. Dr No has come to it after being a Chinese Tong leader. (He fled from them with $10 million in gold.) He considers that Bond might have been a worthy addition to their ranks. (Bond would be interested in the Revenge part.)

The Americans are in the midst of their Mercury flights, with mission MA7 set to achieve a lunar orbit.

Canadian producer Harry Saltzman had optioned the rights to the books about 007 from Ian Fleming in 1961, with the exception of *Casino Royale*. He teamed up with Albert R. 'Cubby' Broccoli to form Eon ('Everything or Nothing') Productions and, in June 1961, they made a deal with United Artists for the first James Bond film.

The writer Johanna Harwood received a telegram from Saltzman just after the deal was concluded, saying: 'HAVE CONCLUDED BOND DEAL WITH UNITED ARTISTS PRODUCTIONS OCTOBER 15 STOP URGENT DO SCREEN TREATMENT BREAKDOWN THUNDERBALL STOP DOCTOR NO OR THUNDERBALL PROBABLY FIRST SUBJECT STOP'. This clearly shows that the producers had not decided which of the two films to make first and were keeping their options open. They ended up settling on *Thunderball*, but a few months later Kevin McClory's court case against Ian Fleming over the ownership of *Thunderball* worried them enough that their efforts were turned towards *Dr No* instead.

When involved with Ivar Bryce and Kevin McClory on *James Bond of the Secret Service* (see the entry on the novel of *Thunderball*) Ian Fleming had favoured David Niven as Bond. Others under consideration at that time were James Stewart, Patrick Allen and Richard Burton. By 1961 he was in favour of Roger Moore as the first 007, but he was too identified, according to Broccoli, as the Saint by this time (although *The Saint* did not start on television until 1962). The model Peter Anthony was screen-tested. Discussions were also held with Patrick McGoohan and Cary Grant, but neither of them was interested in the role. Director Terence Young has stated that George Baker (who later played Sir Hilary Bray in *OHMSS*) was also under consideration. Sean Connery himself was chosen by readers of the *Daily Express* (which was running the Bond comic-strip adaptations) as the perfect Bond.

However, contrary to popular opinion, Sean Connery was not the first big-screen James Bond. The stunt coordinator, Bob Simmons, is the behatted agent who turns and fires at the gun barrel in the opening title sequence.

Bryan Forbes and Guy Hamilton were both asked to direct *Dr No*, but both refused. Hamilton later returned to direct a number of Bond films.

Monica Van der Syl dubbed the voice of Ursula Andress, and many of the later Bond women, including Claudine Auger (Domino Derval).

Lois Maxwell, who went on to play Miss Moneypenny for a further thirteen years, was originally offered the part of Sylvia Trench, later taken by Eunice Gayson. Ian Fleming complimented her at the wrap party at the end of filming: 'I envisioned a tall, elegant woman with the most kissable lips in the world. You are her!'

Ian Fleming suggested that his neighbour in Jamaica, Noël Coward, might make an ideal Dr No for the film, but Coward declined; Fleming also thought his cousin, Christopher Lee (later to play Scaramanga), would be an excellent choice. Lee revealed that Eon Productions didn't contact him.

A number of screen stories were penned. In an early draft by Wolf Mankowitz and Richard Maibaum, 'Buchfield' was the villain, and Dr No the name of the capuchin monkey perched on his shoulder.

In the end, this is one of the closest adaptations made. The opening sequence is virtually identical, and there are numerous sections taken word for word. Felix Leiter, played by Jack Lord, is an addition, and is quickly written out when Bond travels to Crab Key. Honey's background is adapted (her father disappeared on Crab Key, although this is never followed up). The plots deviate when Dr No and Bond meet

– in the film, the torturous assault course is considerably diminished, and in fact we are not convinced that the film Dr No sets out to torture Bond. The book finishes with Bond facing a giant squid (one of the few set pieces from the Fleming canon not yet used in the official series). Fleming did not use SPECTRE until two books after *Doctor No*; his villain worked for himself.

Rather neatly, one of Fleming's less plausible moments (the ease with which Bond steals a knife from Dr No's table) is corrected.

One version of the script had Bond finding Honey in her room, ready with a bottle of liquor to use as a weapon. She faints in his arms, and he catches both her and the bottle. He then quickly takes a swig before carrying her to safety.

A scene was filmed in which Honey is staked out as human meat for giant land crabs. It was deemed undramatic, and cut out of the finished film.

Two versions were filmed of Dent's death. In the unused version, Dent has one bullet remaining which he fires at Bond as 007 simultaneously shoots him. Other scenes were shot for different markets; Connery's seduction scenes with Zena Marshall (Miss Taro), for instance, were redone with her splendid physique covered up for the more prudish countries . . .

A scene showing Dr No telling Bond to send a fake message to Felix Leiter claiming that Crab Key was 'clean', and promising a less painful death for Bond and Honey after they have seen his scheme succeed, was deleted at the editing stage.

During the filming of the scene where Honey Ryder rises from the waves, Ian Fleming and his friends Stephen Spender, Peter Quennell and Nöel Coward are hiding behind a nearby sand dune, having wandered along from Fleming's house while filming was in progress.

The music for the film is credited to Monty Norman, with 'The James Bond Theme' recorded by the John Barry Seven. Although the notes are based on a song Norman wrote, the distinctive plucked-guitar sound is Barry's contribution.

The opening shot of Bond, seen from behind until he

introduces himself to Sylvia Trench, echoes the 1939 film *Juarez*, where the central character does the same. To get Sean Connery in the right frame of mind, director Terence Young made him sleep in a Savile Row suit and tie.

In Italy, the film was entitled *Licence to Kill*, thereby leading to a problem 27 years later! After its release, the Vatican issued a special communiqué expressing its disapproval at the film's morality.

Locations: Jamaica, London and Crab Key.

My Name Is . . . Bond . . . James Bond. Regularly.

James Bond, Fashion Victim: A very unflattering pair of white pyjama bottoms. Maybe the pyjama-coat would have been a better idea?

Bond's Past Life: Bond has carried a Beretta for ten years, and has never missed with it. However, on the last occasion he used it during a mission, it jammed and he spent six months in hospital as a result. (In the books, this is a reference to the end of *From Russia With Love*.)

Toys for the Boys: M mentions a Self-Destructor Bag, which will contain his mission briefing. The Armourer replaces Bond's Beretta with a Walther PPK, and a very clumsy Geiger counter is delivered to Bond in Jamaica. (Given that by this stage Fleming had written *Thunderball*, in which a Geiger counter was concealed in a camera, this really does seem a bit large to us!)

Villainous Foibles: Dr No has steel hands, as a result of his experiments with radioactivity. He is a collector of fine art, including Goya's portrait of the Duke of Wellington, which had, at the time of production of the film, only recently been stolen in real life. (Originally, his choice ran to Picasso, until Johanna Harwood suggested the Goya.)

Sadism: Numerous examples. The assassins let Strangways' secretary see who they are before shooting her. Quarrel is overly persuasive of the photographer, and she breaks a flashbulb to scratch his face.

Bond allows Professor Dent to fire all his bullets, and make an abortive attempt to shoot Bond, before cold-bloodedly shooting him twice (cut from six times by the censors). He kills one of Dr No's guards in the swamp, much to Honey's disgust. Quarrel is burnt to death by 'the dragon'. Bond and Honey are then treated very roughly.

Bond is softened up by No's guards before being placed in the cell, escaping from which he is electrocuted, nearly drowned and burnt. He then kills another guard in the decontamination room.

Single Entendres: 'What gives?' Bond asks Moneypenny. 'Me – given half a chance.'

Lines to Rewind For: 'Are you looking for shells?' Honey asks, as she stands in a white bikini by the water. Bond answers for many of us: 'No, I'm just looking.'

'Unfortunately, I misjudged you,' Dr No tells Bond dismissively. 'You are just a stupid policeman – whose luck has run out.'

It's Only a Movie: Although there's some cod-martial music as Felix arrives with the Navy at the end, it's all played extremely straight. There is almost a documentary feel about Bond's investigations on Jamaica, and it delves into fantasy only once, as Bond and Honey are taken into Dr No's headquarters.

Mistakes Can Be Fatal: Why do the assassins walk to the Queen's Club to shoot Strangways when there's a hearse ready to pick them up and take them to his house?

Head of Signals asks for the MI6 security patrol, rather than MI7.

Why has M's office got a sign saying: UNIVERSAL EXPORTS on the door? Isn't it a secure building? Or are they just taking their cover story a little too far?

Felix Leiter's suit changes colour from the establishing shot at the airport.

The dashboard of Bond's car in Jamaica keeps changing colour, from red to black and back again.

What does 007 get up to between seeing Dent in the morning and returning to his hotel that night?

The glass sheet that the tarantula is walking on over Connery's skin is clearly visible in the scenes when Connery's face is in shot. Bob Simmons had no such protection for the close-ups!

Miss Taro's address changes from 239 Magenta Drive to 2171.

While Bond awaits Professor Dent, his necktie appears and disappears. Dent is actually carrying a Colt ·45 (which fires seven shots), not a Smith and Wesson. Then again, Bond himself is using a Browning 1910 ·32 calibre weapon, rather than the Walther.

Bond is worried that Dr No has picked up the sails of Honey's boat on his radar, as indeed the good Doctor has, but radar systems cannot detect cloth. They can't detect wood either, so the boat masts and hulls would have been undetectable as well.

When Dr No's guard turns to give his instruction to the captain of his boat, it still sounds as if he is using the loudhailer.

Quarrel refers to Bond as 'Cap'n' consistently after their introduction by Felix – except for when Bond is washing in the river, when he's suddenly 'Mr Bond'!

Why doesn't the water that floods down the shafts come out into the decontamination lab?

Why was Honey chained on to the ramp? If she really was taken for the guards' amusement, surely one of the 'mink-lined prison' beds or rooms would have been more . . . suitable?

James Bond Will Return In . . . Who knew?

FROM RUSSIA WITH LOVE (1963)

Starring: Sean Connery as the hero – James Bond
Lotte Lenya as the villainess – Rosa Klebb
Robert Shaw as the villain –
Donovan 'Red' Grant
Daniela Bianchi as the love interest –
Tatiana Romanova

Written By: Richard Maibaum, 'adapted by Johanna Harwood'

Directed By: Terence Young

Tag Lines: 'James Bond is Back.'
'Meet James Bond, secret agent 007. His new incredible women . . . His new incredible enemies . . . His new incredible adventures . . .'

Relevance of Pre-Title Sequence? We think we see 007 being killed. In fact, it sets up Grant as a killer, and introduces SPECTRE Island.

Theme Song: Opening music is an orchestral version of the theme seguing into 'The James Bond Theme'; Matt Monro sings the vocal version over the end titles.

Cringe-Worthy Title Sequence: The titles are projected on to the stomach of a bellydancer. They're by Robert Brownjohn, Maurice Binder's assistant, as there was a dispute between Binder and Eon over logos at that stage.

Plot: Kronsteen, master plotter for SPECTRE, has devised a scheme to steal a new decoder, the Lektor, from the Russians, and embarrass the British Secret Service, along the way gaining revenge for SPECTRE for the death of Dr No. Rosa Klebb, former head of operations for SMERSH, and now a SPECTRE agent, is placed in control by the mysterious No. 1. Klebb assesses Donovan Grant, a psychopath training on SPECTRE Island, and recruits a

Russian cypher clerk, Tatiana Romanova, from the Istanbul Consulate.

In London, the trap is sprung. Tatiana will defect to the British with the Lektor, only if James Bond, with whose picture she has fallen in love, will collect her. Bond plays along, and works with Kerim Bey, head of Station T in Turkey. SPECTRE heats up the Cold War in Istanbul by killing and attacking the Russians and the British, through their respective agents, the Bulgars and the Gypsies. Bond gets caught up in this, and helps Kerim kill Krilencu, a murderous Bulgar.

Tatiana comes to Bond's room, where unbeknown to them, they are photographed making love. He gets enough information out of her for London to agree that the Lektor sounds genuine, so he engineers her escape from the Consulate with the machine, and they race on board the Orient Express. However, Grant, who has been following Bond since his arrival, on one occasion saving his life, is also on board. Kerim Bey is killed, and Bond decides to stay on the train, rather than cross country. He gets a message to London asking for help to smuggle the Lektor across the border, and is met at Zagreb by Captain Nash – or rather, by Grant, who has quickly disposed of the British agent, and taken his place.

Bond is suspicious of Nash when he sees him doctor Tatiana's drink, but is surprised when Nash reveals that he is from the opposition. Tatiana is to be killed, alongside Bond, and a letter threatening to blackmail 007 will be found with a reel of film of the lovemaking. Bond manages to appeal to Grant's greed, and uses a booby trap in the briefcase to turn the tables. After a vicious fight, Bond garrottes Grant, collects Tatiana and hijacks Grant's escape route.

SPECTRE realise what's happened, and send a helicopter and later a flotilla of boats after Bond as he and Tatiana travel by sea to Venice. Bond disposes of them, and reaches Venice, where Rosa Klebb appears, masquerading as a cleaning woman. Tatiana distracts her, and then shoots her as she attacks Bond. Tatiana returns Bond's ring, as he looks at the reel of film he's taken from Grant, and throws it in the water.

Observations: Bond has brown eyes and drives a green Bentley (as he does in the early books), which is equipped with a phone to the office. He doesn't know that much about cryptography. He has a scar on the small of his back. He drinks his coffee medium sweet, and black. He speaks a few words of Turkish.

As well as being the Armourer, Q is the Equipment Officer. Peter Bernard was asked to return as Major Boothroyd, but was committed to another film. Desmond Llewellyn was cast instead, and cinematic history was made. Station T is in Turkey.

We learn more about SPECTRE – its leader, known here as No. 1, and credited in the closing titles as 'Ernst Blofeld', operates from a boat, and wears a ring with an octopus symbol on his little finger (see **Mistakes Can Be Fatal**). His pets include Siamese fighting fish, as well as a white Persian cat which sits on his lap. Although no actor was credited, Anthony Dawson (who played Professor Dent in *Dr No*) was the body, while Eric Pohlmann supplied the voice.

As with *Dr No*, Fleming's basic plot is retained, except another layer of deception has been added with SPECTRE's involvement with the plot. After the death of Grant, there's a chase sequence added which owes more to Hitchcock's film *North by Northwest* than to Ian Fleming. The Spektor decoding machine was renamed the Lektor, to avoid confusion with the new principal villains. SPECTRE are after revenge for the death of their agent, Dr No; Sylvia Trench says she hasn't seen Bond since he flew off to Jamaica six months previously.

The German actress Elga Gimba-Anderson was Terence Young's first choice for the part of Tatiana Romanova, but, Young claimed, there was pressure from the studio not to use her. The second choice, Daniela Bianchi, had been Miss Universe 1960. Ingrid Bergman's daughter Pia Lindstrom was also tested for the part. Also considered were Sally Douglas, Lucia Modogno, Margaret Lee, Sylvia Koscina and Magda Kronopka.

Barbara Jeffoed dubbed the voice of Daniela Bianchi. The

receptionist at the Istanbul hotel is voiced by Monica Van der Syl, who dubbed Ursula Andress in *Dr No*.

Eunice Gayson makes her second and final appearance as Bond's London girlfriend, Sylvia Trench. (Her planned return in *Goldfinger* was cancelled when Guy Hamilton replaced Terence Young as director.) M and Moneypenny also appear. Ian Fleming visited the set in Istanbul, and persistent legend has it that he can be seen fleetingly in the train station sequences. We can't see him.

According to Young, Len Deighton, later co-writer of *Warhead*, wrote the first draft of the screenplay, and accompanied him on his location recce trip.

A sequence was filmed in which Hasan Ceylan, as the mustachioed Bulgar agent, tails Bond to the Bosphorus ferry where he's due to meet Tatiana, but is then killed in a car 'accident'. However, as Terence Young's twelve-year-old son pointed out just before the film was set for release, Ceylan's character was already dead – murdered by Grant in the mosque! The scene was cut.

When Grant tells Bond about the roll of film of him and Tatiana making love, he comments, 'What a performance!' This line was cut before release, making a nonsense of Bond's later remark: 'He was right, you know.'

Given how much later play was made of the fact that 'Sean Connery IS James Bond', it is rather amusing that the one principal actor whose name does not feature in both the American and British trailers for the film is . . . Sean Connery!

The version of the theme music used on the opening credits is not that released on the soundtrack album.

Locations: SPECTRE Island, Venice, London, Istanbul, through the Balkans on the Orient Express.

My Name Is . . . David Somerset, married to Mrs Caroline Somerset, *née* Tatiana Romanova.

Bond's Past Life: At some point, he and M were on a mission together in Tokyo. He also has a scar on his lower back, which may have been caused by turning his back on a woman.

Toys for the Boys: With the advent of Desmond Llewellyn as Q, the toys begin. Bond is equipped with an ordinary black leather case, with twenty rounds of ammunition 'here and here', a flat throwing knife in the side and fifty gold sovereigns in it. He also has an AR7 ·25 folding sniper's rifle, with infrared telescopic sights, and a tin of talcum powder with a tear-gas cartridge inside, which is magnetically fixed to the inside of the case, and which will explode if the case is opened incorrectly. Additionally he carries a small device to check if the phone is bugged.

Patronising Lines: 'Your mouth is the right size . . . for me, that is.'

Villainous Foibles: Blofeld strokes a white Persian cat, and keeps Siamese fighting fish (at least until they start killing each other, and he feeds the survivor to the cat). Rosa Klebb has lesbian tendencies (although less obviously than in the original novel). Grant is a sadistic psychopath who drinks red Chianti with sole. Kronsteen, as befits a master planner, is a chess master.

Sadism: The ersatz Bond is garrotted in the pre-title sequence. The girl fight was criticised for being overlong and overly sadistic, although it seems positively tame nowadays. After the attack on the gypsy encampment, the gypsies torture one of the Bulgars. Bond hits Tania, while Grant smacks Bond over the head, and then plans to shoot him unless he crawls across the floor of the carriage and kisses his boot.

Single Entendres: 'From this angle, things are shaping up nicely!'

Lines to Rewind For: 'You may know the right wines,' Grant tells Bond, 'but you're the one on your knees.'

It's Only a Movie: Matt Monro's theme for the film is playing on the radio when we first meet Bond.

The poster through which Krilencu tries to escape is for *Call Me Bwana*, a Bob Hope comedy produced in 1963 by a certain Harry Saltzman and Albert R. Broccoli.

Mistakes Can Be Fatal: There are two mistakes in the credits: Martine Beswick gains a sex change to Martin (which would make the title sequence of *Dr No* very interesting were it true!), and the composer of the James Bond theme has become Mont*e* Norman.

The ring on Blofeld's little finger switches from his left to right hand in different shots.

When Tatiana enters Bond's room, he is about to have a shower. He never goes and turns it off . . .

How did Grant know to be on the Orient Express?

Why didn't Bond get off the train with Tatiana after Kerim's death anyway, since Kerim had bribed the conductor already?

Come to that, why does he assume Kerim and Benz killed each other?

In the opening sequence, M explains that the briefcase is standard issue for '00' agents. But Captain Nash has one. Is he a 00? If so, he's very easily taken.

Why does Bond run away from the SPECTRE helicopter? Why not just shoot it from the truck?

James Bond Will Return In . . . Let's quote this one in full:

The End.

Not Quite The End.

James Bond Will Return
In The Next Ian Fleming Thriller
Goldfinger

GOLDFINGER (1964)

Starring: Sean Connery as the hero – James Bond
Gert Frobe as the villain – Auric Goldfinger
Honor Blackman as the love interest –
    Pussy Galore

Written By: Richard Maibaum and Paul Dehn

Directed By: Guy Hamilton

Tag Lines: 'James Bond is back in action!'
'James Bond 007 back in action!'
'Everything he touches turns to excitement!'

Relevance of Pre-Title Sequence? Absolutely none (it's the first time the pre-title sequence has been completely divorced from the rest of the movie, and it derives from a throwaway line at the beginning of Ian Fleming's novel where Bond is slightly disgruntled after having killed a Mexican).

Theme Song: Sung by the incomparable Shirley Bassey. It was originally meant to have been sung by Anthony Newley (a recording exists of his version).

Cringe-Worthy Title Sequence: Robert Brownjohn designed a title sequence in which scenes from the film to come are projected on to the golden bodies of scantily clad women. Iconic is the word: odd considering that there was little or no involvement from Maurice Binder.

Plot: While Bond is on holiday, M asks him to look into the activities of the millionaire industrialist and gambler Auric Goldfinger. Bond discovers that Goldfinger cheats at cards and at golf, and discovers that the CIA – in the shape of his old friend Felix Leiter – are interested in the man.

    Bond tracks Goldfinger to Switzerland, where late one night he sneaks into a factory belonging to Goldfinger and discovers Goldfinger's Rolls-Royce being melted down. Its bodywork is fabricated from eighteen-carat gold, and if Goldfinger makes six such trips a year he must be making a hefty profit out of smuggling. Attempting to escape with this information, Bond is captured by Goldfinger and taken to Kentucky, USA, where Bond overhears Goldfinger explaining to a group of American hoodlums that he intends robbing Fort Knox. Each of the hoodlums has provided something – nerve gas, manpower, a laser cutter – and expect a hefty return on their investment. Instead, Goldfinger kills the hoodlums and reveals to Bond that he is being paid by the Red Chinese to detonate a nuclear device in Fort Knox in order to irradiate the entire gold supply of the USA. Cue economic chaos and the sudden increase in value of Goldfinger's gold reserves.

Goldfinger uses Pussy Galore's Flying Circus of female pilots to spread what he thinks is nerve gas across the Fort Knox military base, but Bond has managed to subvert Pussy Galore and get a message out to Felix Leiter: the nerve gas has been replaced with something harmless and the troops who fall over as if dead are actually faking.

Goldfinger's people invade Fort Knox and burn their way into the vault. Goldfinger has an atomic bomb wheeled into the gold reserve and chains Bond to it. The 'dead' troops attack, and manage to disrupt Goldfinger's operation, but Goldfinger activates the bomb and escapes in the uniform of a US General, killing his Chinese liaison as he goes. Bond attempts to defuse the bomb, fighting off and killing Goldfinger's henchman Oddjob while he does so. In the end, an expert disarms the bomb.

On his way to meet the President of the USA, Bond is hijacked by Goldfinger but manages to kill him in a scuffle.

Observations: Bond refers to his Bentley (as seen in *From Russia With Love* and used in the novels). Q says it's had its day. During his initial conversation with Felix Leiter, played here by Cec Linder, Bond makes reference to the events of *Dr No*. M threatens to have Bond replaced with 008 if he turns the Goldfinger operation into a personal vendetta. Moneypenny makes her usual flirting appearance.

Goldfinger has been planning Operation Grand Slam for fifteen years, and has a golden gun (does Scaramanga know?).

Theodore Bikel (recently seen in the *Babylon 5* TV movie *In the Beginning*) auditioned for the part of Goldfinger. Gert Frobe was dubbed by the actor Michael Collins.

Austin Willis was originally cast as Felix Leiter and Cec Linder as Goldfinger's gin rummy partner: the two actors were asked to swap roles shortly before filming began. Nadja Regin, who appears as Bonita (the dancer in the pre-title sequence), previously played Kerim Bey's lover in *From Russia With Love*. Michael G. Wilson, later to become co-producer of the Bond films, plays one of the technicians at the airfield in Kentucky from which Pussy Galore's Flying Circus take off.

The film maintains a close association with the plot of Ian Fleming's book for most of its length, although Goldfinger's plan is different (he's irradiating the gold rather than stealing it). M's asking Bond to look into Goldfinger while he's gambling comes from Ian Fleming's novel *Moonraker*, in which M asks Bond to investigate Hugo Drax's suspected cheating at cards. Fleming himself died shortly before the film's release. The producers were worried enough about the implications of the name 'Pussy' Galore that they considered changing it to 'Kitty' for the film.

Terence Young, director of *Dr No* and *From Russia With Love*, began pre-production work on *Goldfinger* and contributed to early drafts of the screenplay with a view to directing it, but he could not come to an agreement over the terms of his contract and left the project. Paul Dehn, who co-wrote the script with Richard Maibaum, was a British writer and poet who was also responsible for scripting or co-scripting four of the *Planet of the Apes* films.

Watch the title sequence carefully – it consists of scenes from the film projected over the gold-painted bodies of various seminaked women. One of the scenes shown doesn't appear in the film itself – it was cut out before release. It consists of Bond, in Q's laboratory, passing by a Royal Mail van which suddenly opens up to reveal an area which a sniper or a machine-gunner could use as a firing platform. Although the scene was cut, the van is still visible in the background when Q demonstrates the Aston Martin to Bond in the film proper. Other scenes in the title sequence (such as Bond being attacked by a helicopter and putting Sylvia Trench in Bond's flat) are taken from the two previous films.

The count on the atomic bomb clock was originally filmed stopping at 003, but the producers insisted that a shot be inserted showing it stopping at 007. This leads to a slight continuity cock-up (see **Mistakes Can Be Fatal** below).

A sign at Fort Knox states: WELCOME TO FORT KNOX GENERAL RUSSHON. This is an acknowledgement of the hard work undertaken by Charles Russhon, who acted as technical adviser (for which, read unofficial military liaison) on the film.

Locations: The film is set in England (the Home Counties), Switzerland (the area around Geneva) and the USA (Miami, Kentucky and Fort Knox) during 1964 (the year in which it was released).

James Bond, Fashion Victim: Bond wears a rather disreputable hat while playing golf with Goldfinger. Fair enough: Goldfinger wears plus fours and a cardigan, and was wearing what appeared to be yellow pyjamas in Miami earlier on.

Toys for the Boys: Parking meters that spray gas and an Aston Martin DB5 with bulletproof glass, a homing-device detector, a smoke screen, an oil-slick reservoir, Boadicea-type blades that project from the wheel hubs, bulletproof screen in the rear, twin machine guns and a passenger ejector seat. He also sports shoes with a homer built into the heel.

Goodbye, Mr Bond: We have to suffer through Goldfinger's 'Goodnight, Mr Bond,' and 'Good morning, Mr Bond,' before we get, 'Goodbye, Mr Bond.'

Sadism: Well, Oddjob kills girls with his metal-brimmed bowler, and Goldfinger likes suffocating other girls with gold paint.

Single Entendres: Bond's explanation of why he's in bed with Jill Masterson when he should be having dinner with Felix Leiter: 'Something big's come up.'

Pussy Galore: 'My name is Pussy Galore.' Bond: 'I must be dreaming.' (The original script had Bond replying 'I know you are, but what's your name?', but this was judged too much.)

Lines to Rewind For: Q: 'I never joke about my work, 007.'

The classic: 'You expect me to talk?' from Bond strapped beneath a laser. 'No, Mr Bond – I expect you to die,' from Goldfinger.

Goldfinger: 'Forgive me, Mr Bond, but I must arrange to separate my gold from the late Mr Solo.'

Goldfinger: 'Good morning, Mr Bond – for once you're exactly where I want you.'

Mistakes Can Be Fatal: Q demonstrates the switches for the left and right front-wing machine guns – why is the 'right' control on the left and vice versa?

When Oddjob chops the statue's head off outside the golf club, the arm starts falling down with it, but then bounces back. It's spring-loaded (for some bizarre reason).

When Oddjob drives Goldfinger's car away from the golf club, Goldfinger has mysteriously vanished from the back, even though he was sitting there a few minutes before.

The homing device shows Goldfinger is travelling north from Geneva. How come the mountains in the long shots are on his right (the mountains are to the west!)?

So why does Goldfinger gas all the hoodlums to death *after* telling them his plan? Why bother? Why does he arrange to kill the hoodlum named Solo separately? Why not kill them all at the same time in the same place? And what happens to the engine in Oddjob's car before Solo is compacted in it? It's not there!

Time keeps flicking back in the nuclear-bomb disarming scene – if you count the seconds as they tick down, they don't match the count on the clock when we keep cutting back to it.

'Three more ticks and Mr Goldfinger would have hit the jackpot,' says Bond, but the clock stops on a count of 007 (see above).

James Bond Will Return In . . . *Thunderball*.

THUNDERBALL (1965)

Starring: Sean Connery as the hero – James Bond
Adolpho Celi as the villain – Emilio Largo
Claudine Auger as the love interest –
    Dominique (Domino) Vitali

Written By: Richard Maibaum and John Hopkins, based on a story by Kevin McClory, Jack Whittingham and Ian Fleming (see **Observations** below)

Directed By: Terence Young

Tag Line: 'Look Up! Look Down! Look Out! Here comes the biggest Bond of all!'

Relevance of Pre-Title Sequence? Not much, although we later discover that Colonel Jacques Boitier, the man who is killed by Bond in the pre-title sequence, is a SPECTRE agent. Largo tells Bond on their first meeting that he has already been told about him – presumably by Blofeld.

Theme Song: Sung by Tom Jones (but see **Observations** below).

Cringe-Worthy Title Sequence: Among all the usual Maurice Binder overheated teenage imagination stuff, we get a sil-houetted skin diver firing a spear gun between the legs of a naked swimming woman. We know that sometimes a cigar is only a cigar, but . . .

Plot: While at a health farm, Bond decides that another patient – the mysterious Count Lippe – is hiding something. Indeed he is: Lippe is an agent of SPECTRE and is in the midst of carrying out a plan to blackmail the Western world. He has with him at the health farm a SPECTRE agent named Angelo who has undergone plastic surgery to make him look like a NATO pilot named Derval. Under Bond's nose they kill Derval and substitute Angelo, who then flies on an RAF Vulcan bomber carrying nuclear bombs, kills the crew and crash-lands the aircraft in the shallow waters of the Bahamas. Bond discovers Derval's dead body, but Count Lippe is killed by SPECTRE before Bond can investigate further.

SPECTRE's chief sends a ransom demand to the UK and US leaders: pay £100 million or a major city will be blown up. Bond recognises a photograph of Derval, makes the connection with the blackmail plot and is sent by M to investigate Derval's sister – Domino – in the Bahamas. Bond soon realises that Domino's lover, Emilio Largo, is also a member of SPECTRE. Bond locates the crashed Vulcan and determines that the bombs will be loaded on to Largo's boat, the *Disco Volante*. Bond calls in reinforcements, and one of the bombs is recovered during an underwater battle. Largo escapes with the other bomb, but Bond intercepts him. Largo dies in a fight, and the bomb is recovered.

Observations: When James Bond arrives in M's outer office, he makes to throw his hat on to the hat stand as usual, except that someone has moved it so that it is next to the door.

Station C covers Canada.

M has called all the available 00 personnel to a briefing. When Bond arrives, there are nine seats at the table. He takes the seventh one – the only gap. This indicates that there are only nine 00 agents. The man sitting in seat number six, by the way, looks nothing like Alex Trevalyan (006 from *GoldenEye*). The folder Bond is given to read is stamped

TOP SECRET, and, interestingly, O.H.M.S.S. (On Her Majesty's Secret Service).

Secret Intelligence Service operatives appear to be equipped with poison capsules in case of capture – Bond's Nassau assistant Paula takes one to evade interrogation by Largo's thugs.

SPECTRE's HQ is in Paris in this film, hiding behind the International Brotherhood for the Assistance of Stateless Persons. They provided consultation on the Great Train Robbery (1963). Count Lippe, their agent, who arranges for the replacement of the NATO pilot, has a Tong tattoo. This is a leftover from the original McClory/Fleming plotting which is redundant now, apart from being a mechanism for getting Bond interested in Lippe. SPECTRE agents appear to wear a large ring with a representation of an octopus on it, as worn by Blofeld in *From Russia With Love*.

Thunderball was to have been the first Bond film, but the legal problems surrounding it at the time put paid to that. During the filming of *Goldfinger*, Broccoli and Saltzman had intended to make *OHMSS* as the next Bond film (and Sean Connery gave interviews at the time saying that he was under contract for two more films – *OHMSS* and one other). At the same time, Kevin McClory was trying to raise interest in an alternative Bond film based on *Thunderball*, for which he had retained the film rights as a result of the court case against Fleming. Having failed to get *Thunderball* off the ground as his own project (apparently he wanted either Laurence Harvey or Richard Burton as Bond), McClory approached Broccoli and Saltzman. As a result *Thunderball* was made as a Connery Bond film with McClory as producer (see the entry on the novel(isation) of *Thunderball* for a discussion of the legal problems).

Guy Hamilton, who had directed *Goldfinger*, was asked to direct *Thunderball* as well, but turned it down. Paul Dehn, who wrote *Goldfinger*, was asked to write the script, but also declined. One of the eventual writers – John Hopkins – had started out in the BBC writing for *Z Cars*.

For the first time, Sean Connery plays the walking and firing agent at the very top of the film. It had previously been played by stuntman Bob Simmons, but a new sequence had to be filmed as *Thunderball* was shot in CinemaScope.

Blofeld's voice is provided by Joseph Wiseman (he who played Dr No in the first Bond film). Claudine Auger is dubbed by another actress for the entirety of the film. Some, but not all, of Adolpho Celli's lines are dubbed by Robert Rietty, who also dubbed Tetsuro Tamba (Tiger Tanaka) in *You Only Live Twice*. Most of the other actors sound as if they have done extensive overdubbing for their own parts in post-production.

Julie Christie, Faye Dunaway and Luciana Paluzzi were among the hundreds of actresses who auditioned for the part of Domino, as were Yvonne Monlaur and Gloria Pau. Raquel Welch was awarded the part and signed a contract, but she was released as a favour from Broccoli to Richard Zanuck at Twentieth Century Fox in order to appear in *Fantastic Voyage*. The part eventually went to a former Miss France – Claudine Auger – but Luciana Paluzzi was cast as Fiona Volpe instead.

Rik van Nutter, who played Felix Leiter, was signed up for the next few Bond movies as well, but when the scripts for *You Only Live Twice* and *OHMSS* were written there was no obvious point at which Leiter could be introduced, and so Nutter was dropped. Martine Beswick – Bond's ill-fated Secret Service companion in Nassau – also appeared in *From Russia With Love* as the battling gypsy Zora. She was also one of the dancers in the title sequence of *Dr No*.

The usual suspects also turn up – Bernard Lee, Desmond Llewellyn and Lois Maxwell as M, Q and Miss Moneypenny. Producer Kevin McClory appears briefly in the film. When Bond enters the Nassau casino, he passes a seated man who is smoking a cigar. That's McClory.

Ricou Browning, Director of Underwater Photography, was the man in the Gill-Man suit in the three *Creature From the Black Lagoon* films. The well-known cult film director André de Toth shot some second unit footage for the scenes of the US Marines parachuting from an aircraft into the sea.

Since in many ways Fleming's book is actually a novelisation of the original McClory–Whittingham script, the book and script can be seen as being identical for all practical purposes. The book does simplify the SPECTRE plot slightly – rather than use plastic surgery to impersonate a NATO pilot, they just bribe the original pilot – and there is an additional sequence in which Bond and Leiter follow the *Disco Volante* in a nuclear submarine.

Richard Maibaum's original idea for the pre-title sequence was similar to that used in the final film – in that Bond was tracking down an enemy agent disguised as a woman – but was set in a gambling den in Hong Kong.

The character of Fiona Volpe was referred to as Fiona Kelly in early drafts of the screenplay, while Paula Caplan was originally Paula Roberts.

Three separate theme songs were recorded for this film. The first two were both versions of the same song – 'Mr Kiss Kiss Bang Bang' – as sung by Shirley Bassey and Dionne Warwick, respectively. 'Mr Kiss Kiss Bang Bang' was what James Bond was known as in Italy, and the producers wanted to acknowledge that in the theme song. There is a rumour that the producers actually wanted the fourth Bond film to be called *Mr Kiss Kiss Bang Bang*, but this seems unlikely given their adherence (at that time) to Fleming's novels. Since the phrase didn't crop up anywhere in the film itself, the name of a nightclub in the Nassau section was quickly changed from the Jump Jump Club to the Kiss Kiss club. It was only at the last minute that the producers decided they had to have the film title in the theme song, so Tom Jones was brought in to sing 'Thunderball'. That, by the way, is why John Barry's music for the film is built around the 'Mr Kiss Kiss Bang Bang' theme, rather than the 'Thunderball' theme – he had almost finished scoring the film when the decision to switch theme songs was made. Tom Jones fainted at the recording session when he completed singing the final top note.

There are various alternative versions of *Thunderball* with slight changes in dialogue (including Bond's). This is almost certainly a result of the extensive post-production overdubbing on the film, rather than actual shooting of alternate scenes. A scene of Largo showing Bond over the *Disco Volante* was filmed but never used in the final cut and, according to Desmond Llewellyn, a decision was taken to cut back the number of scenes in which Rik van Nutter (Felix Leiter) appeared. As one of them involved Q, Desmond Llewellyn's scenes were cut as well.

There's a lot of great travelogue-type photography in this film, but we have a particular fondness for two shots. One is of Bond and Domino in full aqualung gear slowly sinking behind a rock with their limbs entwined. The other is a shot from above of Bond and Leiter's helicopter, showing how shallow the sea is around those parts.

The film was awarded an Academy Award for Best Visual Effects.

The card table over which Bond beats Largo at chemin de fer is the same one at which Bond met Sylvia Trench in *Dr No*.

Locations: France, London briefly and the Bahamas.

James Bond, Fashion Victim: He does wear a straw hat in Nassau, but at least it doesn't say 'Kiss Me Quick'. Q, however, wears a shirt covered with brightly coloured pineapples for which there is no excuse.

Toys for the Boys: Bond escapes from the thugs in France using a rocket backpack. 'Yes, very practical,' his female companion murmurs. They then drive away in his Aston Martin DB5, complete with a bulletproof shield that pops up from the rear boot and water jets that . . . er . . . dampen the opposition (note that the control panel is different from that shown in *Goldfinger*). Later Q gives him a Geiger counter disguised as a watch, and another disguised as a camera, an underwater camera with infrared film, a miniaturised Very flare, a miniaturised air cylinder with four minutes' worth of air and a radioactive tracer pill (completely harmless, of course) and a propeller-driven scuba tank that fires explosive harpoons. SPECTRE have all the big gadgets – a motorcycle that fires rockets and a luxury yacht that converts into a hydrofoil.

Patronising Lines: Bond to Domino: 'Most girls just paddle around. You swim like a man.'

Villainous Foibles: Largo is a typical Italian mafioso type – he even kisses his SPECTRE ring when ordering the death of one of his men for incompetence. Blofeld still has his white cat, but (as in *From Russia With Love*) we do not get to see his face.

Sadism: Largo tortures Domino with an ice cube and a cigar (something to do with the scientific application of cold and heat, we are told).

Single Entendres: Domino: 'What sharp little eyes you've got.' Bond: 'Wait till you get to my teeth.'

Bond to Fiona Volpe when she picks him up in her car: 'How far do you go?'

Lines to Rewind For: 'Was there ever a man more misunderstood?' Bond sighs at one stage.

It's Only a Movie: During the carnival sequence, one group of revellers in the parade are carrying yellow signs that read '007' in large red letters (look for the scene with the pissing dog in the middle of the street – they're passing by behind it). This happened because local islanders were asked to build their own costumes for the parade, and some of them got into the spirit of the film a bit more than the producers would have liked.

After she is revealed to be a villainess, Fiona Volpe taunts Bond by saying, 'James Bond, who only has to make love to a woman and she starts to hear heavenly choirs singing: she repents and then immediately returns to the side of rights and virtue – but not this one.' This is a knowing reference on the part of the scriptwriter John Hopkins back to the character of Pussy Galore in *Goldfinger*.

Mistakes Can Be Fatal: Why does the stretching machine in the Shrublands health farm have a highly dangerous full-on setting? Why not just have safe settings?

Why do SPECTRE, who are presumably not short of a bob or two, send agent Angelo to Shrublands to recuperate after his plastic surgery? Why can't they look after him in a safer location where passing secret agents won't discover their plans? Don't their doctors make house calls (or perhaps SPECTRE Island calls)?

When he's at Shrublands, Bond enters a room marked MASSAGE to confront Count Lippe. When he leaves, the door is marked SITZ BATH & HEAT TREATMENT.

Count Lippe and Bond both have licence plates on their cars when they leave Shrublands. During the chase leading up to Lippe's death, neither car has a licence plate. When Lippe's flaming car careers off the road and into the bushes, it's miraculously regained its licence plate again.

Knowing that Count Lippe is closely linked to the theft of the nuclear bombs, why does Bond then go off to investigate Domino? He has no reason to suspect her of being involved. Why not investigate Count Lippe's background?

When Bond first meets Domino while swimming, he is wearing flippers. He escorts her to her boat, and when he floats there talking to her he isn't wearing flippers. He swims the short distance to his own boat, and suddenly he's wearing flippers again.

Shortly after Domino and Bond have had dinner together, Largo arrives to take her away. As they leave, in the background Bond turns to the following figure of Felix Leiter and says something. At this point in the film, they have not met yet. The error occurred because some scenes were swapped around during the editing to make the flow of the story clearer.

Sneaking out of the cellar of Largo's house after finding Paula's body, Bond leaves the hatch open. Moments later, when Largo passes it, the hatch is closed.

Leiter's clothes change between trousers and shorts when he and Bond are sitting in the helicopter looking for the crashed Vulcan bomber.

When Domino steps on a poisonous spine, it's her right heel that's affected. When Bond sucks the spine out, he sucks it from her left heel.

Escaping from Fiona and Largo's thugs at the Junkanoo, Bond is shot in the right leg. During the subsequent chase the wound is in his left leg.

During the underwater fight scenes late in the film, Bond has his (blue) mask snatched off by a passing SPECTRE agent. He takes a replacement (black) mask from a dead SPECTRE thug. Moments later, he is wearing a blue one again.

The *Disco Volante* explodes into flames with a nuclear bomb on board. Won't this scatter radioactive material far and wide? Doesn't anyone worry about this?

Actor Paul Stassino is credited as playing Palazzi in the film's end credits. In fact, he plays Derval and also Angelo disguised as Derval. The name Palazzi is a holdover from a previous draft of the script.

James Bond Will Return In . . . It's not said on screen, although legend has it that the original prints of the film said 'James Bond Will Return in "On Her Majesty's Secret Service".' The line was allegedly removed when it was decided to film *You Only Live Twice* next.

YOU ONLY LIVE TWICE (1967)

Starring: Sean Connery as the hero – James Bond
Donald Pleasence as the villain –
    Ernst Stavro Blofeld
Akiko Wakabayashi and Mie Hama as the
    love interests Aki and Kissy

Written By: Roald Dahl (although Harold Jack Bloom is credited in the titles before Dahl with providing 'additional story material', which presumably means all those elements of the plot not deriving from Ian Fleming's book – and, let's face it, that's most of them)

Directed By: Lewis Gilbert

Tag Line: '. . . and "TWICE" is the only way to live!'

Relevance of Pre-Title Sequence? It sets up SPECTRE's theft of the American space capsule pretty nicely. Bond's supposed death at the hands of machine-gun-wielding thugs is later referred to by Blofeld.

Theme Song: Sung by Nancy Sinatra.

Cringe-Worthy Title Sequence: Pretty tame by Maurice Binder standards: a series of Japanese girls overlaid against shots of spurting volcanoes and dribbling lava flows. Actually, perhaps it's not that tame after all.

Plot: An American space capsule is engulfed by a mysterious unmarked spacecraft. America blames the Soviet Union, but England has tracked the mysterious craft to the Sea of Japan.

Bond is sent to Tokyo to investigate, but the SIS Head of Station – Henderson – is murdered before he can pass on any useful information. Bond kills the assassin and, substituting himself for the assassin in the escape car, is taken to a building owned by Osato Electrical and Engineering Company. He finds there an order form for liquid oxygen – a key component of rocket fuel – and a photograph which directs him to a ship named the *Ling Po*. While Bond investigates Osato Co. more fully there are several attempts on his life, culminating in his kidnap by Osato.

In space, the situation escalates when a Soviet space capsule is also engulfed by the same unmarked craft.

Bond escapes from Osato Co. and, together with Kissy Suzuki – an agent working for M's Japanese equivalent, 'Tiger' Tanaka – investigates the Japanese island where the *Ling Po* has been seen stopping and unloading. He and Kissy discover that the dormant volcano at the heart of the island is actually a secret base occupied by SPECTRE and its leader, Ernst Stavro Blofeld. SPECTRE are being paid by the Chinese government to start a war between America and the Soviet Union. To accomplish this, they have been stealing space capsules and hoping each side will blame the other. Bond averts the taking of a second American craft – a situation that would certainly have resulted in the USA taking military action against the Soviet Union – and 'Tiger' Tanaka's Ninja troops attack the base. In the confusion, Blofeld escapes.

Observations: M, Q and Moneypenny all appear. Blofeld, still wearing his octopus ring, reappears, and we see his face for the first time. Czech actor Jan Werich was originally cast as Blofeld in this movie, but he left after filming a couple of scenes (supposedly because of illness) and Donald Pleasence was cast instead. Various options were tried to make Pleasence look villainous, including a limp and a hump, but eventually the producers settled on a nasty scar across his eye.

The voice of actor Robert Rietty was used to dub the part of 'Tiger' Tanaka (as played by Tetsuro Tamba). Rietty had previously dubbed Largo (Adolpho Celi) in *Thunderball*. Originally Mie Hama was cast as Aki and Akiko Wakabayashi as Kissy, but Wakabayashi picked up the English language much more quickly than Hama and was recast in the role with more dialogue (but less relevance to the plot).

Bert Kwouk, who plays one of Blofeld's mission controllers in this film, previously appeared as Goldfinger's Chinese liaison in *Goldfinger* (and was shot by Goldfinger, so we assume he's not meant to be playing the same character).

One of the two Hong Kong policemen who find Bond's 'dead' body is Anthony Ainley, who later went on to play the Master in BBC TV's *Doctor Who*.

It had been intended that *OHMSS* was to be the film to follow *Thunderball*, but plans were changed late in the day and *You Only Live Twice* was selected instead. The film bears almost no relationship to Ian Fleming's novel (which was generally believed to be almost unfilmable). The characters of Blofeld, 'Tiger' Tanaka, Kissy (Suzuki) and (Dikko) Henderson are reused, as is the Japanese location and some odd little details such as Blofeld's piranha fish, but all else is new. The original screenwriter Harold Jack Bloom claims to have invented the majority of the plot for the film, although he later left the film for reasons that remain unclear and Roald Dahl took over the scripting. Peter Hunt (later to direct *OHMSS*) had hoped to direct *You Only Live Twice* after his success editing the previous films, but it was not to be.

Director Lewis Gilbert's final cut of *You Only Live Twice* ran to around 135 minutes. Something like twenty additional minutes were removed by the second-unit director, Peter Hunt, before the film was released.

A different theme song, written by John Barry and Leslie Bricusse and sung by an unknown singer, was written for this film but never used. It can be found on the *James Bond 30th Anniversary* double-CD collection.

Mie Hama's character is never named in the film itself and credited only as Kissy on the end credits. In the book this film is based on, she is called Kissy Suzuki. It's worth pointing out that Bond's marriage to Kissy is not a legal marriage, as he is pretending to be a poor Japanese fisherman and has thus given a false name to the Shinto priest.

Cinematographer Johnnie Jordan lost his foot during the helicopter/autogyro chase sequence when one of the SPECTRE helicopters got too close to the helicopter he was filming from and its rotors sliced through his lower leg and his helicopter's landing skids. Filming was abandoned, and remounted later.

Locations: Hong Kong, Japan and, of course, Space.

My Name Is ... Mr Fisher, Managing Director of Empire Chemicals.

James Bond, Fashion Victim: Bond wears his Naval uniform.

Bond infiltrates the Osato building wearing spats, but he's disguised as the assassin who killed Henderson, so he can be excused. His later grey tracksuit can be put down to the Ninja, rather than Bond's own, wardrobe.

Bond's Past Life: Bond tells Moneypenny that he took a First in Oriental languages at Cambridge. Raymond Benson, in his novelisation of *Tomorrow Never Dies*, claims that Bond is fibbing, but in Benson's own *Zero Minus Ten* Bond speaks fluent Cantonese. In this film he does actually speak Japanese pretty well, although he claims he has never been to Japan before.

Henderson gives Bond a vodka Martini that's been stirred, not shaken, but Bond is good enough not to make a fuss.

Bond has used *Little Nellie*, the autogyro, before.

Toys for the Boys: Q brings Bond an autogyro with twin machine guns, rocket launchers with heat-seeking air-to-air missiles, rockets, flame throwers, smoke ejectors and aerial mines. Bond later obtains from 'Tiger' Tanaka some cigarettes that fire small rockets when lit.

Patronising Lines: Bond: 'Why do Chinese girls taste different from all other girls?'

Tiger Tanaka tells Bond: 'In Japan men always come first. Women come second.' 'I might just retire to here,' Bond says wistfully.

Goodbye, Mr Bond: A classic one from Donald Pleasence as he prepares to shoot Bond. He's prevented from doing so when 'Tiger' Tanaka impales his wrist with a sharp-edged martial-arts throwing star.

Sadism: Blofeld has a tank full of piranha fish that he uses to dispose of people he doesn't like (does his cat ever try to hook them out? one wonders).

Single Entendres: 'I think I will enjoy very much serving under you,' Aki tells Bond.

Lines to Rewind For: 'You can watch it all on TV,' Blofeld tells Bond. Too true: that's how we wrote this book, after all.

It's Only a Movie: One of 'Tiger' Tanaka's Ninja troops attacks the camera ferociously with a sword. Another one karate-chops a watermelon on to the camera lens, splashing pulp and seeds everywhere.

Mistakes Can Be Fatal: All this rigmarole with Bond being buried at sea wearing an aqualung and then recovered by divers to a British submarine, just to convince his enemies that he is dead, is pretty pointless. Why not just use a fake body and smuggle Bond to M in disguise?

According to *From Russia With Love*, M and Bond had been together in Tokyo. So why does he claim he's never been there before?

During a car chase, Bond is amazed to see the thugs' car picked up on the end of an electromagnet dangling from a helicopter owned by the Japanese Secret Service. The helicopter takes the car out into the bay and drops it into the water – a process watched by Bond on a TV screen in the car he's in. The picture he's watching shows the helicopter from above, implying that it's being relayed from a second helicopter flying above the first one, but there's nothing else in the sky. (And doesn't anyone notice the Japanese Secret Service dumping cars?) Similarly, the pictures of Blofeld's spacecraft that he is watching in his volcano headquarters could only be transmitted by another spacecraft.

When Bond is left in a plummeting aircraft by Helga Brandt, the fields beneath the aircraft look suspiciously British (the sequence was actually filmed in Scotland).

Bond and Kissy Suzuki are almost overcome by lethal gas in the caves leading to Blofeld's island, and have to swim underwater to avoid breathing it, but later they manage to swim out on the surface of the water without any ill effects.

Why does Blofeld capture the American and Soviet spacecraft and return them to Earth, keeping their occupants captive. Why not just destroy them in space? Surely it would have the same effect for a lot less outlay on hardware?

James Bond Will Return In ... *On Her Majesty's Secret Service.*

ON HER MAJESTY'S SECRET SERVICE (1969)

Starring: George Lazenby as the hero – James Bond
Telly Savalas as the villain –
    Ernst Stavro Blofeld
Diana Rigg as the love interest –
    Contessa Teresa di Vicenzo (Tracy)

Written By: Richard Maibaum with additional dialogue by Simon Raven

Directed By: Peter Hunt

Tag Line: 'Far up! Far out! Far more! James Bond 007 Is Back!'

Relevance of Pre-Title Sequence? It introduces Lazenby as Bond in a vicious fight sequence which is indicative of what's to come; Tracy appears to be trying to commit suicide but is being watched . . .

Theme Song: An orchestral theme over the opening titles; 'The James Bond Theme' over the closing. The film's theme song, 'We Have All the Time in the World', accompanies the montage of scenes showing Bond and Tracy falling in love. It was performed by Louis Armstrong.

Cringe-Worthy Title Sequence: A glass becomes the sands of time running out with scenes from previous Bond films inset. It's not particularly inspired, but was all part of the 'this really is still James Bond' idea that the producers were keen to promote.

Plot: While on the trail of Blofeld, James Bond's interest is piqued by a young woman driving a fast car who stops at a beach and wades out to sea. His rescue is somewhat marred by two thugs who try to restrain them both, although they separately escape. That evening, he encounters the woman again at a casino, when she makes a reckless bet and he has to bale her out as she has no money. She introduces herself as Contessa Teresa di Vicenzo, better known as Tracy, and invites Bond to her suite for repayment. However when Bond goes there, one of the thugs awaits him. After dealing with him, he tries to get answers out of Tracy, who won't talk – and the thug leaves them alone when he realises that Tracy is all right.

The next morning, she's gone, and Bond is 'invited' on a trip at gunpoint to the headquarters of Marc-Ange Draco, of the Union Corse. Tracy is his daughter, a wayward child, and Draco offers Bond £1 million to marry her. Bond agrees to see Tracy, if Draco can help locate Blofeld. In London, Bond is relieved from the search for Blofeld, and he resigns in disgust – although Moneypenny changes his request from resignation to two weeks' leave. As ever, Tracy comes home for Draco's birthday, and forces her father to give Bond the information he seeks without payment – although Bond makes it clear that it is no hardship to spend time with her. After a whirlwind courtship, they end up in Geneva, where Draco has discovered a lawyer, Gumbold, with connections to Blofeld. Bond breaks into Gumbold's office, and finds documents from the College of Arms in London addressed to Blofeld.

With M's reluctant permission, Bond works with Sir Hilary Bray of the College, and masquerades as the genealogist on a visit to Blofeld's headquarters on top of an Alp at Piz Gloria in Switzerland. He is met by Irma Bunt, a strict Fraulein, who keeps the Count's 'patients' under control. Blofeld has pretensions of being the Comte de Bleuchamp, and is also working on allergy research, with a group of attractive young women as his patients. Bond discovers that he is using hypnotic conditioning on the women to make them love items they previously loathed. However, his bed-hopping ways, and a mistake in Bray's briefing, give him away, and he is hauled before Blofeld. Bond manages to escape, and is pursued down the mountain by Blofeld and his men. By luck, he runs into Tracy, who helps him escape, and as they rest that night Bond asks her to marry him.

The next day, the chase is on again, and Blofeld triggers an avalanche, apparently killing Bond but sparing Tracy, whom he captures. He then delivers his ultimatum: a pardon for past crimes, and recognition of his title, or he will destroy strains of plant and animal life. In the short time remaining before the UN capitulate, Bond and Draco combine forces and attack Piz Gloria, freeing Tracy and destroying Blofeld's command centre. Blofeld gets his neck caught in a tree as he tries to avoid Bond on a bobsleigh run.

Bond and Tracy marry at Draco's estate, but, as they are heading for their honeymoon, Blofeld, his neck in a brace, drives past, and Irma Bunt opens fire. Bond cradles Tracy's dead body as his enemies race into the distance . . .

Observations: James Bond likes Dom Perignon '57 (he was drinking the '53 in *Dr No*), and knows his caviar and perfumes. He takes his Martini shaken not stirred, still uses the cigarette case first seen in *Dr No*, and remains mockingly superstitious about the 13th (see *From Russia With Love*). He's heard of Marc-Ange Draco, head of the Union Corse, and is willing to give up being in the Secret Service for Tracy, knowing that the life of a married man and his sort of agent aren't compatible. Their wedding is attended by 'Their Royal Highnesses, My Lords, Ladies and Gentlemen' – friends of Draco's, we assume. We see Bond's office for the first, and so far only, time in the film series, when he looks through souvenirs of past cases (but see **It's Only a Movie** below).

The cover for the SIS is now Universal Exports (London) Ltd. Operation Bedlam is the code name for the hunt for Blofeld, which has been going on for two years since *You Only Live Twice*. M, Moneypenny and Q are all guests at Bond's wedding, as well as making brief appearances earlier. The relationship between M and Moneypenny is more symbiotic than previously, while Bond is definitely more forward with Moneypenny, pinching her backside. M has a beautiful house in the countryside, where he keeps his collection of butterflies.

An Australian chocolate-bar advertisement 'star', George

Lazenby, bluffed his way into an audition for Bond, claiming to be a playboy who raced cars for a living. He tested against the Australian singer Trisha Noble. He was up for the role against John Richardson, star of *One Million Years BC* (the male lead that hardly anyone gets a chance to notice once Raquel Welch is on screen); and three British actors: Anthony Rogers, Robert Campbell and Hans de Vries. His filmed test was the scene in Tracy's hotel suite, where Bond is surprised by Che Che. His performance won him the role.

Two of Lazenby's eventual successors were also considered for the part, alongside Ian Ogilvy (later to star as the Saint on television), Adam West (TV's Batman), and Richard Burton once again. Roger Moore was offered the part when Sean Connery left during *You Only Live Twice*. At that time, there was a possibility that the next film might have been set partly in Cambodia. However, Moore was contractually tied to the TV series *The Saint*, and could not take the opportunity. Co-Producer Cubby Broccoli then offered the part to Timothy Dalton (then best known for his role in *The Lion in Winter*), but Dalton turned it down, believing himself to be too young aged 25.

The producers considered explaining Bond's change of face by making reference to plastic surgery, although the idea was dropped quite early. However, never ones to let a good idea go to waste, they incorporated it into the start of *Diamonds Are Forever*. The title sequence features friends and enemies from the past, and there are numerous nods (see below) to the series' past.

Brigitte Bardot was Peter Hunt's first choice for the part of Tracy, but she signed up to play opposite Sean Connery in *Shalako*. The second choice was French actress Catherine Deneuve, who did not see herself as a Bond girl, no matter how different.

There was a lot of voice dubbing going on in this film. David De Keyser spoke for Gabrielle Ferzetti, while George Baker dubbed George Lazenby for the sequences where Bond was masquerading as Bray. Robert Rietty, who dubbed Largo in *Thunderball*, appears in this film as the Chef du Jour.

Angela Scoular, who plays Ruby, played Buttercup, the seductive enemy agent after Sir James Bond, in *Casino Royale*. Other girls included the absolutely fabulous future *New Avenger*, Joanna Lumley, the children's TV hostess Jenny Hanley, and *Space: 1999*'s metamorph, Catherine Von Schell. Draco's pilot was RAF officer Captain John Crewdson, who previously flew the SPECTRE helicopter destroyed by Bond in *From Russia With Love*.

An early idea for the script saw Blofeld's headquarters on the Maginot Line (the defensive fortifications along the Franco-German border), while at one point Bond was going to chase Blofeld on a snow shovel rather than on a bobsleigh. The ski-jump which later opened *The Spy Who Loved Me* was also under consideration as a mode of escape for Blofeld.

The most important change discussed was for the climax of the film. It was originally planned that *OHMSS* would finish on an upbeat note (and the death of Tracy form the pre-title sequence of *Diamonds Are Forever*), but Peter Hunt, quite rightly in our opinion, fought for it to remain as written by Fleming. He then kept George Lazenby locked in his trailer all day to ensure that the requisite emotion was portrayed.

Although this is commonly regarded as the closest adaptation of Fleming's originals, there are key differences. Blofeld's motivation changes and Tracy accompanies Bond on his escape from Piz Gloria, subsequently being held hostage there, which gives Draco and Bond much more reason to attack. However, in terms of feel and attention to detail (particularly the reconstruction of M's home, Quarterdeck, down to the cannon in the drive), this is Fleming.

OHMSS is the longest film in the canon at 140 minutes, and was saved from further editing by George Pinches, the booking manager for the Rank Organisation (one of the principal cinema chains in Britain at the time), who saw it and found it so fast-paced that he didn't think it should be cut.

However, at least two scenes didn't make it: when Bond buys Tracy's wedding ring in the closing sequences, we saw Irma Bunt watching surreptitiously; and a long sequence in which Bond chases an eavesdropper from Sir Hilary Bray's office across the rooftops of London was also dropped.

Not unusually for Bond films, we don't learn the name of Bernard Horsfall's character, Campbell, until the end credits. The scene where he tries to gain access to Piz Gloria at the ski lift is regularly cut from television and European theatrical showings.

On American television, *OHMSS* was originally shown in two parts, with an ersatz Bond introducing the second part with a commentary.

Locations: The Italian Riviera, the South of France, London, Geneva and the Swiss Alps, from September 1969 to just after Christmas.

My Name Is . . . Sir Hilary Bray, baronet.

James Bond, Fashion Victim: We just love the kilt.

Toys for the Boys: Q proffers some radioactive lint to M at the start of the film, a ridiculous item that demonstrated how reliant on gadgetry Bond seemed to have become. For the rest of the film, he uses his wits rather than gadgets, with the exception of a handy safe-cracker-cum-photocopier that opens Gumbold's safe in Switzerland, and a miniature camera with which he photographs Blofeld's map. But this time, as he tells Q, 'I've got the gadgets and I know how to use them.'

Blofeld seems to have hired a Q Branch, though, with his hypnotic sleep centres, and the make-up compacts containing miniature radios.

Patronising Lines: The pick-up lines from 'Sir Hilary Bray' are bad enough the first time round – but twice? Maybe this should be listed under sadism.

'Just keep my mind on your driving!'

Villainous Foibles: Blofeld's dreams have come down somewhat. Instead of millions of dollars, he simply wants an amnesty for past crimes, and the recognition of his title. The ultimate proof of madness, we think.

Sadism: All the fights in *OHMSS* are very realistic. Tracy is frogmarched by what we later discover are her father's men; Bond hurts her arm when she holds a gun on him, and smacks her; come to that, even her father knocks her out. It's really not her few months. Bond himself is beaten up by Blofeld's men, and dishes out some vicious blows. In the battle for Piz Gloria, flame throwers are used to dispose of people!

Single Entendres: When Irma Bunt checks Bond is OK after Ruby has written on his thigh in lipstick, Bond deadpans, 'Just a slight stiffness coming on . . .'

'You're an inspiration,' Bond tells his second female conquest of the night, and under his breath adds, 'You'll need to be.'

'I hope my big end can stand up to this!'

Lines to Rewind For: 'She likes you,' Draco tells Bond. 'I can see it!' 'You must give me the name of your oculist!'

It's Only a Movie: At the end of the pre-title sequence, Bond turns to camera and says, 'This never happened to the other fellah!' This was the writer's deliberate nod to the audience that Connery had been replaced, as was the scene when Bond goes to his office after 'resigning'. He picks up souvenirs from his previous films – none of which he could have had (Dr No took Honey's knife; Bond didn't pick up the garrotte watch from Grant's body in *From Russia With Love*; and he lost the rebreather in *Thunderball*).

As Bond is escorted to Marc-Ange Draco, he passes a janitor who's whistling Shirley Bassey's title song from *Goldfinger*.

Mistakes Can Be Fatal: Bond wakes after an expensive night with Tracy with immaculately combed hair. And from where did Tracy get the chips that she uses to repay Bond?

Sir Hilary tells Bond that the Bond coat of arms has three bezants (gold balls) on it. When Bond as Bray is displaying his knowledge, he claims there are four. Either way, it's a mistake, because Bond should be talking about Bray's arms, not his own! And originally Lazenby says 'three' – the mistake was 'added' at the voice-over stage.

The backs of the cards change colour in the casino from white to red.

Irma Bunt comments that 'here at least is no avarice', but Bond doesn't pick up the implication that there *is* deceit.

The colour of the sofa in Sir Hilary Bray's room changes from orange to white from shot to shot.

Why doesn't Blofeld recognise Bond? They were face to face in *You Only Live Twice*, and in *OHMSS*. Bond isn't even wearing his disguise when they first encounter one another. Is his snobbery making him that blind?

If Bond and Tracy's car battery is dying on them, how come the lights are still so bright?

Why does Blofeld assume that Bond has died, if he knows that Tracy is alive?

Why don't Bond and Marc-Ange use the headsets to talk to each other in the helicopter?

The long shot of Blofeld caught in the tree shows him holding on by his hands.

James Bond Will Return In . . . *Diamonds Are Forever*.

DIAMONDS ARE FOREVER (1971)

Starring: Sean Connery as the hero – James Bond
Charles Grey as the villain –
    Ernst Stavro Blofeld
Jill St John as the love interest – Tiffany Case

Written By: Richard Maibaum and Tom Mankiewicz

Directed By: Guy Hamilton

Tag Line: Strangely, none on the posters.

Relevance of Pre-Title Sequence? Well, following Blofeld's murder of Bond's wife Tracy in *OHMSS*, Bond tracks him

163

down and (or so he thinks) kills him in the pre-title sequence of *Diamonds Are Forever*. This supposedly sets up Bond's motivation to stop him later in the film when he turns up very much alive – as if saving the Western world wasn't enough.

Theme Song: Sung by Shirley Bassey.

Cringe-Worthy Title Sequence: Actually, it's not too bad.

Plot: The SIS are brought in on a simple smuggling matter – someone appears to be hoarding diamonds, and the Government are worried that the stability of the diamond market might be threatened if all the hoarded diamonds are released at the same time. Bond infiltrates the smuggling ring and follows it to Las Vegas. In parallel, he discovers that whoever is running the smuggling is closing the operation down and killing everyone who was working on it. He tracks the diamonds to a laboratory belonging to millionaire Willard Whyte in the Arizona desert, where it would appear that they are being fitted into a satellite which is ready for launch.

Breaking into Whyte's penthouse suite in the hotel he owns (the Whyte House), Bond discovers that Whyte has been abducted and Ernst Stavro Blofeld is running everything. Blofeld's plan is to launch a satellite with a powerful laser on board (for which he needs the diamonds). Once it's launched, he will blackmail the world. Blofeld tries to kill Bond, who escapes and releases Whyte, but in the interim Blofeld's satellite is launched and Blofeld destroys a US missile base in North Dakota, a Russian submarine and a Chinese missile base. He intends holding an international auction with nuclear supremacy as the prize. When the US launch an attack on his base – a converted oil rig – he tries to destroy Washington, DC, but Bond destroys his base and apparently kills him again.

Observations: Bond has a membership card for the Playboy Club, membership number 40401 (if we were really sad, we would try to find out who *really* has this membership number). Tiffany Case has obviously heard of Bond – a legend in small-time smuggling circles, perhaps. Or has Blofeld spread the word that his people are to look out for Bond? Bond claims he knows a good tailor in Hong Kong. Well, he was there in *You Only Live Twice* (and beforehand, according to the dialogue of *From Russia With Love*).

George Lazenby had signed a Letter of Intent to appear in *Diamonds Are Forever*, and was even sent an initial instalment of his salary, but he returned the money. Following his departure from the Bond franchise, the search was on to find a new Bond. Director Guy Hamilton favoured Burt Reynolds, but it was John Gavin who finally signed a contract to become the cinema's third 007. Gavin was a reasonably well-known American actor who had played Sam Loomis in *Psycho* and Julius Caesar in *Spartacus*. His career had slipped fractionally since then, to the point where he had played a spoof version of Bond in a cheap Italian flick entitled *O.S.S. 117 Double Agent*. Oddly (for those of us with that sort of mind), his co-stars were Luciana Paluzzi (Fiona in *Thunderball*) and Curt Jurgens (later to play Stromberg in *The Spy Who Loved Me*). Suddenly, however, Sean Connery was back on the scene, and Gavin's contract was quietly bought out for a sum said to be around $50,000.

Connery's motives for returning for what he was already saying was his final Bond film were threefold – first, his fee of $1.25 million plus a percentage of the film's profits, all of which he was donating to a Scottish charity that he was involved with; secondly, a fee of $10,000 per week for any overrun on the shooting schedule; and thirdly, United Artists' agreement that they would support any two films Connery wanted to make afterwards (either as actor or director).

M, Q and Moneypenny all turn up, as does Felix Leiter (played in this – his fourth appearance – by the charisma-less Norman Burton). Ernst Stavro Blofeld returns for his fifth appearance, played this time by Charles Grey, who previously appeared as Dikko Henderson in *You Only Live Twice*.

Shane Rimmer (a NASA technician) was in *You Only Live*

Twice, while this film contains a rare example of the actor David De Keyser appearing himself, rather than overdubbing someone else's voice (he's Blofeld's plastic surgeon). Jill St John was originally cast in the bit part of Plenty O'Toole, but director Guy Hamilton was sufficiently impressed by her to give her the larger part of Tiffany Case.

During the filming of *OHMSS*, Harry Saltzman had planned to film *Moonraker* as the next Bond film. This was almost certainly in order to capitalise on the success of the SF movie *2001: A Space Odyssey* (1968) and the worldwide interest in the Apollo 11 moon landing (July 1969). Saltzman approached TV puppet-master Gerry Anderson during the making of his TV series *UFO* and asked him to submit a proposal. Anderson and *UFO*'s script editor Tony Barwick turned in a seventy-page draft which involved a villain named Zodiac (whose three identical henchmen are named Tic, Tac and Toe) threatening to destroy the nuclear submarines of the Western world powers if they do not pay him a great deal of money. The situation was additionally complicated by the fact that Michael Billington – one of the actors in *UFO* – had been suggested as a replacement for George Lazenby. In the end, and for reasons that remain unclear, the Anderson–Barwick proposal was never taken up (although it did result in a brief flurry of legal activity around the time of *The Spy Who Loved Me*) and *Diamonds Are Forever* was chosen as the next film. Maybe a small carry-over from this planning was the astronauts in the 'moonwalk' sequences at the Nevada installation, but can anyone explain to us what they are practising and why they are moving in slow motion?

Other initial ideas revolved around having the brother of Goldfinger as the villain, with a laser cannon housed in a supertanker as his superweapon (shades of *The Spy Who Loved Me*). Gert Frobe was allegedly approached to play the part. The Blofeld plastic-surgery idea was originally intended to explain why Bond's face had altered in *OHMSS*. Director Guy Hamilton has stated that France was considered as a location for the film. The reclusive billionaire Howard

Hughes, the basis for Willard Whyte, allowed the producers to film inside his casinos and at his other properties in exchange for one 16mm print of the film.

Ian Fleming's book is about Bond tracking down a group of Mafia-related diamond smugglers. Apart from the basic diamond-smuggling plot that motivates the first half of the film, there's no real relationship. Initial drafts of the script had Bond and Blofeld in a dramatic chase across Lake Mead, also involving various bizarre craft from the local casinos, which culminated in a finale on the edge of the Hoover Dam. The finale as filmed – with Blofeld attempting to escape from his oil rig in a submarine – was to have continued with Bond chasing him by hanging from a weather balloon, following him ashore and cornering him in a salt-mining plant in Mexico. Mmm-hmm?

In an early draft of the script, Bond swooped in on the sunbathing Marie in a hang-glider in the pre-title sequence. This idea was eventually used in *Live and Let Die* as Bond's method of infiltrating Mr Big's base. An earlier script version of the final fight scene between Bond, Wint and Kidd had the fight occurring below decks on the ship. While Kidd's death would have been much the same as the one we saw, Wint was to have been stabbed with an ice sculpture. Although the scripts refer to Blofeld's men as SPECTREs, there is no direct reference to the organisation.

For those people wondering exactly why Plenty O'Toole turns up dead in Tiffany Case's pool, a sequence filmed but cut from the final print involved a humiliated Plenty returning to Bond's room, finding Bond and Tiffany making love, noting Tiffany's address from an item in her discarded handbag, then later arriving at Tiffany's house to confront her but bumping into Wint and Kidd, who mistake her for Tiffany and kill her. Poor girl – an earlier scene of her having dinner with Bond was also cut. 'Entertainer' Sammy Davis Jnr had played a cameo role during filming, but even his scenes were cut out of the final film. We also should have seen frogmen approaching Blofeld's rig from below: this also was cut, but explains their presence on the film poster.

A prose adaptation appeared in the *Daily Express* from 18 to 24 December 1971, written by their film correspondent Vic Davis, to tie in with the release of the film in the UK. It appears that the space allotted was curtailed suddenly, as it describes the climactic rig sequence – from Willard Whyte's 'I don't have anything in Baja' to the scene on the *QE2* – in 57 words!

Locations: Japan, Egypt, Amsterdam, South America, South Africa and London (all briefly), plus the area in and around Las Vegas, America.

My Name Is . . . Bond impersonates the smuggler Peter Franks in order to infiltrate the diamond-smuggling ring, and the technician Klaus Hergersheimer to infiltrate Professor Doctor Metz's laboratory. He and Tiffany Case book into a hotel under the names Mr and Mrs Jones.

James Bond, Fashion Victim: Bond wears a white tuxedo jacket when he visits the casino. Humphrey Bogart might have got away with it in *Casablanca*, but nobody in the higher echelons of British society would dare. He later wears a white suit with a pink tie that even Roger Moore would have turned his nose up at, and a plaid jacket over a polo-neck. The costume designer on this film should have been shot. And the less said about the sight of Blofeld escaping in drag, the better.

Bond's Past Life: Bond is an expert sherry-taster – hardly the sort of thing one picks up by accident.

Toys for the Boys: Bond uses surprisingly few gadgets in this film. However, in the background of Q's laboratory, technicians can be seen fitting missiles into the Aston Martin DB5 (missiles that aren't used in the film). Bond has a piton-firing gun, and Q later turns up with a voice-changing device and a magnetic thingie which can cause one-armed bandits to pay out every time.

Patronising Lines: M to Bond when Bond admits he doesn't know much about diamonds: 'Refreshing to hear there's one subject you're not an expert on.'

Goodbye, Mr Bond: Well, Blofeld says, 'Good *night*, Mr Bond.'

Sadism: While Bond is looking for Blofeld, he assaults a woman with her own bikini top. Is there no end to the man's bullying?

Single Entendres: 'Hi, I'm Plenty,' says a woman as she introduces herself to Bond. 'Of course you are,' he replies, looking at her bust. 'Plenty O'Toole,' she adds. 'Named after your father, no doubt,' he says.

'I'm afraid you've caught me with more than my hands up,' a naked Bond says to Tiffany Case when he finds her in his bed, holding a gun.

Lines to Rewind For: Blofeld gets all the best lines. 'Science was never my strong suit,' he admits at one stage, and later, 'I do so hate martial music.' Some of his lines suggest a previously unsuspected talent as a stand-up comedian. 'Surely you haven't come to negotiate, Mr Bond?' he asks at the climax of the film. 'Your pitiful little island hasn't even been threatened.' 'If we destroy Kansas the world may not hear about it for years,' he later tells one of the scientists who work for him, and, as Tiffany Case tries to get out of his control room with the tape of his satellite control instructions shoved in the back of her bikini bottoms, 'We're showing a little more cheek than usual, aren't we?'

Mistakes Can Be Fatal: During the fight in the lift with Bond, the *real* Peter Franks manages to pick up a huge shard of glass and attempts to slice Bond open with it, without cutting his hand.

During the chase between the motorcycles and the moonbuggy, a tyre rolls into view from off screen. It's not the right size for the motorcycles, and looks more like it came off the moonbuggy, but when we next see the buggy all of its wheels are intact.

Why, after Blofeld has gassed Bond into unconsciousness in the lift, do Wint and Kidd take him out into the desert and leave him in a section of pipe so he gets buried beneath the

Nevada sands? Why not just . . . kill him? Where is the light coming from in the pipe when Bond wakes up?

Why does Burt Saxby turn up to kill Willard Whyte? The instruction was given to a vocally disguised Bond!

Bond is told at one point that the first laser used a diamond. It didn't – it used a ruby (Theodore Mainen built it in 1960). Besides that, Blofeld's diamond-*encrusted* satellite is useless – the laser light has to be generated inside the crystal, not reflected from it. It fits with Blofeld claiming he's not a scientist, but in *OHMSS* he very definitely was one!

James Bond Will Return In . . . *Live and Let Die*.

LIVE AND LET DIE (1973)

Starring: Roger Moore as the hero – James Bond
Yaphet Kotto as the villain – Kananga
Jane Seymour as the love interest – Solitaire

Written By: Tom Mankiewicz

Directed By: Guy Hamilton

Tag Line: None (again!)

Relevance of Pre-Title Sequence? Well, although Bond doesn't actually appear in it (the first time that's happened since *From Russia With Love*) it covers the death of all three British Secret Service agents – the events that spark off Bond's interest in Kananga.

Theme Song: Paul McCartney and Wings.

Cringe-Worthy Title Sequence: Skulls, naked black women and flames: a rather cheesy evocation of voodoo spoilt only by the fibre-optic lamp backdrop.

Plot: Three British Secret Service agents are killed within the space of a few hours – one in New York, one in New Orleans and one on the island of San Monique in the Caribbean. The only connection appears to be a man named Kananga – he's the Prime Minister of San Monique, and the agent in New York was shadowing him on behalf of the CIA (the man in New Orleans was investigating odd activities at a restaurant named Filet of Soul).

Bond travels to New York and tails Kananga to another in the Filet of Soul chain of restaurants, but is taken captive by a black gangster named Mr Big and sentenced to death. Escaping, he and Felix wonder what the connection is between the Prime Minister of a Caribbean island and a Harlem gangster.

Bond travels to San Monique in search of answers, and falls in with CIA agent Rosie Carver. After an attempt on Bond's life, and the exposure of Rosie as a double agent on Kananga's payroll, Bond infiltrates Kananga's cliff-top fortress and seduces his 'ward' Solitaire. They escape together and discover that Kananga is growing vast fields of poppies under nets to escape prying eyes. Kananga is obviously producing and smuggling heroin at a vast rate. They head for New Orleans, where Bond still wants to discover the connection between Kananga and the British Secret Service agent's death, but they are taken captive by Mr Big's men again. Bond escapes, is recaptured and confronts Mr Big, who turns out to be Kananga himself. Kananga grows the poppies, produces the heroin and then distributes it (as Mr Big) through his chain of Filet of Soul restaurants. He intends giving away the heroin until he has cornered the market, thus driving the Mafia out of business.

Bond manages to destroy Kananga's heroin-refining operation in New Orleans and escapes along the Louisiana bayous. Hearing that Kananga has returned to his island realm with Solitaire, he follows and finds that Kananga is having Solitaire sacrificed at a voodoo ceremony. While he rescues her, Leiter's CIA agents blow up the poppy fields.

Bond and Solitaire penetrate Kananga's underground heroin-refining plant on San Monique and Bond kills Kananga in hand-to-hand combat. A last-minute attack by Kananga's henchman, Tee-Hee, is averted, and Bond and Solitaire are safe.

Observations: James Bond has moved: his flat is not the one he occupied in *Dr No*. He knows at least a smattering of Italian, and has a friend in San Monique – Quarrel Jnr (presumably son of the Quarrel killed in *Dr No*), who now appears to be working for the CIA.

Bond uses trickery to get Solitaire to sacrifice her virginity to him and tell him what Kananga is up to. Isn't this a trifle . . . manipulative? Still, at least he tells her, so that's OK, isn't it?

The official title for Q Branch is the Special Ordnance Section.

After Sean Connery turned down an offer of £5 million to return once more, the Eon machine swung into action to recast the part. United Artists apparently wanted someone of the stature of Burt Reynolds or Paul Newman. The eventual short list included, rather bizarrely, Jeremy Brett (later to play another quintessential British hero, Sherlock Holmes, on television), Julian Glover (later to appear as the villain in *For Your Eyes Only)* and young actor Michael Billington. This was Billington's first actual screen test for the role, although he had been under consideration by Broccoli and Saltzman since *OHMSS*. Billington eventually turned up as Soviet agent Sergei in *The Spy Who Loved Me*. When *Live and Let Die* had been confirmed as the next Bond film after *Diamonds Are Forever*, but before Sean Connery had said he would not return as Bond, tentative plans had been set in motion to ask Ursula Andress to return as Honey Ryder (from *Dr No*). When Roger Moore was cast, it was decided not to saddle him with any hangovers from previous films. In fact, unlike *OHMSS*, where the producers went to great lengths to persuade the audience that here was more of the same, in *Live and Let Die* there's a distinct sense that they are trying to avoid anything that reminds us of the old Sean Connery films. There is no briefing scene in M's office (M comes to Bond instead), Bond is never seen in a tuxedo, he never orders a

Martini (in any form), there's no Q scene at all and John Barry isn't doing the music.

It's been said that Bernard Lee's indisposition almost prompted his replacement as M by actor Kenneth More. This strikes us as implausible: More's screen persona is of a cuddly, warm human being, not a crusty retired admiral with damnably clear grey eyes.

A fairly late draft script for the film has the part of Solitaire to be played by a black actress and the part of Rosie to be played by a white actress. Following the switch in race, Catherine Deneuve, who had turned down the role of Tracy in *OHMSS*, was apparently seriously considered for the part of Solitaire.

There's a distinct whiff of Shane Rimmer's voice about the overdubbing on the CIA agent in the pre-title sequence. Shane Rimmer previously appeared in *You Only Live Twice* and *Diamonds Are Forever*.

Little of Ian Fleming's novel survives Tom Mankiewicz's adaptation. Mr Big, Fleming's villain, is revealed to be a false identity used by Kananga (named after a stuntman who also owned the crocodile farm used during the filming), and the treasure-hunting plot is jettisoned in favour of the heroin production. Only the characters – Mr Big, Solitaire, Felix Leiter – remain.

Cuts to the script included references to Quarrel Jnr's dad and *Dr No*, the setting up of the shark gun, and a section in the pre-title sequence that would have explained Bond's Italian mission. The hang-glider that Bond used to infiltrate Mr Big's base was originally scheduled for the pre-title sequence of *Diamonds Are Forever*, where Bond would have used it to swoop in on the sunbathing Marie. The keelhauling sequence which finishes the novel was considered for the movie, and eventually turned up in *For Your Eyes Only*.

Live and Let Die marks the second time that the theme song has been performed as a real song within the main body of the film (the first was Matt Monro's 'From Russia With Love'). George Martin persuaded Paul McCartney to write the theme song, but McCartney told the producers that he would allow its use only if he performed it. Accordingly, a compromise was reached whereby B.J. Arnau gave it a feminine rendition mid-film.

Locations: New York, New Orleans, London, San Monique (a fictional island in the Caribbean).

James Bond, Fashion Victim: Bond's overcoat and gloves are rather more Head Prefect than Secret Agent. And Bond starts smoking a cigar that must be all of twelve inches long (sometimes, of course, a cigar is just a cigar).

Toys for the Boys: Given the absence of Q himself, it's all a bit thin. We get a radio in a hairbrush, an electronic bug detector, a compressed-gas shark gun and a watch that also acts as a powerful magnet and a buzz-saw, but the latter just appears, with no previous set-up, to save Bond's life.

Bond's Past Life: Bond has just returned from Rome, where he has been on a mission with the Italian Secret Service.

Villainous Foibles: Kananga's henchman, Tee-Hee, has a metal arm. The original was bitten off by a crocodile.

Single Entendres: Rosie: 'I'm going to be completely useless to you.' Bond: 'I'm sure we'll be able to lick you into shape.'

Bond to Solitaire when she asks him not to leave: 'Absolutely. There's no sense in going off half cocked.'

Lines to Rewind For: Bond, when M appears at his door early one morning: 'Insomnia, sir?' M, tersely: 'Instructions.'

Bond, hearing the voice of Felix Leiter coming out of a loudspeaker hidden in a lighter in the dashboard of a CIA car: 'A genuine Felix Lighter – illuminating.'

Bond, when Rosie discovers the snake he's killed in the bathroom: 'You should never go in there without a mongoose.'

Bond, when Rosie discovers the voodoo symbol in her room: 'It's just a hat, darling, belonging to a small man of limited means who lost a fight with a chicken.'

Rosie, when Bond threatens to kill her after a bout of

afternoon sex: 'But you couldn't – you wouldn't – not after what we've just done.' Bond: 'I certainly wouldn't have killed you before.'

Sheriff J.W. Pepper to Bond: 'What are you – some kind of doomsday machine?' And on hearing Bond is working for the Secret Service he wails: 'On whose side?'

Lines to Fast-Forward Past: Mr Big: 'Names is for tombstones, baby.'

It's Only a Movie: Solitaire's tarot cards have an 007 motif repeated in the design on the back.

M tells Bond that 'Hamilton' has been killed in New York – Guy Hamilton directed the film, of course.

Geoffrey Holder as Baron Samedi keeps grimacing at the camera.

Mistakes Can Be Fatal: Bond follows the killer of his CIA driver into a shop called Oh Cult. Distracting the woman at the till, he follows the man through the back into a car park. He then sees Kananga, Solitaire and their bodyguards pass through the car park and he tails them to Harlem. As he leaves Oh Cult, the woman at the till picks up a radio and tells someone that he is leaving. We assume she's telling one of Kananga's people, but it later turns out that she's with the CIA. So why doesn't Leiter know a lot more about what's going on than he appears to, if he has a CIA agent in place in Kananga's rear entrance (as it were)?

So who exactly sends the tarot card to Bond that tips him off about Rosie's treachery? Solitaire? And if so – why?

Why didn't Felix Leiter tell Bond that he had an agent in San Monique? Also, if Rosie's loyalties are with Kananga rather than Felix, why does she stop Quarrel when she thinks he's trying to kill Bond? Surely she must think he's also working for Kananga.

'Three men and a girl have been killed in the last four days,' says Bond. He's wrong – it's four men and a girl if you include the CIA driver who picks Bond up at the airport. Or perhaps he doesn't count, as he's just a functionary.

When Baron Samedi attacks Bond with a machete during the sacrifice of Solitaire, why does Bond pick up another machete and fight him, rather than just shooting him? Machismo?

We see, during the fight on the train between Bond and Tee-Hee, that Tee-Hee's false arm has no joints from the claw up to the elbow. So how come, earlier in the film, he can bend it at the wrist?

James Bond Will Return In . . . *The Man With the Golden Gun.*

THE MAN WITH THE GOLDEN GUN
(1974)

Starring: Roger Moore as the hero – James Bond
    Christopher Lee as the villain –
     Francisco Scaramanga
    Britt Ekland as the love interest –
     Mary Goodnight

Written By: Richard Maibaum and Tom Mankiewicz

Directed By: Guy Hamilton

Tag Line: 'The World's Greatest Villains Tried To Kill James Bond. Now It's Scaramanga's Turn To Try.' (US only.)

Relevance of Pre-Title Sequence? It establishes Scaramanga's Fun House, and his regard for 007. As with *Live and Let Die*, Bond as such does not feature.

Theme Song: A pretty nondescript offering from Lulu. The end-title version is unusual in that the opening picks up from Bond's last line – 'Good night, good night. Sleep well, my dear. No need to fear: James Bond is near . . .' – then goes back to the main song.

Cringe-Worthy Title Sequence: Girls swim and dance in water and against fireworks with a golden gun appearing from time to time. Nothing to stay awake for.

Plot: A golden bullet arrives in London, with 007's number engraved on it, the trademark of Francisco Scaramanga, an assassin who charges $1 million per victim. Bond is useless to M on his current assignment, searching for a missing solar-engineering expert, until this situation is resolved, so he goes to Beirut, where 002 was apparently shot by Scaramanga in 1969. With some difficulty, he obtains the bullet, and it's analysed by Q Branch. The gold/nickel content indicates it's probably been made by Lazar, a gunsmith based in Macao.

Bond persuades Lazar to tell him how Scaramanga collects his merchandise, and follows statuesque Miss Anders from a casino in Macao across to Hong Kong, where he meets with fellow agent Mary Goodnight. Further not so gentle persuasion of Anders gains the information that Scaramanga will be at the Bottoms Up club. He is – but Bond isn't the target. Gibson, the solar-engineering expert, is, and Scaramanga's midget henchman, Nick Nack, relieves the corpse of the solex, the key piece of the system. Bond is arrested by Lieutenant Hip and taken across Hong Kong Harbour, where he escapes on to the wreck of the *Queen Elizabeth*, which turns out to be a naval intelligence base. There M assigns Goodnight to act as liaison between Bond and Hip while they investigate a new lead: Hai Fat, a wealthy Thai businessman, who could have afforded Scaramanga's fee.

Gambling that Hai Fat and Scaramanga won't have met, Bond, masquerading as the assassin, visits Hai Fat, and gets an invitation to dinner. Unfortunately the two are well acquainted and a trap is laid for Bond. He wakes in a karate school from which he escapes with Hip and his two karate-kicking nieces' help. Hai Fat decides he will lie low, but Scaramanga kills him.

Miss Anders reveals that she sent the bullet to Bond: 007 is the only person Scaramanga fears. He even has a model of him in his Fun House. She agrees to get the solex and Bond will then deal with the assassin. They arrange to meet at a boxing tournament, but when Bond arrives she's already dead. Scaramanga warns Bond off, but Bond finds the solex and gets it to Goodnight, who then follows Nick

Nack. Unfortunately, Scaramanga is following her and she is captured.

Bond gives chase, accompanied inadvertently by Sheriff J.W. Pepper, but Scaramanga's car becomes a plane and he flies off. Q's homing device in Goodnight's dress works, showing she's in Red Chinese waters. Unofficially, Bond strays into their territory, and arrives on Scaramanga's island. Scaramanga shows off his solar complex, complete with laser, with which he destroys Bond's plane. He then challenges Bond to a duel: his golden gun against Bond's Walther PPK. Bond accepts, and Nick Nack appears to help him. Eventually Bond replaces his own mannequin and shoots a very surprised Scaramanga. Goodnight, meanwhile, has dealt with Scaramanga's maintenance man, although, by tipping him in a vat of liquid helium, she's ensured that the place will explode. Bond retrieves the solex; he and Goodnight steal Scaramanga's junk and, after dealing with Nick Nack, who's stowed away, they take a slow boat from China . . .

Observations: Bond smokes cigars throughout this film, and prefers Dom Perignon '62 (odd, considering he was drinking the '53 in *Dr No* and the '57 in *OHMSS*). He has a good working knowledge of solar energy. He's 'never killed a midget before'. Agent 002, Bill Fairbanks, died in Beirut in 1969. The *Queen Elizabeth I*, which sank under mysterious circumstances in Hong Kong Harbour in 1971, is used as a spy base by the British. M, Moneypenny and Q all appear, with M and Q sniping like two old women. The Chief of Staff also turns up, but is uncredited.

Britt Ekland originally auditioned for the part of Andrea Anders, but it was eventually taken by the future Octopussy, Maud Adams. The role of Scaramanga was originally offered to Jack Palance.

Sheriff J.W. Pepper of the Loueeesiahna State Poh-lice is on holiday in Bangkok and gets caught up with Bond. Clifton James's character was evidently so popular after his appearance in *Live and Let Die* that he was featured in the trailer.

The central villain has the same name as in Fleming's

novel, and became a killer for much the same reason (his pet elephant was shot); Mary Goodnight is the heroine; but otherwise Fleming wouldn't recognise it. His Scaramanga is organising a conference between the Mafia and the KGB in Jamaica. The film's version would more likely be hired to take them out!

The elephant hunt that appears in *Octopussy* was originally planned to appear in *The Man With the Golden Gun*.

The first draft of the script saw what became the Beirut nightclub scenes set in a brothel, with Saida as a raddled old whore whom Bond reluctantly beds.

The sequence at the karate school originally took place at a martial-arts academy, where Hip and his nieces are watching the 'display', complete with running commentary from the headmaster. In the escape, Bond is accompanied by one of the girls, Nara (giving him an audience for his quips). Bond also has a different sidekick for the car chase. Rather than Sheriff Pepper (and why would an American tourist be wanting a demonstration of an American car in Bangkok?), it's just an ordinary member of the public (as Mrs Bell was in *Live and Let Die*).

Scaramanga's maintenance man was originally Hai Fat's henchman, Merdan, who was removed from the earlier sequences. In an early draft of the script, Hai Fat was to have a partner called Lo Fat. No doubt nowadays he would have been called 'I Can't Believe It's Not Fat'.

Bond was also going to be masquerading as an ornithologist (a nice tip of the hat to the birdwatcher after whom Fleming named the character in the first place).

The duel on the beach between Bond and Scaramanga was supposed to be much longer. Scaramanga hides in the rocks, and he and Bond exchange insults. Bond then fashions a Molotov cocktail, which the assassin shoots out of the sky. Bond therefore thinks that Scaramanga has no more bullets, but he's revealed to have an extra one in his belt buckle. At the end of the gunplay, Bond would be down to one bullet only as well.

Alice Cooper's *Muscle of Love* album features a song with

the film's title. The CD alleges that this was to have been the film's theme song but that the producers backed out.

The spiral jump that Bond and Sheriff Pepper make was done for real. Stunt driver 'Bumps' Willard sat in a re-designed American Motors Hornet and followed exactly the set speed that would allow him to take off, describe a 360-degree circle and land on the specially designed ramps (disguised for the purposes of the film as bits of a broken bridge). Eon Productions took out a two-year option on the stunt, which was worked out on the computers at Cornell University. It was originally going to be followed by the police cars trying the same thing. Instead, now, we assume they just went back a mile and a half or so.

A prose adaptation of *The Man With the Golden Gun* appeared in the *Daily Express* from 19–24 December 1974, penned, like that of *Diamonds Are Forever*, by Vic Davis. It's much smoother than its predecessor, although Calthorp is named Boothroyd (as he was in the original script), and Lieutenant Hip disappears entirely. The battle between Bond and Scaramanga on the beach is novelised in its entirety.

Locations: Scaramanga's island in Red Chinese waters, London, Beirut, Macao, Hong Kong, Bangkok.

My Name Is . . . Scaramanga (when he visits Hai Fat).

James Bond, Fashion Victim: What a wonderful check sports jacket 007 wears as he arrives on Scaramanga's island. Not.

Bond's Past Life: He knew Mary Goodnight two years previously, before she was stationed in Hong Kong. (Whether they were lovers then is ambiguous: in the books, Goodnight was Bond's secretary, and *The Man With the Golden Gun* is the first time they become lovers.) Bond has been searching for Gibson and his missing solex for some time before the movie begins.

Toys for the Boys: Well, of course the main one is the Golden Gun itself, manufactured by Calibri Lighters. It consists of a ballpoint pen, a cigarette lighter and its case, and a cufflink, with the bullet being secreted in Scaramanga's belt buckle.

Q has a rocket launcher disguised in a camera and supplies a third nipple for Bond to 'disguise' himself as Scaramanga (Hai Fat finds him 'quite titillating'). Bond also uses a special rifle adapted for a fingerless hoodlum.

For the girls, Q Branch designs their dresses. The bottom button has a homing device in it.

One toy didn't make it. Originally Q gives Bond a camera with 'gas ejection: instant solidification . . . liquid non-adhesion . . .' and a self-destruct mechanism. It didn't get used operationally by Bond, even in the first draft of the script.

Patronising Lines: Bond's relationship with Mary is totally patronising. It starts with, 'Madam, would you be kind enough to move this bloody bedpan,' and deteriorates from there. Our favourite, though, is his comforting words after he has turfed Mary out of bed in favour of Miss Anders: 'Your turn will come'!

Villainous Foibles: Scaramanga has a third nipple above and slightly to the right of his left one; he has a butterfly collection as part of his Fun House, a masochistic training ground to which he allows his midget servant, Nick Nack, to import hired killers; he uses a special 4·2mm golden gun. He has a love of golden jewellery. He makes love only before he kills and it's clear from one scene that the gun is a penis substitute.

Sadism: To counter Roger Moore's natural urbanity, the writers placed him in situations where he had to show Bond's darker side. The fight in the Beirut nightclub is reminiscent of *The Saint* at its best, while later he twists Anders's arm before smacking her round the face and threatening her with a blow to the neck. In the fight in Hai Fat's garden, he tightens one of the sumo wrestlers' G-strings. When Bond goes to school, there is an unpleasant display between two of the students culminating in one of them dying.

Single Entendres: 'You have no idea what that [the bullet] went through to get here.'

'Speak now, or forever hold your piece.'

'He must have found me quite titillating.'

'I'll keep the wine chilled' – 'And everything else warm.'

And finally, 'She's just coming, sir . . .'

Lines to Rewind For: 'Who would pay $1 million to have me killed?' Bond asks. 'Jealous husbands, outraged chefs, humiliated tailors . . . the list is endless,' M replies.

It's Only a Movie: As Bond passes Sheriff Pepper on the river, the soundtrack plays the five-note theme from *Live and Let Die*.

Mistakes Can Be Fatal: How does Rodney (the hoodlum) arrive on Scaramanga's island for the pre-credits sequence? In that clear an area, sound would travel easily, if nothing else.

How does one shot from Rodney's gun take two arms off the Al Capone mannequin?

Why is Calthorp at Bond's initial briefing?

And why does Bond go to all the trouble of finding the bullet used against 002? He's got a bullet there in London, for crying out loud. The whole sequence in Beirut could be cut, if someone just thought of analysing the golden bullet 'Scaramanga' has been kind enough to send to them!

Although Anders indicates clearly where Scaramanga's third nipple is, Bond puts it on the wrong breast at the wrong height.

Although this is a criticism of most of the Roger Moore movies, we'll say it just the once here: What sort of secret agent is he if everyone knows him all around the world? And, worse, he's proud of that?

Why are Hip's nieces with him when he comes to the karate school? And why doesn't Hip stop when the girls tell him Bond isn't in the car? Doesn't his car have a reverse gear?

If Scaramanga's bullets are so expensive, how come he doesn't notice that Anders has purloined one and sent it to London?

It's not at all clear who owns the island Scaramanga is based on. Hai Fat tells him to go to the plant, implying the island, we believe; while later Scaramanga tells Bond that 'he does his landlords [the Red Chinese] an occasional favour'.

There's a hastily inserted line, but it does seem like Kraus gets forgotten when Scaramanga talks about just him and Nick Nack on the island.

Nick Nack taunts Bond that he has only three bullets left, but he's fired only twice (that we've seen – see **Observations** above).

The control console reads COMPUTERS CONTROLLED LOCK IN. Goodnight follows it with her finger, and reads out 'Computer Interlock'. Maybe she did deserve everything Bond was saying about her?

How does M get Scaramanga's phone number? (In the first-draft script, M states that they tried to ring him first.)

James Bond Will Return In . . . *The Spy Who Loved Me*.

THE SPY WHO LOVED ME (1977)

Starring: Roger Moore as the hero – James Bond
    Kurt Jurgens as the villain – Carl Stromberg
    Barbara Bach as the love interest –
     Major Anya Amasova

Written By: Christopher Wood and Richard Maibaum (but see **Observations** below)

Directed By: Lewis Gilbert

Tag Line: 'It's the biggest. It's the best. It's Bond. And Beyond.'

Relevance of Pre-Title Sequence? It sets up the theft of the British submarine (important to the plot of the film) and the fact that Bond has killed Anya Amasova's lover.

Theme Song: Sung by Carly Simon. The end version begins with a rugby-club rendition of the first verse, before Ms Simon retrieves it.

Cringe-Worthy Title Sequence: A silhouetted Bond-figure in a tuxedo trampolining across the screen, and a naked woman performing gymnastic tricks around a terribly phallic scaled-up gun barrel.

Plot: Two nuclear submarines – one British and one Russian – have been stolen. A mysterious person offers the submarine detection device for sale to the highest bidder. Bond is sent to Egypt to negotiate with businessman Max Kalba, who is known to be representing the seller, but has to go through a middleman, Fekkesh, first. Two things become very clear very quickly – first, the Russians are also bidding, in the shape of Major Anya Amasova, and secondly someone wants to frustrate the sale, and does so by killing both Kalba and Fekkesh. Bond and Anya chase the assassin – a giant of a man with metal teeth – but he escapes.

During a conference between M, General Gogol, Bond and Major Amasova, Bond realises that the small piece of the plans for the submarine detection device that they obtained from Max Kalba before he was killed contain a clue pointing to the millionaire shipping magnate Carl Stromberg. Bond and Anya travel undercover to Stromberg's oceanic home in Sardinia to investigate, but he sees through their disguise and tries to have them killed. Investigating more openly in an American nuclear submarine, Bond and Anya are stunned when the submarine is incapacitated and swallowed up by one of Stromberg's oil tankers – actually a seagoing submarine stealer. Both the British and the Russian submarines are already inside her capacious body.

Stromberg explains that, tired of the corruption of civilisation, he intends using the nuclear missiles taken from the submarines to provoke a Third World War between the Soviet Union and the United States of America, devastating the land so that mankind will have to live beneath the sea. Without Stromberg's knowledge, one of his employees had tried to sell the plans of his submarine tracking equipment, and he had sent Jaws to recover the plans and eliminate anyone involved in the foolish scheme.

Stromberg fires the missiles, but Bond has retargeted them so that they destroy the submarines that fired them rather than their original targets of New York and Moscow. Bond follows Stromberg back to his Sardinian undersea base, where he has taken Major Amasova, and shoots him. Bond and Anya escape in a life capsule.

Observations: After the downplaying of previous Bond elements in Moore's first two films, a brief reference is made by Anya to Bond's ill-fated marriage (see *OHMSS*).

Bond has learnt how to defuse nuclear bombs (he had no idea in *Goldfinger*).

The Spy Who Loved Me marks the first appearances of the Minister for Defence (played by Geoffrey Keen) and General Gogol (played by Walter Gotell, who had previously played Morzeny in *From Russia With Love*). Bernard Lee and Desmond Llewelyn as M and Q seem to have patched things up, with Lois Maxwell making an all-too-brief appearance as Miss Moneypenny.

The late Kurt Jurgens (or Curd Jürgens), who played Stromberg, was a well-known German stage and screen actor. George Baker, who plays Captain Benson, previously appeared in *OHMSS* as Sir Hilary Bray (and dubs George Lazenby's voice for some of the film). Shane Rimmer was previously in *You Only Live Twice* and *Diamonds Are Forever* in minor roles. Robert Brown, as Admiral Hargreaves, was to return to the series six years later in *Octopussy*, as M following the death of Bernard Lee.

Guy Hamilton was originally going to direct *The Spy Who Loved Me*, but left to join *Superman: The Movie* (on which he was later replaced by Richard Donner).

Dave Prowse (Darth Vader in *Star Wars*) and Will Sampson (the actor who played Jack Nicholson's Native American friend in *One Flew Over the Cuckoo's Nest*) were both considered for the part of Jaws. Cubby Broccoli claimed that he discovered Richard Kiel and told the writers to create a part for him in the film.

Milton Reid, who plays Sandor (the man Bond holds up by the tie), was previously one of Dr No's guards, and one of Mata Bond's attendants in *Casino Royale*. Watch out for Valerie Léon, stalwart of numerous 1970s comedy series (including *The Two Ronnies*) and that well-remembered Hai Karate! aftershave advert, as a hotel receptionist.

The film's cinematographer is Claude Renoir – grandson of the famous painter and nephew of the famous film director.

The music for the film was written by Marvin Hamlisch – an odd choice, considering the fact that he was better known as a writer of musicals such as *A Chorus Line*. The lyrics of the theme song were written by Hamlisch's then partner, Carole Bayer Sager.

When Fleming sold the rights of *The Spy Who Loved Me* to Albert Broccoli and Harry Saltzman, he made it a condition of the deal that they were not to use any of the plot of his book – just the title.

There are at least thirteen significant correspondences between the plots of *The Spy Who Loved Me* and the previous Bond film, *You Only Live Twice*. Lewis Gilbert directed both films. Although only two writers are credited with the screenplay, twelve or so worked on it at one time or another. The situation is confusing – made more so by the fact that the various orders of events as reported by different Bond reference books are not consistent. Briefly: Roald Dahl (writer of the script for *You Only Live Twice*) recommended the American comic writer Cary Bates, who turned in a draft involving nuclear submarines which was based on *Moonraker* and set at least partially around Loch Ness. Hugo Drax would have been the villain; Tatiana Romanova (from *From Russia With Love*) the love interest. Later writers – including former Bond writer Tom Mankiewicz, novelist Ronald Hardy, well-known film writer and Irwin Allen collaborator Stirling Silliphant, film director John Landis (best known for *The Blues Brothers*, *Trading Places* and *An American Werewolf in London*), thriller writer Derek Marlowe and, bizarrely, that grand old man of English literature, Anthony Burgess – kept various elements of that original idea but failed to make the script gel.

Richard Maibaum introduced the notion of reusing SPECTRE as the villains, under the control of a villain named Stavros, but his script was rewritten by the incoming writer Christopher Wood, and one of the changes was to drop all references to SPECTRE in order to avert possible legal action from Kevin McClory, who had co-written the plot of *Thunderball* with Ian Fleming and who had an arguable claim on the copyright of Blofeld and SPECTRE now that the ten-year period after *Thunderball* had elapsed (see File 007). Stavros was also renamed Stromberg to avoid similarity with Ernst Stavro Blofeld.

Gerry Anderson brought legal action against the producers when he discovered that aspects of the script bore a resemblance to a *Moonraker* proposal that he and Tony Barwick had been asked to submit in the late sixties (for more details, see the film entry on *Diamonds Are Forever*). Anderson was persuaded to drop his case, and rights to his proposal were purchased by the producers.

The Spy Who Loved Me is the first film to have been produced by Cubby Broccoli alone. His relationship with Harry Saltzman had been deteriorating for some time, and the two men had been almost alternating production duties on the films. Following the rather lacklustre performance of *The Man With the Golden Gun*, United Artists bought out Saltzman's share in the Bond phenomenon.

Lois Chiles, later to play Dr Holly Goodhead in *Moonraker*, was under consideration for the role of Anya Amasova. She refused, saying that she was temporarily in retirement.

Until shortly before filming, the pre-title sequence involved Bond making love on a raft somewhere offshore in an exotic location. Following the 'pager' message from M, he surfs ashore. Some of the draft scripts following the introduction of Anya Amasova's character also have a Soviet equivalent of Q – named P! – while in one early draft of the script, Bond and the Russian goons fought in the Cairo Museum of Antiquities (this sequence was moved to *Moonraker*). The backgammon match between Bond and Kamal Khan in *Octopussy* was originally intended to be here between Max Kalba and Bond. Jaws originally died when he fell into a furnace in Stromberg's watery fortress.

Christopher Wood's novelisation of the script (*James Bond and the Spy Who Loved Me*) counts as a decent Bond novel in its own right, and is certainly more stylish than many of the later volumes. Some interesting differences exist between the book and the final version of the film, probably reflecting cuts or changes in the script: Stromberg's ship is called the *Lepadus*, not the *Liparus*; Jaws's real name is Zbigniew Krycsiwiki; Anya Amasova's boss is Colonel-General Nikitin (head of SMERSH, and a character from Ian Fleming's novel *From Russia With Love*) rather than General Gogol; and Bond is tortured early on by having electrodes attached to his wedding tackle and a large voltage applied. Interestingly (or perhaps not) we are told that Bond is a Scorpio. However, Wood does commit one cardinal blunder: he indicates that Bond has never seen a nuclear submarine before, whereas Bond actually spent some time on one in Ian Fleming's novel *Thunderball*.

Locations: Austria, Egypt, Sardinia and a momentary glimpse of Scotland (although the film makers chose to use Canada's Baffin Island as a stand-in for Austria, because it suited the requirements for the parachute ski-jump stunt, and strangely the Bahamas as a stand-in for the undersea sections of Sardinia).

My Name Is ... Robert Sterling (supposedly a marine biologist).

James Bond, Fashion Victim: Blazer and white trousers (hello, sailor). Tan safari jacket, blue shirt and beige slacks. Brown suit and striped shirt. Note also that this is the second film in which we see Bond in his Naval uniform.

Bond's Past Life: Bond was at Cambridge University. Later, when he served in the Royal Navy, he was assigned to the *Ark Royal*. He speaks fluent Arabic, and he knows the Minister of Defence well enough to call him Freddie.

Toys for the Boys: Q demonstrates a hovering metal tea tray that can accelerate along a tabletop and slice someone's head off, a spring-loaded cushion, a saddle with a spring-loaded dagger in a sensitive area, a hookah that fires bullets and a sprayer that dispenses what looks like liquid concrete.

Bond uses a watch that receives messages and passes them on via a dymo printout, a ski-stick that fires rockets, and a water-cycle. He also drives a submersible Lotus Esprit fitted with a concrete sprayer, missiles, mines and what appears to be an octopus-like ink-cloud dispenser.

Patronising Lines: Bond runs through a whole string of patronising put-downs about Major Amasova's driving, culminating in, 'Would you like me to drive?'

Goodbye, Mr Bond: Once, plus one 'Farewell, Mr Bond.'

Villainous Foibles: Stromberg, the primary villain, has webbed fingers (clearly visible in at least two points in the film, but never referred to). Jaws, his hulking assassin, has metal teeth which he uses to bite through chains and necks with equal ease.

Sadism: Bond suspends a villain above a long drop, gets the information he wants from the man, then lets him fall anyway. Later, Bond shoots Stromberg four times in cold blood.

Single Entendres: Anya, when she finds out that Bond has an injury: 'Why don't you lie down and let me look at it?'

The Minister for Defence, having pulled Bond's escape capsule from the sea and being about to discover a naked Bond and Major Amasova locked in an embrace inside: 'Do you think there's any chance of the bends?' Moments later, he exclaims, 'Bond, what do you think you're doing?', to which Bond replies, 'Keeping the British end up, sir.'

Lines to Rewind For: Stromberg: 'Farewell, Mr Bond. That word has, I must admit, a welcome ring of permanence about it.'

It's Only a Movie: Considering the fact that this film is seen as marking the place where the rot began to set in, it's actually remarkably free of in-jokes. Bond's parachute in the pre-title sequence has a Union Jack pattern, of course (so much for going undercover), and, when he and Major Amasova are trekking across the Egyptian desert, the soundtrack is playing the theme from *Lawrence of Arabia*.

Mistakes Can Be Fatal: When Stromberg's stolen submarines fire their missiles, their progress is shown on a large, translucent globe in his control centre. Unfortunately, the lights representing the missiles describe huge semicircles on the globe, going thousands of miles out of their way – as if someone drove from Glasgow to London via Dublin. It's as if their ballistic trajectories have been projected down on to the surface of the globe.

The Captain of the HMS *Ranger* is alternately referred to as Captain and Commander Talbot.

James Bond Will Return In . . . *For Your Eyes Only* (but the next film was actually *Moonraker*).

MOONRAKER (1979)

Starring: Roger Moore as the hero – James Bond
Michael Lonsdale as the villain – Hugo Drax
Lois Chiles as the love interest –
     Holly Goodhead

Directed By: Lewis Gilbert

Written By: Christopher Wood

Tag Lines: 'Other films promise you the moon. Moonraker delivers.'
    'Where all the other Bonds end . . . this one begins!'

Relevance of Pre-Title Sequence? We see the Moonraker shuttle being hijacked, and Bond being thrown out of a plane. However, what works as a very effective sequence is destroyed when Jaws reappears and lands without benefit of a parachute on a circus tent, which folds in. We suppose it's relevant in that it warns you what's coming up!

Theme Song: A very insipid song that even the great Shirley Bassey could do very little with.

Cringe-Worthy Title Sequence: We see Roger Moore relievedly floating to Earth on his parachute, then it's the normal naked girls and pseudo-agents accompanied by shots of Earth from space. It's one of the better ones. Shame about the song, though.

Plot: Bond is assigned to discover why there is no wreckage of a Moonraker space shuttle at the site of the crash of the RAF plane which was transporting it over to Britain. His first port of call is Drax Industries in California, run by Hugo Drax, a billionaire obsessed with the conquest of space. Attempts on Bond's life make him suspicious and, with the help of Drax's assistant Corinne, he breaks into Drax's safe, where he discovers blueprints for custom-made glassware from Venini Glass in Venice. He also meets Dr Holly Goodhead, an attractive scientist who doesn't take much of a shine to Bond. Bond leaves, and Drax has Corinne killed.

In Venice, Bond finds containers that match the blueprints being made, and runs into Holly Goodhead again. Another attempt is made on Bond's life on the Venice canals, which he survives (although his credibility doesn't), and that night he returns to the glass factory, where he discovers a scientific laboratory manufacturing a chemical and placing it into globes. In his hurry not to be caught, Bond leaves out a phial of the chemical, which one of the scientists knocks over, releasing a gas, which proves fatal to humans, but not to the laboratory animals and plants. Drax's henchman, Chang, attacks Bond, but 007 defeats him and goes to his rendezvous with Holly. She admits that she's CIA, also concerned about Drax, and they agree to join forces.

Bond calls in M and Frederick Gray, the Minister of Defence, but when they go into what was a laboratory it's been transformed into a palatial room, with Drax awaiting them. Bond is given two weeks' leave by M to pursue the case unofficially, and goes to Rio de Janeiro, home of C & W, whose packing cases he had found in Venice. Investigating C & W's warehouse that night, during the carnival, Bond finds it empty save for an air-freight sticker – and runs into Jaws again. Stromberg's henchman has replaced Chang, but 007 and local agent Manuela escape.

Monitoring Drax Air Freight's planes from a vantage point, Bond runs into Holly yet again, and this time they agree to team up properly. The cable car they ride down on is attacked by Jaws, from whom they escape again, although they are then captured by Drax's men in a phoney ambulance. Bond escapes, but Holly is still a prisoner.

Q has analysed a phial of the toxin that 007 took from the laboratory and traced it to a black orchid in the upper reaches of the Amazon. Bond finds it guarded by Drax's men, as well as Jaws. Using a hang-glider, Bond evades them and follows a beautiful woman into an ancient temple – Drax's headquarters. Bond is brought before Drax, whose Moonrakers are lifting off. Drax intends to fire globes of the toxin in orbit around the world to destroy the world's human population, and then repopulate the planet with perfect genetic specimens he has gathered together. Bond and Holly are reunited in the blast chamber of Moonraker 5, from which they escape and hijack Moonraker 6.

Blasting off, they are brought on automatic pilot to Drax's space station, built high above the Earth, invisible because of radar jamming. Bond and Holly destroy the radar jammer, allowing the US and USSR to see it, and the US launch the Space Marines. The agents are meanwhile brought before Drax, who orders Jaws to expel them from the airlock. Bond persuades Jaws that there won't be a place for him or his new girlfriend in this genetic paradise, and he changes side. The marines attack, although Drax has managed to launch three of his deadly globes. Bond eliminates Drax; then he and Holly use the laser in Moonraker 5's nose to destroy the three globes before they can release their toxin.

Observations: As increasingly became the case over the Roger Moore years, we learn little more about either 007 or the Secret Service in each film. Here we discover that Bond speaks fluent Italian and still drinks his Martinis shaken, not stirred, M is answerable to the Minister of Defence and Station VH is in Rio de Janeiro. However, in Bond's world in 1979, things are very different: the Americans have a space shuttle at Vandenberg which is used by the US Space Marines under Colonel Scott.

M (Bernard Lee, sadly for the last time), Moneypenny and Q turn up, alongside Frederick Gray. General Gogol (Walter Gotell) and his assistant Rublevitch (Eva-Rueber Staier) make a brief appearance. The amazed man on the beach from *The Spy Who Loved Me* makes a cameo in St Mark's Square . . .

And, of course, Jaws (Richard Kiel) is back. *Moonraker* is criticised for being slapstick, yet if you remove Jaws from the pre-credits and the riverboat chase, and totally remove his girlfriend, the film stands up much better. Funnily enough, this is exactly what Christopher Wood did when he wrote the official novelisation (released as *James Bond and Moonraker*). We're not aware of Jaws' presence until after Chang's death – giving his entry far more of an impact. But he is here, complete with deadly dentistry – and a steel groin, from the look on James Bond's face when he punches him there.

Moonraker was a Franco-British co-production made by Les Productions Artistes Associés (Paris) and Eon Productions Ltd (London). This explains the high proportion of French cast and crew as well as the locations. The star Michel (the correct spelling of his name) Lonsdale was delighted with the opportunity, as there weren't similar opportunities to play such parts in France normally. Earlier, James Mason was offered the part of Hugo Drax, and Louis Jourdan, who later played Kamal Khan in *Octopussy*, was also under consideration but was committed to another film at the time. Lois Chiles had previously been considered for the role of Anya

Amasova in *The Spy Who Loved Me*, but said she was temporarily in retirement.

It has been alleged that Kate Bush was asked to sing the theme tune of the film, but refused.

The producers felt that Ian Fleming's book wasn't relevant. We may be biased, but a nuclear bomb falling on London is still a pretty frightening idea. They retained Drax's name, the name of the rocket, and the scene where Bond and the heroine are trapped beneath the rocket's exhausts – then threw most of the rest away. There's one lovely throwaway line, though, from Frederick Gray: 'I play bridge with this fellow Drax', a key element of the Fleming novel. The final version is a comparative rarity: a Bond film without Richard Maibaum's name on it, although his later co-writer and producer of the franchise, Michael G. Wilson, did some uncredited rewrite work on the script. The centrifuge sequence is very reminiscent of the traction table in *Thunderball*.

Even up to the month when filming began, it was intended that Barbara Bach return in a cameo appearance as Major Anya Amasova (from the previous film, *The Spy Who Loved Me*). She was to have been seen in bed with General Gogol. The fight between Chang and Bond in the Venice Glass Museum was first designed to appear in *The Spy Who Loved Me* in the Cairo Museum of Antiquities 'mummy room'. Corinne Dufour started life as Trudi Parker (a name she retains in Christopher Wood's novelisation). Originally, Bond and Holly were going to trail the planes from Rio airport in mini-Acrostar planes (as later used in the pre-credits of *Octopussy*). After some aerial acrobatics, they would be attacked by a fleet of Vampyre jets sent by Drax. The stunt was dependent on the water level at the Angel Falls at the time of shooting, and, unfortunately, the river bed was dry, so no stunt.

A scene was edited out in which Drax holds a meeting in the blast chamber beneath Moonraker 5. It would explain why such an elaborate set was built.

The product placement in *Moonraker* is perhaps the most obvious of all the movies, particularly the sequence where the ambulance carrying Bond and Holly is driving up a mountain road, passing huge advertising hoardings for each one!

Interestingly, Drax states that he *has* created a dynasty for the new race to look up to. Does this mean there are little baby Draxes (Draxi?) around somewhere?

The fight scene atop the cable cars just doesn't work. The blue screen work is very poor compared with a lot of the effects used later in the film.

Locations: London, California, Venice, Rio de Janeiro, the Amazon and 'Outer Space'.

James Bond, Fashion Victim: The dart gun must have created havoc for his tailor.

Bond's Past Life: Bond is on his way back from 'an African job'.

Toys for the Boys: This is the film where the gadgetry really runs wild. M's office is now equipped with a computer screen. Q is issuing a wristgun activated by nerve impulses, with five blue darts (armour-plated) and five red (cyanide-tipped). Bond uses an X-ray machine inside his cigarette case, and a miniaturised camera personalised for 007 (the second 0 is the lens). In Venice he has a gondola which can become motorised, and which also has a hovercraft cushion underneath, in which secret agents, anxious not to blow their cover, can parade around St Mark's Square. How *does* Q get the money for his section?

He also provides Bond with what the script calls the Q-Craft, which can eject mines and torpedoes from the rear as well as becoming a hang-glider when the button 'roof' is pressed.

At the workshop hidden in Brazil, Q is testing exploding bolas, a sombrero-wearing dummy that opens up to reveal a machine gun, and a laser pistol, which is later used to deadly effect in outer space. Without warning earlier in the film, Bond's Seiko wristwatch conceals a fuse and explosive.

The CIA are getting in on the act, too. Holly is equipped with a pen with a poison nib, a diary that fires darts from the spine, an atomiser that shoots flames, and a radio in her handbag.

Patronising Lines: Bond's assumption that Dr Goodhead is male, and his attempts to come back from that, are pretty patronising.

'Play it again, San,' Bond says to an Asian assassin.

Goodbye, Mr Bond: 'Mr Bond, Dr Goodhead, I bid you farewell.' We'll let Drax off. He's French.

Sadism: Corinne's death is beautifully shot and pumps up the tension. The fight between Chang and Bond gets quite vicious.

Single Entendres: 'I like to keep abreast of things,' Bond tells Holly.

'Can I interest you in something?' he's asked at the glass museum. 'I'm tempted to say yes immediately,' he replies.

'I think he's attempting re-entry, sir.' At least Q is looking at his instrumentation at that stage.

Lines to Rewind For: 'Look after Mr Bond. See that some harm comes to him.'

'Mr Bond, you defy all my attempts to plan an amusing death for you.'

'James Bond – you appear with the tedious inevitability of an unloved season.'

'At least I shall have the pleasure of putting you out of my misery.'

And, of course, the classic exchange as Drax prepares to shoot Bond with a laser gun: 'Desolated, Mr Bond,' and, as Bond shoots Drax through the heart with a cyanide-tipped dart, 'Heartbroken, Mr Drax.'

Lines to Fast-Forward Past: Drax: 'Allow me to introduce you to the airlock chamber.'

It's Only a Movie: The hunters' retreat is the opening notes from Richard Strauss's *Also Sprach Zarathustra* (better known as the theme from *2001: A Space Odyssey*). The theme from *Close Encounters of the 3rd Kind* is the key to opening Drax's scientific lab in Venice, while the Magnificent 007 is accompanied by Elmer Bernstein's theme from the western.

Mistakes Can Be Fatal: For safety reasons, let alone the weight of a ton of fuel, why on earth are the RAF transporting a shuttle that's fuelled?

Drax's henchman sounds like he's called Char, yet in the titles he's listed as Chang.

Holly Goodhead is an astronaut and therefore presumably fully fit. Why does she have a packet of Marlboro cigarettes in her hotel drawer? (Yes, we know: it's called product placement . . .)

Why does Bond think it better to go on to the top of the cable car rather than wait inside?

The snake that attacks 007 in the pool is very obviously rubber.

OK, we can accept that the space station has a radar-jamming system. But how did they disguise all the shuttle launches that must have gone on beforehand, or the station itself during construction? We know that the shuttles aren't equipped with radar jamming, as they show up on each other's radar screens.

It's an old mistake, but since much was made of the involvement of NASA experts as technical advisers to the film it's worth mentioning. In a vacuum you can't hear sound. It's all very well for the laser beams from the weaponry to carry on into space, as they would, but not accompanied by a distinctive whoosh!

The layout of the station doesn't fit with the way they've set up their zero-gravity sections.

How did Jaws get his girlfriend up to the station?

Bond kills Drax with the dart gun. But he wasn't wearing it when he entered Drax's temple hideout (his wrist clearly doesn't have anything on it when he knocks out the Moonraker 6 pilots). When did he get it back?

James Bond Will Return In . . . *For Your Eyes Only* (this time for real).

FOR YOUR EYES ONLY (1981)

Starring: Roger Moore as the hero – James Bond
                Julian Glover as the villain – Ari Kristatos
                Carole Bouquet as the love interest –
                   Melina Havelock

Written By: Richard Maibaum and Michael G. Wilson

Directed By: John Glen

Tag Line: '(When It Comes To Action, Adventure, Romance . . .) No One Comes Close To James Bond 007.'

Relevance of Pre-Title Sequence? Since it was intended to introduce audiences to a new Bond, it's more a continuity feast with the return (and death?) of one of Bond's old enemies. Since the legal battle was raging between Eon Productions and Kevin McClory at the time over the ownership of SPECTRE and Blofeld, we think this was an amusing way of once and for all ensuring that any other Bond film would definitely not be official – how could it be with its main villain dead? It has no relevance to the rest of the movie whatsoever.

Theme Song: 'For Your Eyes Only', written by Bill Conti and Mick Leeson, and sung by Sheena Easton, was nominated for an Oscar for Best Song, but lost to the theme from *Arthur*.

Cringe-Worthy Title Sequence: Sheena Easton is the only title singer, to date, who appears in the title sequence. Depends whether you like her or not, then.

Plot: The spy ship *St Georges*, equipped with the ATAC communications device, is sunk accidentally by a mine in the Ionian Sea, and both the British and the Russians are after it. Marine archaeologist Sir Timothy Havelock's daughter Melina returns home and sees her parents murdered by Hector Gonzales, a Cuban hitman. Bond is briefed by the Chief of

Staff that the Havelocks were looking for the ATAC. He therefore travels to Madrid, where Gonzales is staying, and witnesses Gonzales being paid by a ruthless-looking man. Gonzales is killed by a crossbow bolt fired by Melina, and Bond helps them both escape. Melina is set on revenge, although Bond tries to dissuade her.

Bond identifies the paymaster as Emile Leopold Locque, a Belgian enforcer last seen in Cortina, northern Italy. Bond liaises with the local agent, Ferrara, who introduces him to Ari Kristatos, his contact among the Greek underworld. Kristatos tells Bond that Locque works for his rival, Colombo. Kristatos is sponsor to Bibi Dahl, a young ice skater, and 007 agrees to take her to the biathlon. Bond spots Melina, who was lured to Cortina by a fake telegram from 007, and saves her life before packing her off back to Corfu.

Bond and Bibi watch Erich Kriegler, an East German champion, perform in the biathlon. Bond sees rather more of him when Kriegler, alongside Locque's thugs, try to kill him in an extended ski chase, although he evades them. Another attempt is made when he says goodbye to Bibi, after which he discovers Ferrara dead clutching a white dove, Colombo's sign.

Bond travels to Corfu and meets Kristatos, who points out Colombo to him. To find out more about Bond, Colombo's mistress, Countess Lisl, makes an unsubtle play for him to which he responds, but the next morning she is killed by Locque. Bond is saved by men wearing the white dove. He awakes in Colombo's headquarters, where the smuggler persuades him that Kristatos is really the enemy, and will prove it during a raid on a factory in Albania. This he does, and at the end Bond kills Locque.

Bond and Melina find the wreck of the *St Georges* and collect the ATAC, although they are attacked by Kristatos's men in both a specially equipped diving suit and a small mini-sub. When they surface, they find Kristatos waiting. He relieves them of the ATAC and plans to take it to St Cyril's to await collection by the Russians. Bond and Melina are keel-hauled but they manage to cut themselves free and use a spare diving tank luckily left on the sea floor. The Havelocks' parrot, Max, repeats the phrase 'ATAC to St Cyril's' to them, and, via Colombo, Bond discovers that this is a monastery at the top of a supposedly unclimbable mountain. Bond climbs it, and lets a basket down to allow Colombo, his men and Melina to come up. Tension is rising in Kristatos's camp, as he tells Bibi and her trainer that they are going to Cuba. They therefore decide to leave, and help Bond and party deal with Kristatos's guards. General Gogol arrives to collect the ATAC, but before he can get it Bond throws it off the mountain. He stops Melina from killing Kristatos, but Colombo deals with him anyway . . .

Observations: James Bond speaks Spanish, and is an expert on orchids. Interestingly, Gonzales identifies Bond through his Walther PPK, and infers that the whole British Service has a licence to kill.

Bernard Lee, who played M in every film, died of cancer while preparing for his part, and the script was rewritten stating M was on leave. A very acerbic Chief of Staff (James Villiers) replaced him alongside a grunting Minister of Defence. Tanner had featured in the original script, sharing the lines with M. The scene in the Greek confessional was originally going to feature M rather than Q. As an aside, the Marvel Comics adaptation still features M.

For a long period after *Moonraker*, Roger Moore insisted that he would not be returning to the part of 007. *For Your Eyes Only* was therefore the focus for another round of Bond auditions, with James Brolin, Lambert Wilson and Timothy Dalton all under active consideration. Mel Gibson has said he was offered the part (as he was regularly afterwards) but turned it down. Maryam D'Abo (who later played Kara in *The Living Daylights*) screen-tested against the actors. As happened with Sean Connery in *Diamonds Are Forever*, only at the last minute was a deal struck with Roger Moore for him to return for the fifth time.

One legacy of all this toing and froing is the pre-credits sequence, showing Bond at his wife's graveside, which was supposed to be an immediate continuity link for audiences seeing a new actor in the role. As it turned out, the reverse approach was actually taken when Timothy Dalton assumed the role in 1987.

Carole Bouquet, who played Melina Havelock, had visited the set of *Moonraker*, from where Albert Broccoli and John Glen remembered her.

A bald man (played by John Hollis) wearing a neck brace stroking a white cat appears in the pre-credits sequence? No, we can't say that this rings any bells with us at all . . . Hollis had played a Thai monk in *Casino Royale*.

General Gogol (Walter Gotell) makes a brief appearance at the start and finish, accompanied originally by Eva-Rueber Staier in her traditional comforting role. Miss Moneypenny has acquired a make-up drawer in her filing cabinet, all the better to be ready for James. Q makes his customary appearance with an assistant, Smithers, played by Jeremy Bulloch, who was previously one of the British submariners in *The Spy Who Loved Me*. And that amazed man who followed Bond from *The Spy Who Loved Me* to *Moonraker* turns up here as well, as one of the guests whose dinner is skied through.

One of the Bond girls, Tula, later turned out to be a transsexual.

Noel Johnson, who played the first eponymous incarnation of radio's *Dick Barton – Special Agent*, appears as the Vice Admiral. And yes, that is Charles Dance playing one of Kristatos's henchmen. Michael G. Wilson plays the priest who flits across the screen at the marriage ceremony at St Cyril's. John Wells, who mugs it up as Denis Thatcher, played Fordise, Q's assistant in *Casino Royale*. Cassandra Harris, who plays Countess Lisl, was Pierce Brosnan's wife.

Sadly, stuntman Paolo Gigon was killed during the bobsleigh chase.

The theme of the Havelocks' daughter (in the original named Judy) seeking revenge for her parents' death at the hands of Gonzales, and exacting it with a crossbow, comes from the title short story from Fleming's 1960 collection, *For Your Eyes Only*. The Kristatos–Colombo rivalry, Bond being recruited by both camps, and the raid on the factory (which in the book culminates with the death of Kristatos, here with the death of Locque) are from 'Risico', which was published in the same collection, *For Your Eyes Only*. The keel-hauling sequence is taken from *Live and Let Die* (in which film it was originally intended to appear), except there Bond and the woman escape because the villain's boat blows up before they are cut to shreds on the coral.

John Glen revealed that Jaws was considered for *For Your Eyes Only*, but was not felt right for the new mood of the film. Glen visited Athens and the Acropolis as a potential location, but decided against it.

Early versions of the script included a frostiness between Bond and Melina since she won't sleep with him until she has gained revenge, Bond dropping a huge pile of snow and ice on to the hockey players at the end of the fight in the ice rink, more overt references to both Kristatos's and Brink's sexual interest in Bibi, and Kriegler stepping on a loose floorboard during the final fight, which knocks him in the crotch.

Locations: The Ionian Sea, Madrid, Cortina, Corfu.

My Name Is . . . James Bond, writing a novel about drug smugglers.

Toys for the Boys: Bond has a Lotus with a rather drastic burglar preventative (it explodes!). On his way to use the Identigraph, which allows him to build up a picture of a suspect and then tap into the databases of the friendly security services, he passes through Q's lab, where he sees a fake plaster cast spring out with great force and an umbrella with razor-sharp ribs. Bond also has a wristwatch with a digital display and walkie-talkie capability, with which Max the parrot can talk to Margaret Thatcher.

Goodbye, Mr Bond: Blofeld gets one last try: 'Goodbye, Mr Bond – I trust you had a pleasant . . . fright!'
'Farewell, Mr Bond, but not goodbye . . .' says Bibi.

Villainous Foibles: As Julian Glover noted, 'As an actor I have to be fairly good as Kristatos because he has no noticeable

eccentricities . . . He's a human being, a recognisable person.'
OK, he has lascivious eyes for Bibi Dahl (say her name out
loud and it makes awful sense), but so do a lot of people.

Sadism: Bibi seems to be on the receiving end: both
Kristatos and Kriegler smack her across the face. Otherwise
there are the normal Bond fights, none of which are
particularly nasty. Only Kristatos and Colombo's final battle
seems to have any real venom in it.

Bond, of course, commits murder when he pushes Locque
off the cliff.

Single Entendres: 'A lady in your position would get to
know many things.'

Lines to Fast-Forward Past: Blofeld's unbelievable offer of
'I'll buy you a delicatessen in stainless steel' before he's
dropped into the chimney. It's not in the original script so we
can only assume that someone thought it was funny on set!

Mistakes Can Be Fatal: How does Blofeld get hold of a
Universal Exports helicopter?

Chief of Staff refers to Melina as 'Sir Havelock's' daughter:
it should be either 'the Havelocks' ', or 'Sir Timothy's'. It's
what can happen when Americans write British films!

How can Kriegler abandon the biathlon just like that to
pursue Bond? And what appointment was Bond going to
when he left Bibi?

It doesn't say much about Luigi Ferrara's intelligence (or
that much about the British checks) that Kristatos is able to
fool them for so long.

Bond tells Melina to talk only when necessary when they're
in the wreck of the *St Georges*. So why does he provide a
running commentary, even to the extent of reading out what is
clearly printed on the card he's holding?

The wound on Bond's arm from the JIM diving suit
disappears for some time before reappearing when he's on the
deck of the *Triana*.

James Bond Will Return In . . . *Octopussy.*

OCTOPUSSY (1983)

Starring: Roger Moore as the hero – James Bond
Louis Jourdan as the villain – Kamal Khan
Maud Adams as the love interest – Octopussy

Screen Story and Screenplay By:
George MacDonald Fraser and Richard
Maibaum and Michael G. Wilson (*sic*)

Directed By: John Glen

Tag Line: 'James Bond's All Time High.'

Relevance of Pre-Title Sequence? None at all. It's terrific fun, though, as Bond uses a miniature Acrostar jet to evade the Cuban Air Force and complete his mission to destroy a new plane by getting their own missile to blow it up.

Theme Song: 'All-Time High', sung by Rita Coolidge. The lyricist Tim Rice was pleased not to have the challenge of a song about Octopussy, although the *Tomorrow Never Dies* composer David Arnold says that k.d. lang would have been interested in having a go!

Cringe-Worthy Title Sequence: One of the better ones. The addition of the octopus theme clearly inspired Maurice Binder.

Plot: Agent 009 dies bringing a fake Fabergé egg across the Berlin Wall, alerting the Secret Service to a possible funding source for Russian agents in Britain. Four eggs have been sold in recent months. Bond accompanies an art expert, Jim Fanning, to the auction to see if he can spot the seller. In Russia, the Praesidium are divided between General Gogol's dovelike approach to the talks with NATO and General Orlov's desire for conquest. Orlov is involved in an intricate scam with the Kremlin Art Repository, faking eggs. However, with the fake egg lost, and an inventory coming up, he needs the real egg back, and orders his agent in Britain to buy it back at the auction.

At Sotheby's, Bond switches the fake for the real egg, while forcing Kamal Khan, a rather shady character, to show his hand and buy the egg. Bond follows Khan to India to find out more about him. He plays backgammon against him, and cheats the cheat, showing Khan he has the real egg, as well as winning 200,000 rupees. Khan's henchman, Gobinda, tries to get the egg back, but Bond evades him, and gets Q to place a homer inside it. Khan's assistant, Magda, tries to persuade Bond to hand the egg over, which he won't do, so she seduces him instead. In bed, he sees the tattoo of an octopus on her back – 'my little Octopussy' – a sign he has seen on the boat Khan arrived on. Magda takes the egg, while Bond is knocked out and taken to Khan's Monsoon Palace.

Khan's partner, Octopussy, recognises Bond's name, and wants him brought to her. That evening, Khan, Gobinda and General Orlov meet. Bond hears part of their conversation involving Karlmarxstadht, then manages to escape, despite being hunted by Khan. Identifying the tattoo as the sign of the Octopus cult, Bond visits Octopussy's island, where she wants him to team up with her. She is well disposed to him since Bond had allowed her father an honourable death some years earlier. She is involved in jewellery and gold smuggling, as well as running various other sidelines, including circuses. Khan is displeased that Octopussy won't let him kill Bond, and hires yo-yo-wielding assassins to do so. Killing Bond's Indian contact, Vijay, along the way, the assassins try to carry out their task but fail. Bond falls in the water and is believed eaten by crocodiles.

Bond travels to Karlmarxstadht and masquerades as one of Octopussy's circus crew. Meanwhile, the fake jewellery is discovered in Moscow and General Gogol gets on Orlov's trail. Bond discovers that Orlov is switching a container with the real jewels, which Octopussy was going to smuggle across into West Germany, with an atomic bomb which has the signature of an American one. Orlov hopes this will force the US to disarm in Europe unilaterally, allowing the Russians to walk in. General Gogol catches up with Orlov as he desperately makes a bid for the West and is shot by the border guards. Despite being forced off the train, Bond manages finally to get to the circus at its new site in a US Base in West Germany, and defuses the bomb before it goes off. He and Octopussy return to India and settle their score with Khan, who knew of Orlov's scheme and had run out on her.

Observations: General Gogol (Walter Gotell) is pivotal to the action, acting as the counterbalance to General Orlov's fanaticism, eventually organising the investigation into Orlov's crimes. Rublevitch (Eva-Rueber Staier) accompanies him as usual. On the British side, Miss Moneypenny is assisted by Penelope Smallbone, an idea that wasn't repeated. Following Bernard Lee's death, Robert Brown (who played Admiral Hargreaves in *The Spy Who Loved Me*), takes over as M. Frederick Gray and Q appear again, and Smithers, Q's assistant played by Jeremy Bullock, returns from *For Your Eyes Only*.

Maud Adams, of course, was Scaramanga's girlfriend, Andrea Adams, in *The Man With the Golden Gun*.

Louis Jourdan was previously considered for another Bond villain, Hugo Drax in the Franco-British co-production of *Moonraker*.

Hidden under the clown make-up of 009 at the start of the film is Andy Bradford, who played one of Kristatos's guards in *For Your Eyes Only* (he's the one who is shot by the crossbow during the assault on the mountain).

Playing Sadruddin, Head of Station I in Udaipur, is Albert Moses, who was the bartender at Max Kalba's club in *The Spy Who Loved Me*. Producer Michael G. Wilson is one of the passengers on the riverboat.

It would be wrong of us to point out the starring role played by our fellow Virgin author Gary Russell as one of the teenagers who refuses to give Bond a lift. So we won't.

The auction sequence at Sotheby's is taken from Fleming's 1963 short story 'The Property of a Lady'; the events of Fleming's 'Octopussy' occurred, suitably updated, to Octopussy's father. George MacDonald Fraser, the author of the Flashman series of historical novels, and an acknowledged expert on India, drafted the original screenplay and then a story conference was held with Cubby Broccoli. Richard Maibaum and Michael G. Wilson then added certain touches to the script (leading to the credit as above).

The backgammon match between Bond and Khan was originally to take place in *The Spy Who Loved Me* in Max Kalba's club, and the pre-credits Acrostar sequence in *Moonraker*. The elephant hunt started life in an early version of *The Man With the Golden Gun*. At one stage, Octopussy was going to be a villainess, who would use her knowledge of Tracy's death to get Bond on her side against SPECTRE. Up to the start of shooting and the casting of the tennis star Vijay Amitraz, Bond dealt with only one agent in India (Sadruddin). Presumably the producers felt that Amitraz would look too young to be a credible Head of Station.

Many people have speculated that the film makers got lost as to who had the real and who the fake eggs during the course of *Octopussy*, claiming that it is a mistake when Orlov destroys the real egg. Watch Kamal Khan's face: he knows it's the real egg that Orlov is destroying, even though Orlov thinks it's a fake. It's a nice piece of acting by Louis Jourdan.

Locations: Cuba, East Berlin, London, Udaipur and surrounds (India), East and West Germany.

My Name Is . . . Colonel Luis Toro, one of Castro's men; and Charles Morton, a manufacturer's representative from Leeds visiting factories in the East.

Bond's Past Life: Bond travelled to Sri Lanka twenty years after the Korean War to deal with Octopussy's father, Major Dexter Smythe, after the latter was found responsible for the theft of Chinese gold from North Korea, and the murder of two guides.

Toys for the Boys: Bond has a briefcase with a false bottom, allowing explosives to be placed within it. The miniature Acrostar jet is hidden within the rear end of a mechanical horse. The Indian company car has a souped-up engine, prepared no doubt at the Indian Q branch, where Q is working on a rope trick and a door knocker that sends the door smashing against the visitor. He equips the Fabergé egg with a homing device, which Bond can track on his watch, and gives 007 a pen with concentrated nitric and hydrochloric acid. He's also using the most up-to-date liquid-crystal TVs, one of which Bond again has in his watch, and provides Bond with a fake crocodile.

Patronising Lines: We can't understand how Bond's line to Sadruddin, 'That'll keep you in curry for a few weeks', ever got through!

Goodbye, Mr Bond: One 'Good evening' from Octopussy, and one 'Good night'. Nobody says goodbye any more!

Villainous Foibles: Kamal Khan is incredibly urbane – his dinner conversation may be of such things as the incipient torture 007 is about to undergo, but his manners never falter. He cheats at backgammon, though.

Sadism: Vijay's death is very nasty, and Gobinda is not at all pleasant to Octopussy. Otherwise, the fights are standard Bond, even, sadly, the one in the Indian market, where the humour robs the piece of tension.

Single Entendres: 'Having problems keeping it up, Q?'

Lines to Rewind For: Both from Kamal Khan: 'Mr Bond is indeed a very rare breed – soon to be made extinct;' 'You have a nasty habit of surviving.'

It's Only a Movie: Vijay plays 'The James Bond Theme' when he is waiting for Bond to recognise him. Vijay Amitraz is in fact a world-class tennis player, and in the film he claims to 'play a bit myself' as well as using a tennis racket to fend off Gobinda's thugs in the 'car' chase.

During the hunt, Bond faces down a tiger with Barbara Woodhouse's famous dog-training command, 'Sit!', and then emits a Tarzan yell as he goes through the trees.

Mistakes Can Be Fatal: Radar systems do not light up when they operate. Even in Cuba.

Wouldn't the Russians notice that Fabergé eggs are being sold through Sotheby's?

When Bond puts his jacket back on in the Indian Q Branch, he forgets to put his holster on first.

Let's get this right. Bond has the *real* Fabergé egg and Kamal Khan has the fake one. Khan sends the beautiful Magda to seduce Bond and steal the egg, which she does. Khan *then* sends Gobinda to knock Bond unconscious and bring him to Khan's palace. Er . . . why not just fetch the egg at the same time? Why go through all the seduction routine?

Be that as it may, Gobinda knocks Bond out in his hotel room, and transports him to the Monsoon Palace. Doesn't anyone notice that his watch is acting as a tracking device rather than a timepiece?

How does Bond get to his crocodile suit without being eaten by genuine crocodiles when he is in the water outside Octopussy's window – and come to that, how did the assassins manage not to get eaten on the way over?

And we suppose we'd better just accept that Bond could get in and out of the gorilla suit . . .

James Bond Will Return In . . . *From a View to a Kill* (he lost the 'From').

Well, as far as audiences were concerned, that wasn't the case. Later that year, the original 007 was back . . .

NEVER SAY NEVER AGAIN (1983)

Starring: Sean Connery as the hero – James Bond
Max Von Sydow and Klaus Maria Brandauer
as the villains – Ernst Stavro Blofeld and
Maximillian Largo
Kim Basinger as the love interest –
Domino Petachi

Written By: Lorenzo Semple Jnr (but see **Observations** below)

Directed By: Irvin Kershner

Tag Line: '007 is Number One. The excitement Never stops. And the thrills Never end.'

Relevance of Pre-Title Sequence? We don't actually get a pre-title sequence. How disconcerting.

Theme Song: Sung by Lani Hall.

Cringe-Worthy Title Sequence: It's actually rather sophisticated and very un-Bond, running over the war game 007 is playing.

Plot: The new M is worried that Bond's reflexes are slowing down, so he sends him to a health farm. While there, Bond stumbles unwittingly across a plot to replace the cornea of a drug-addicted USAF officer named Jack Petachi with a replica of the cornea of the President of the United States. This will enable SPECTRE – the organisation behind the plot – to use Petachi to authorise the replacement of two dummy warheads with real nuclear warheads in a cruise missile flight test.

The missiles are fired – with the real warheads – and SPECTRE intercept them in mid-flight. They also kill Petachi, just to cover their tracks, and send a blackmail demand to the governments of the world – they want a sum equivalent to 25 per cent of the sums paid for oil by the members of NATO.

Bond is sent to the Bahamas to make contact with Petachi's sister, Domino, but is identified by SPECTRE agent Fatima Blush. SPECTRE attempt to kill Bond, and Bond realises that Domino's lover, Maximillian Largo, is involved with SPECTRE and is probably responsible for stealing the nuclear warheads.

Largo imprisons Bond, attempts to sell Domino off to a group of nomads and puts SPECTRE's plan into effect, moving one nuclear weapon to a position beneath the White

House in Washington, DC, and attempting to move the other one to a location in North Africa close to the Middle East's oil fields through a series of flooded underground tunnels. Bond realises that a pendant given to Domino by Largo, the Tears of Allah, gives a clue as to where Largo is moving the second weapon. He and Felix Leiter, along with a detachment of Marines, intercept Largo's men and, during a pitched underwater battle, Domino kills Largo.

Observations: Bond is drinking Absolut vodka and smokes cigars (though not foot-long ones). In a vague attempt not to contradict the 'official' Bond films, it is clearly stated that M (Edward Fox) is new, and has recently replaced his predecessor. Moneypenny (Pamela Salem) and Q (Alec McCowen), of course, are here although not as we knew them, along with Blofeld and Largo. And a black Felix Leiter, played very effectively by Bernie Casey. At one stage McClory had announced that Orson Welles would play Blofeld against Trevor Howard's M, while Gabrielle Drake was on the verge of signing as Miss Moneypenny.

This film contains a rare example of the actor Robert Rietty appearing himself, rather than overdubbing someone else's voice (he's a diplomat who reacts badly to Blofeld's blackmail attempt). Rietty had previously dubbed the voices of many of the early Bond villains, including Goldfinger and the original Largo, and had appeared in a minor role in *OHMSS*. Valerie Léon previously appeared in *The Spy Who Loved Me*.

The first assistant director of the film was David Tomblin – he previously directed various episodes of *The Prisoner*, *Space: 1999* and *U.F.O.* for British television, and then moved to Hollywood to act as first assistant director on many blockbuster films such as *Raiders of the Lost Ark*. Ricou Browning supervised the underwater sequences on this film, as he previously did on *Thunderball*.

This film has a chequered history. The outcome of the court case between Kevin McClory and Ian Fleming (for which, see the entry on the novel of *Thunderball*) was that Fleming kept the literary rights to the *Thunderball* plot while McClory kept complete copyright on the material he and Fleming had co-written (which, McClory was later to say, was enough to cover three separate films). McClory tried to get *Thunderball* under way as his own film project, in competition with the then nascent Broccoli–Saltzman series, but ended up as co-producer with them on the first version of *Thunderball*, starring Sean Connery. Part of the terms of his agreement with them was that he would not try to make any other films based on the material for another ten years. Just over ten years after the release of *Thunderball*, on 28 April 1976, Kevin McClory announced that he would be making a new film, based on that material, under the title *James Bond of the Secret Service*. The script for the film had been written by McClory, Sean Connery and the thriller writer Len Deighton, and it was anticipated that Connery would return to the part of James Bond. The intention was to film in the Bahamas, New York and Japan. The title was altered to *Warhead*, and filming was scheduled to start in February 1977. Things rapidly became complicated: McClory took out an injunction to stop the filming of *The Spy Who Loved Me* when he discovered that it was intended to feature SPECTRE, while Broccoli took out an injunction to stop the filming of *Warhead*. *The Spy Who Loved Me* got made; *Warhead* didn't. Sean Connery later said that he walked away when the legal wrangling got too intense. McClory obviously kept plugging away, of course – and this is the result. (For more details of *Warhead*, see **File 007**.)

The credited writer, Lorenzo Semple Jnr, is an old alumnus of the 1960s *Batman* television series – and it shows. Sean Connery, however, had script approval, and one can presume that some of the lines were actually written by him. In addition, Connery asked that British comedy writers Dick Clements and Ian La Frenais be brought in to freshen up the humorous elements in the script. Jack Schwartzmann's brother-in-law, Francis Ford Coppola, also apparently performed some uncredited script doctoring on the film.

Unsurprisingly, it's fairly close to the novel of *Thunder-*

ball. The Vulcan has been replaced with a more hi-tech alternative (cruise missiles), Fatima Blush is a new addition (although apparently based on an idea by Ian Fleming) and the ending has been subtly rearranged so that Bond and Largo confront each other underwater rather than on Largo's ship, but it's all very familiar. Largo's first name has been changed from Emilio to Maximillian.

A pre-credits sequence was planned, set at a medieval pageant, at which one knight kills another with a metal-bladed, tipped lance. A third knight takes off his helmet to reveal 007, who chases after the knight on horseback, leading to a steeplechase across a car park. It was deemed too expensive. Shame.

Another lost scene saw Blofeld killed by his cat's poisoned claws, and a number of scenes between Bond and Moneypenny never made it to the final print.

Locations: The Home Counties, the South of France and the Bahamas.

James Bond, Fashion Victim: Bond's clothes sense in this film is a disaster. He wears a pair of dungarees over nothing else, and he has to disguise himself as a jogger by stripping off to his vest and jockey shorts. And Bond in a pullover – please! Where are the pipe and slippers?

Bond's Past Life: This is a new Bond – he *has* no past life. This version is known to SPECTRE, and has spent his time teaching rather than doing since the new M joined.

Toys for the Boys: SPECTRE are using remote-controlled sharks to guard the cruise missiles. This is a holdover from the robot sharks of McClory's *Warhead* script. Bond and Leiter use human torpedo capsules. Q supplies Bond with a rocket-propelled motorcycle, a laser-equipped watch and a fountain pen with special capabilities.

Sadism: Well, Bond throws acidic urine into the face of a villainous thug at the end of a very vicious fight, and Largo is a certifiable nutter.

Single Entendres: Bond's advice to Fatima Blush: 'Going down, one should always be relaxed.'

Lines to Rewind For: Q sums up the feelings of the audience perfectly when he says: 'Good to see you, Mr Bond. Things have been awfully dull around here ... Now you're on this, I hope we're going to have some gratuitous sex and violence.'

'Do you lose as gracefully as you win?' Largo asks Bond, to which he replies, 'I wouldn't know – I've never lost.'

Bond to Domino: 'Your brother is dead. Keep dancing.'

It's Only a Movie: Lord Alpert (mentioned as such in dialogue, but credited as Lord Ambrose) may be a nod towards the trumpeter Herb Alpert, who contributed the trumpet solo on the opening theme song.

Sean Connery turns and winks at the camera at the end of the film. Thanks, Sean. We waited long enough for you to come back – the least you could do is not spoil the illusion.

Mistakes Can Be Fatal: Anthony Sharp's character, Lord Alpert, is credited as Lord Ambrose.

James Bond Will Return In ... Another remake of *Thunderball* at some later date – possibly called *Warhead 2000*.

A VIEW TO A KILL (1985)

Starring: Roger Moore as the hero – James Bond
Christopher Walken as the villain –
  Max Zorin
Tanya Roberts as the love interest –
  Stacey Sutton

Written By: Richard Maibaum and Michael G. Wilson

Directed By: John Glen

Tag Line: 'Has James Bond finally met his match?'

Relevance of Pre-Title Sequence? Bond recovers a microchip resistant to electromagnetic interference from the body of 003, who retrieved it from a Soviet research institute. This provides the lead-in to the main plot – Max Zorin is meant to be the only person making these chips – but gets forgotten about very quickly.

Theme Song: Sung by Duran Duran.

Cringe-Worthy Title Sequence: It's the pits. Women covered in luminous paint fire crudely animated laser beams at each other while writhing in ultraviolet light. It's *so* cheap that shots of Roger Moore have been repeated from the title sequence of *The Spy Who Loved Me* in a forlorn attempt to liven it up a bit. It's as if *French and Saunders* had decided to pastiche the Maurice Binder title sequences, only it's worse than that.

Plot: Agent 003 is on a mission in Siberia, investigating reports that the KGB have obtained computer chips resistant to electromagnetic pulses. With these chips they can build computer equipment that will work after a nuclear explosion, but the only factory making these chips is in the West and is owned by Zorin Industries – a company owned by the wealthy industrialist Max Zorin. Agent 003 is killed, but Bond retrieves the sample chip he had stolen from the KGB. If there is a leak to the KGB from somewhere, then Zorin Industries is the place to start.

Bond investigates Zorin's operations in England, then follows Zorin to his stables in France. He discovers a secret laboratory beneath the stables, and evidence indicating that Zorin is the product of Nazi genetic experimentation. Zorin becomes aware of Bond's investigations and attempts to have him killed.

Zorin heads for San Francisco, and Bond follows. Joining forces with seismologist Stacey Sutton, Bond discovers that Zorin plans to use a massive amount of explosive to flood a series of oil wells he owns along the sides of the San Andreas fault. The subsequent seismic activity would cause the fault to slip, sending California's Silicon Valley plunging into the ocean. The primary manufacturers of computer chips would be destroyed, and the value of Zorin's company (safe elsewhere) would shoot through the roof. Bond and Stacey intercept the trigger bomb, aided by May Day – the henchwoman Zorin abandons – and ensure it explodes far from the main mass of explosive. Zorin kidnaps Stacey and whisks her away in his escape airship, but Bond gives chase and confronts Zorin atop the Golden Gate Bridge, from where Zorin plunges to his death.

Observations: Bond drinks Stolichnaya vodka and is awarded the Order of Lenin at the end of the film.

The headquarters of the SIS is now in the Old War Office – a building owned in reality by the Ministry of Defence. It's almost certain that Ian Fleming would have attended meetings in this building, even though he never had an office in it. M's office is obviously different from the one seen in previous films.

Q and Moneypenny (played, for the last time, by Lois Maxwell), along with the Minister for Defence and General Gogol, all make an appearance.

Producer 'Cubby' Broccoli had seriously considered David Bowie for the part of Max Zorin, and was quoted as saying, 'We plan to exploit his unique physical oddity – his different-coloured and different-sized eyes.' Tanya Roberts was one of the last of *Charlie's Angels*. Patrick Macnee, who plays Sir Godfrey Tippett, was of course Avenger *par excellence*, John Steed.

Anthony Chinn, who plays the criminal gang leader who falls to his death from Zorin's airship, was previously a SPECTRE operative in *You Only Live Twice*. Maud Adams, the eponymous Octopussy, can be seen briefly in the Fishermen's Wharf sequence. Manning Redwood, who plays Bob Conley, was General Miller in *Never Say Never Again*. Grace Jones's then little-known boyfriend, Dolph Lundgren, has a small part as a KGB heavy.

A View to a Kill begins with a disclaimer stating that

'Neither the name "Zorin" nor any other name or character in this film is meant to portray a real company or actual person.' This was in case Zoran Ladicorbic Ltd, a fashion design company, might consider Zorin's deeds actionable.

Despite the title, *A View to a Kill* (the 'From' disappeared shortly before shooting commenced) bears absolutely no relevance to any Ian Fleming book or plot whatsoever – and it shows. The scene where Zorin lays out his plans to a group of mobsters with the aid of a diorama, one of them leaves and is killed for his trouble is reminiscent of the film of *Goldfinger* (except that *all* the mobsters died in that film).

Early plans for the film had Zorin manipulating the course of Halley's Comet in order to destroy Silicon Valley. A cut scene had Bond being arrested after his car chase (to be fair, a half-car chase) across Paris. Hilarious scenes ensued when the local *gendarmerie* discovered all the Q-provided gadgets in his pockets.

A series of children's books by authors including Goose-bumps writer R.L. Stine, *Find Your Own Fate With James Bond*, was penned based around incidents in this film (see **File 005**).

Locations: Siberia, the Home Counties, France and San Francisco, in and around May 1985.

My Name Is ... James St John Smythe, and later James Stock of the London *Financial Times*.

James Bond, Fashion Victim: Bond wears a blue suede jacket. Timothy Dalton could have got away with it. Pierce Brosnan could still get away with it (just). An elderly Roger Moore could not.

Bond's Past Life: Bond is an expert safe cracker and can ride a horse. He can also cook (although quiche seems to be his favoured dish).

Toys for the Boys: It's a remarkably gadget-free film, but to make up for it we get one of the stupidest gadgets of all time –

the mink-lined SIS submarine disguised as an iceberg with a bed as its central feature and a Union Jack under the hatch. Those other gadgets we do get are almost realistic – a flat-pack photocopier, a credit-card-sized lockpick and a ring that can take photographs. Q has a robot snooper, however (the one that appears so unexpectedly in the 'joke' sequence at the end), and a cut scene had it being used to investigate Zorin's pumping station.

Patronising Lines: Well, the whole thing has an air of patronisation. We're meant to find Bond's humiliation of Sir Godfrey humorous, for instance, and is that funny French taxi driver the most racist thing ever to appear in a Bond film? We think so.

Sadism: Zorin guns down the workers who have laboured so hard to dig through to the San Andreas fault, and he laughs while he's doing it. He also throws a man into a rotating propeller blade. The guy is, quite literally, a psycho – created as a result of Nazi experiments with steroids on pregnant women.

Single Entendres: 'You slept well?' Zorin asks Bond, to which the response from a sexually sated Bond is, 'A little restless, but I got off eventually.'

'Here, put your hand on this!' Bond tells Stacey during a particularly dramatic fire-engine chase. 'The wheel! The wheel!' he adds quickly as she reaches for his groin (in his dreams). Later she asks Bond, 'Do you know what I'm sitting on?' 'I'm trying not to think about it,' he responds.

It's Only a Movie: When Bond is snow-boarding away from the Soviet agents in Siberia, the audience cringes at the sounds of the Beach Boys' hit 'California Girls'. Actually, as a point of information, it's actually a cover version by Gidea Park, possibly indicating an unusual desire to save money on the part of the producers (for more on that, see the discussion of the title sequence earlier).

Mistakes Can Be Fatal: M refers to Sir Godfrey Tippett as

'Tippett' when he should refer to him as 'Sir Godfrey'. A man of M's rank would know that.

Bond has a device that can locate hidden listening devices, but it *makes a loud noise when it is working*! Doesn't that give the game away just a little?

Despite what you might see in this film, computer chips are not shipped out thrown higgledy-piggledy in a packing crate. They are delicate pieces of equipment that need to be protected from damage.

Towards the end of the film, Zorin attempts to make his escape in a large vehicle with his name emblazoned along the side. Not planning on getting very far without being seen, then.

James Bond Will Return In . . . He'll just return.

THE LIVING DAYLIGHTS (1987)

Starring: Timothy Dalton as the hero – James Bond
Jeroen Krabbe as the villain – Georgi Koskov
Maryam D'Abo as the love interest –
  Kara Milovy

Written By: Richard Maibaum and Michael G. Wilson

Directed By: John Glen

Tag Line: None.

Relevance of Pre-Title Sequence? It introduces the new Bond, and the Smiert Spionem plot. Very relevant, we'd say.

Theme Song: 'The Living Daylights' by a-ha and John Barry, about which the Norwegian group complained to trade papers, and even released their own separately mixed version; the Pretenders contributed both 'Where Has Every Body Gone?' (which played incessantly on Necros' walkman) and the closing theme, 'If There Was a Man'.

Cringe-Worthy Title Sequence: It's the usual stuff with girls and guns and explosions but, very unusually, the title of the movie does not come on screen simultaneously with its appearance in the lyrics. Title designer Maurice Binder had worked with composer Bill Conti to change the theme of *For Your Eyes Only* to ensure that the two coincided.

Plot: A straightforward training mission on Gibraltar turns sour for the 00 section when 004 is murdered. Soon after, Georgi Koskov, a senior Russian, is defecting in Bratislava, and wants Bond to act as lookout to ensure his safety. A beautiful cellist catches Bond's eye, and turns out to be the sniper trying to stop Koskov. Against orders, he shoots at the stock of the gun, knocking it out of her hands.

Koskov claims to have defected because his superior, General Pushkin, who has replaced General Gogol, has started a new operation: Smiert Spionem (Death to Spies). Pushkin will be in Tangiers in three days' time, and Koskov suggests that he be eliminated to stop the operation. However, the safe house in which Koskov is being debriefed is attacked, and Koskov is kidnapped by someone he claims is a KGB agent. A label with 'Spiert Spionem' written on it had been found by 004's body so M orders Bond to kill Pushkin. Bond reluctantly accepts. Bond has asked Moneypenny to identify the woman with the cello, and finds her name is Kara Milovy. He therefore travels back to Bratislava, where he discovers that the bullets she was using were fake. He poses as a friend of Koskov's and gets her out of the country.

In Tangiers, General Pushkin tells pseudo-General Brad Whitaker, a weapons dealer and Pushkin's contact in the West, that the deal Pushkin was brokering is off, and the money paid on deposit is to be repaid. Koskov and his 'kidnapper' Necros are guests at Whitaker's house; Koskov is sure he has convinced the British that Pushkin is a threat to them, and therefore they will eliminate him. Another British agent will be killed as a reminder.

In Vienna, Bond discovers from the local agent, Saunders, that Whitaker paid for Kara's cello, which had apparently been a present from Koskov. Saunders is killed by Necros, and Bond heads for Tangiers, where he stalks Pushkin. Bond is still reluctant to kill the Russian, and Pushkin tells him that Koskov was about to be arrested, and that Smiert Spionem was an operation disbanded twenty years earlier. The only way they will find out what is going on is if Pushkin dies. They therefore fake his death at Bond's hands, and, while evading capture, Bond runs into the CIA and his old friend Felix Leiter, who is investigating Whitaker.

Kara meanwhile has contacted Koskov directly, and discovered Bond is not a friend. She drugs his drink, but as he falls into unconsciousness he persuades her that he was on her side. Bond is transported out of Tangiers on a Soviet plane to Afghanistan, along with a fortune in diamonds. Kara changes loyalties but is rewarded by being given to the Russians by Koskov as a defector. Bond and Kara escape from the Russian jail, alongside a dirty, smelly Afghan – who turns out to be Kamran Shah, one of the leaders of the Mujadin, the Afghan resistance.

The next day Bond and Kara attend a trade between the Russians and opium sellers. The sale of the opium in America will allow Koskov and Whitaker to turn a fast profit and carry through their arms deal. After ensuring the Afghans get their diamonds, Bond travels back inside the base alongside the opium, with a bomb. Kara chases after the Russian convoy, and is reluctantly followed by Kamran and his men. Bond places the bomb in the Russian transporter, but is spotted. At that moment, the Afghans arrive and, in the confusion, Bond and Kara manage to fly the cargo transporter away, with the bomb and Necros on board. Bond and Necros fight to the death, then Bond uses the bomb to halt the Russians chasing after Kamran's men.

On his return to Tangiers, Bond faces Whitaker and kills him. His life is saved from Whitaker's bodyguard by Pushkin. Koskov tries valiantly one last time to change sides, but Pushkin orders him returned to Moscow in the diplomatic bag. Kara embarks on a world tour as a solo cellist . . .

Observations: Bond's line to the head of Station V (Vienna), Saunders, 'If he [M] fires me, I'll thank him for it', seems out of character. In the original script, when Bond is reluctant to accept the termination warrant for Gogol, M asks if he is suffering from accidie, a very neat return to the original Fleming. Unfortunately that reference disappeared, but the earlier hint of it remains. We learn that Bond knows his American battles. He doesn't speak Czechoslovakian but does speak a few words of Afghan.

The SIS HQ in London has moved. It was on Whitehall in the Moore films; now it's moved up to the corner of Trafalgar Square and the Mall (the Malaysian tourist office is there at the moment, if anyone wants to check). Universal Exports Ltd owns a safe house at Blayden. Agent 008 is currently in Hong Kong. He doesn't know Pushkin, and will follow orders, not instincts. M and Frederick Gray turn up on parade, although we don't understand why the Minister of Defence is attending the debriefing of a defector; and alongside a new Bond is a new Moneypenny, played by Caroline Bliss. With the change of cast has come a change in taste as well – Miss Moneypenny with a Barry Manilow collection!

Walter Gotell gets a long overdue promotion. General Gogol reappears as a high-ranking foreign-service bureaucrat – although in the early drafts of the script, *he* was Koskov's superior: for Pushkin read Gogol. The change came about because of Walter Gotell's poor health at the time of filming.

After Roger Moore's departure, Albert Broccoli spoke with Timothy Dalton about assuming the mantle of Bond, but he was about to embark on a double bill of Shakespeare plays in London's West End (alongside the then future star of *Doctor Who*, Sylvester McCoy), so declined the role. Pierce Brosnan, then best known as private detective Remington Steele, was approached. His stunt double was hired, and he had apparently shot the gun-barrel sequence before NBC television executives, who had an option on his contract to appear as Steele, decided to make further TV episodes about the character. Brosnan's time was to come eight years later.

The actor Mark Greenstreet revealed to Terry Wogan that he had also auditioned for the part of Bond, re-creating the scene from *From Russia With Love* where Tatiana (played by

Fiona Fullerton, not, as some sources report, Maryam d'Abo) entered Bond's room while he was preparing to shower. Other potential Bonds included Sam Neill and Finlay Light. The run of Dalton's play was curtailed and the actor, who had previously been considered as a replacement Bond for *OHMSS* and *For Your Eyes Only*, became available.

In earlier films, the producers had wanted to introduce a new actor playing Bond by emphasising the familiar around him. In *The Living Daylights*, there is a deliberate obfuscation in the pre-credits sequence: three 00 agents parachute out of the aircraft, and we don't see their faces. Effectively, any of them could be the new 007.

Maryam d'Abo had acted in screen tests against the potential James Bonds auditioned in 1981. Peter Porteous, who plays the gasworks supervisor almost seduced by Julie T. Wallace, previously played the jewel forger Lenkin in *Octopussy*. Nadim Sawalha, the Tangier Chief of Security, was Fekkesh in *The Spy Who Loved Me*.

The first fifteen or so minutes of the film are taken from Fleming's short story 'The Living Daylights' (published in the collection *Octopussy and the Living Daylights*): Bond shoots a Russian sniper, code-named Trigger, on the stock of the gun rather than kill her and scares the living daylights out of her. Smiert Spionem, better known as SMERSH, were the villains of Fleming's novels from *Casino Royale* to *Goldfinger*.

Bond and Kara's escape from Czechoslovakia was originally in a stolen KGB car and then an ice yacht. During the elaborate chase scene over the rooftops in Tangiers, some scenes were filmed that would have suited Roger Moore better than Dalton. To give you an idea of what Moore would have made of it, the scenes included one where Bond throws an oriental rug over a set of telephone wires and 'rides' the rug from one roof to another, looking to the amazed bystanders (and presumably to one drunk who then throws away his bottle in disgust) just like a flying carpet. Not.

Kamran Shah was originally called Ranjit. Between his first meeting Bond in the Russian jail, and when he shows himself in his true colours, the script underwent a number of changes. Bond and Kara get out of the jail cell by using Kara's bra to snag the keys, and Ranjit then leads them towards the Pakistani border, only ten miles away. They then go to a massive bazaar in the Khyber Pass from where they are rescued by the Mujadin. The bazaar finally made an appearance ten years later in *Tomorrow Never Dies*.

The other major change is at the end. Bond and Kara crash-land the plane on a US carrier, and then travel together back to Tangiers. There they are both taken to Whitaker's house, where the confrontation between Whitaker and Bond occurs as in the final version, but since the explosive charge in the keyring was already used in the Khyber Pass sequence, it is left to Gogol to shoot Whitaker.

Bond's line to Scaramanga ('There's a useful four-letter word and you're full of it') is echoed in his line to Koskov ('We have an old saying too – and you're full of it').

Plans for a *For Your Eyes Only*-style ending, but with Prince Charles and Princess Diana instead of Margaret and Dennis Thatcher, were dropped during production. An actor had already been cast as Prince Charles.

Locations: Gibraltar, Bratislava, London, Blayden, Vienna, Tangiers, Afghanistan.

My Name Is ... Jerzy Bondov (on the documents faked by Koskov allowing him to leave Tangier for Afghanistan).

Bond's Past Life: Bond has worked with Rosika Miklos (Julie T. Wallace) before. He is well known at the Sacher hotel in Vienna, and has been to Karachi.

Toys for the Boys: Sanders uses night-vision binoculars, and Bond has a pair of binoculars which sit on an ordinary pair of glasses frames. Q Branch have adapted the cleaning module on the Trans-Siberian Gas Pipeline to carry a man. They are working on a ghettoblaster that fires rockets for the Americans, and a sofa that swallows the person sitting on it. A rake acts as a weapons detector. Bond is armed with a keyring that can release stun gas if he whistles 'Rule Britannia', and detonates plastic explosive if he wolf-whistles. The Aston Martin Volante is equipped with a police scanner, a laser in the wheel hub, missiles in the fog lamps which are controlled on a heads-up display on the windscreen by the heating controls and fired from the cigarette lighter, steel spikes for icy conditions, an outrigger, a rocket boost motor, bulletproof glass – and, the ultimate essential, a self-destructor.

Necros uses exploding milk bottles.

Patronising Lines: Although on the whole Bond is far more favourable to Kara than to previous heroines, he has one marvellous put-down, when she says they're free. 'Kara, we're in the middle of a Russian airbase in Afghanistan!'

Kamran Shah also comes out with 'Women!' but that is expected of his sort of chap, even if he has been to Oxford.

Sadism: The KGB agent allows 004 to see the 'Smiert Spionem' note before he cuts the rope. The kitchen fight between the security guard and Necros is extremely brutal, as is the fight between Bond and the jailors in Afghanistan.

Single Entendres: Kara asks Bond to 'take me on the wheel'. He obliges. The jailor comments that 'I haven't had a woman prisoner for a long time.' Kara *doesn't* oblige.

Mistakes Can Be Fatal: Rosika Miklos speaks perfect English when she first meets Bond, but slips into pigeon English quite quickly.

Obviously there's a major time change between Czechoslovakia and Austria. At 23.00 hours at the Czech border, it's pitch black, but dawn is breaking in Austria as Koskov gets in the fighter.

It's a shame that Maryam d'Abo's soaping of the bow (i.e. making it look as if she is playing the cello) doesn't match the bowing that Stefan Kropfitsch is providing on the soundtrack.

Pushkin tells Bond that Smiert Spionem (SMERSH) was disbanded twenty years ago. In fact, it was more like forty.

The aircraft in the airfield in Afghanistan are all Western aircraft painted with Russian markings. The one Bond and Kara steal at the end is, of course, a Hercules.

The thirty seconds' stun provided by the gas went incredibly quickly. Bond should have asked for a refund.

James Bond Will Return ... They hoped, and they were right.

LICENCE TO KILL (1989)

Starring: Timothy Dalton as the hero – James Bond
Robert Davi as the villain – Franz Sanchez
Carey Lowell as the love interest –
Pam Bouvier

Written By: Richard Maibaum and Michael G. Wilson

Directed By: John Glen

Tag Lines: 'His bad side is a dangerous place to be' (on the advance posters); 'James Bond is out on his own and out for revenge.'

Relevance of Pre-Title Sequence? It introduces the hero and the villain, and defines the relationship between them. Could almost be part of the real film.

Theme Song: Opening theme sung by Gladys Knight; end theme sung by Patti Labelle.

Cringe-Worthy Title Sequence: Not too bad, considering.

Plot: A South American drug czar, Sanchez, is arrested by the Drug Enforcement Agency's Felix Leiter with the help of James Bond. Sanchez escapes custody by bribing a DEA official, Killifer, with $2 million, and returns to kill Leiter's new bride and throw Leiter to the sharks.

Bond kills Killifer, but is chastised by M for taking it all personally. Bond attempts to resign from the SIS, but M refuses to accept his resignation and withdraws Bond's licence to kill. Bond escapes, and manages to disrupt Sanchez's drug-smuggling operation after discovering that Sanchez is smuggling drugs into America through the marine company run by Milton Krest.

Bond teams up with a CIA contract pilot, Pam Bouvier – whose name he discovered in Felix Leiter's files – and together they travel to Sanchez's dominion in Isthmus City, the capital city of a South American country not a million miles away from Mexico. Bond establishes himself as a rich assassin looking for a job, and makes contact with Sanchez. Discovering that Sanchez hides himself away behind two inches of armoured glass, Bond arranges plastic explosive around the rim of the window of Sanchez's office and attempts to kill the drug czar by detonating the explosive to shatter the window and firing at him from across the street. The attempt fails and Bond is taken captive by the SIS operative in Isthmus City, who says that Bond has come close to disrupting a joint SIS and Hong Kong Narcotics Bureau operation. In fact, Bond *has* disrupted it, because Sanchez's forces suddenly attack the SIS safe house and rescue Bond.

Taken into Sanchez's confidence, Bond discovers that Sanchez has obtained four surface-to-air missiles from the Contra rebels and is threatening to shoot down an American airliner if the DEA keep pursuing him. Bond travels with Sanchez to his drug-refining plant – cunningly hidden in a religious retreat which also provides the TV evangelist programming that secretly auctions off the drugs – but is identified by one of Sanchez's henchmen. Bond manages to set fire to the plant, destroying it, but Sanchez escapes with twenty tons of cocaine, $500 million and the four Stinger missiles. Bond gives chase and systematically destroys each of the oil tankers carrying Sanchez's drugs. Sanchez and Bond end up in hand-to-hand combat. Sanchez loses.

Observations: James Bond in a bar-room brawl – it doesn't seem right, somehow. M (Robert Brown), Q and Moneypenny (Caroline Bliss) all turn up, as does Felix Leiter (played once again by *Live and Let Die*'s David Hedison). Q in particular gets a trip to Isthmus City. In fact, we would go so far as to say that this film is Q's finest moment.

The film Felix Leiter, like the book Felix Leiter, has left the CIA, but the film one is currently working for the US Drug Enforcement Agency while the book one went to work for Pinkerton's Detective Agency. Like Bond, he has a very short-lived marriage – maybe it is bad luck when he makes reference to Bond's marriage in *OHMSS*.

One of Sanchez's drug-peddling allies is Professor Joe Butcher, played by Wayne Newton. Newton is an American entertainer. The best analogy for those of us in the UK is to imagine what it would be like if Bruce Forsyth had turned up as a contract killer. Pedro Armendariz Jnr, who plays President Lopez, is the son of Pedro Armendariz who played Kerim Bey in *From Russia With Love*.

Producer Michael G. Wilson has admitted that the rock guitarist Eric Clapton was involved at one stage with the music for the film, possibly in terms of a revised version of 'The James Bond Theme'. This would make sense, given composer Michael Kamen's previous working relationship with Clapton (on the BBC TV series *Edge of Darkness*) but it never came to fruition.

There is precious little relevance to Ian Fleming's novels and short stories here. The only things taken from Fleming's work are the character of Milton Krest and his ship (from the short story 'The Hildebrand Rarity') and Felix Leiter's unfortunate encounter with a shark (from the novel *Live and Let Die*). The latter move caused severe problems for the noveliser John Gardner, who tried to tie *Licence to Kill* in with the Ian Fleming series, and had to resort to the shark biting Felix Leiter's false leg off.

The film was originally entitled *Licence Revoked*, but this was changed late in the day when it became clear that many in the (US) audience didn't know what 'revoked' meant. Some of the advance film posters have the original, rather than the final, title. The original intention was that *Licence Revoked* would be set in China, while still being about a drugs warlord. The idea was dropped in part because the Bernardo Bertolucci film *The Last Emperor* made China a less remote and unknown location. Richard Maibaum collaborated with Michael G. Wilson on the storyline of *Licence to Kill*, but a Writers' Guild dispute meant that Wilson had to write the script himself. Bond's quip when he pushes a man into a tank of maggots – '*Bon appetit*' – is the same quip he uses when throwing Blofeld's henchman into a tank of piranha in *You Only Live Twice*.

The death knell for Timothy Dalton's Bond is the pre-title sequence scene where he is suspended from a helicopter like a trussed turkey, making birdlike motions with his arms. It makes him look ridiculous, but there is a good argument to the effect that the extended finale, with the oil-tanker chase, is the finest piece of action directing and editing in any of the James Bond films.

Since *Licence to Kill* was the Italian title of *Dr No*, this was retitled *Private Revenge* in Italy.

Locations: The USA (Florida), the UK (London) and a made-up country in South America (Isthmus City).

My Name Is . . . In John Gardner's novelisation, Bond carries a passport in the name James Boldman – his standard Gardner false identity.

James Bond, Fashion Victim: Timothy Dalton can carry off most sets of clothes without any problems, but has an odd problem looking confident in evening dress. Still, Franz Sanchez, *de facto* ruler of an entire South American country, wears a cardigan and a pink shirt, so what do we know?

Toys for the Boys: An exploding alarm clock, exploding toothpaste, an X-ray instamatic camera with a laser beam facility and a sniper rifle with an optical palm reader which prevents anyone but the authorised user firing it.

Sadism: Sanchez's henchman, Dario, used to be with the Contras until they threw him out. Too sadistic for an organisation known for its acts of violence? He *must* be bad.

Lines to Rewind For: 'What about the money, *padrone*?' one of Sanchez's henchmen asks after Milton Krest has exploded all over it. 'Launder it,' Sanchez replies.

Lupe Lamora to Bond: 'Don't you know – iguanas are a girl's best friend?' (Watch out for the new James Bond film – *Iguanas Are Forever*.)

It's Only a Movie: When Sanchez is firing at the tanker Bond is driving, his bullets play 'The James Bond Theme'.

Just before the end credits, the stone fish guarding the swimming pool winks at the camera. Just think of all the effort on the part of the props department that went into making it do that, and to what end?

Mistakes Can Be Fatal: During the course of this film Bond attacks M, disrupts a joint SIS–Hong Kong Narcotics operation and screws up a deal that would have put Sanchez into the hands of the American authorities. And they still give him back his licence to kill. What exactly does he have to do to get himself fired – kill the Prime Minister?

James Bond Will Return In . . . Six years.

GOLDENEYE (1995)

Starring: Pierce Brosnan as the hero – James Bond
Sean Bean as the villain – Alec Trevalyan
Izabella Scorupco as the love interest –
  Natalya Simonova

Written By: Jeffrey Caine and Bruce Feirstein from a
story by Michael France (but see
Observations below)

Directed By: Martin Campbell

Tag Lines: 'You know the name. You know the number.' Alternatively, the teaser posters simply said, 'There is no substitute.'

Relevance of Pre-Title Sequence? Completely relevant – it sets up two of the three main villains, and Bond's relationship to them.

Theme Song: Sung by Tina Turner (opening) and Eric Serra (closing).

Cringe-Worthy Title Sequence: It's fine up until the moment where the gun barrel emerges from the woman's mouth. It's not by Maurice Binder, by the way, who had died in 1991.

Plot: Bond and Alec Trevalyan (006) break into a Soviet chemical weapons facility at Archangel. Trevalyan is apparently killed, but Bond destroys the facility and escapes.

Nine years later, at a casino in France, Bond meets Xenia Onatopp – a beautiful woman who, he discovers, is probably a member of the Janus crime syndicate, based in St Petersburg. The head of Janus is a Cossack who apparently lives on an old missile train.

Onatopp kills a Canadian admiral and steals his pass. Using it, she and an associate obtain access to the demonstration of a new helicopter which is hardened against all forms of electromagnetic jamming or radiation. They steal the helicopter and, later, Onatopp uses it to take Ouromov (Head of the Russian Space Division) to a satellite control station at Severnaya. There they steal the control codes for the two highly secret GoldenEye satellites, which use nuclear explosions to form an electromagnetic pulse which can disable and destroy all of the electrical devices in whatever area they are fired at. Ouromov uses one of the satellites to blow up Severnaya itself to cover his tracks – escaping in the protected helicopter while three MiGs sent to investigate crash, their electronics malfunctioning. Ouromov is unaware that a woman – Natalya Simonova – has escaped.

Bond is sent by M to find out what happened. Knowing that Onatopp is somehow involved, he ensures that he comes to the attention of the Janus crime syndicate, but is shocked to discover their head is Alec Trevalyan – formerly 006. Trevalyan is bitter at the treatment of his parents by the British (they were Cossacks returned to Stalin after World War Two) and he intends electronically stealing billions of pounds from London's financial market and then covering his tracks using GoldenEye to wipe all records of the transactions. Bond follows Trevalyan to Cuba, where his satellite control station is located, and blows it up before he can transmit the firing signal. Trevalyan is killed in a fight with Bond.

Observations: Bond is still a commander in this film, despite his promotion in Gardner's 1989 *Win, Lose or Die*. Trevalyan makes reference to Bond's parents dying in a climbing accident – this is taken from Ian Fleming's novels, and is the first time it's been acknowledged in the films. Bond has another Aston Martin DB5 – although, since its number plate is two digits lower than that used in *Goldfinger* and *Thunderball*, we presume it's a replacement.

This film marks the first appearance of the new M as played by Judi Dench. Lois Maxwell, who played the original Miss Moneypenny, had suggested to the producers in 1987 that the new M should be female – in fact, her, adding a different dynamic to the Bond–M relationship. She was told that this wasn't possible as the head of the Secret Service was always a man.

The headquarters of the Secret Intelligence Service in this film is the actual SIS building in Vauxhall. Trevalyan and Zukov definitely refer to the organisation as MI6 – remember that M calls it MI7 in *Dr No*. The character of Bill Tanner, M's Chief of Staff, previously appeared in *For Your Eyes Only* played by James Villiers. Here Bond refers to Bill Tanner as 'Tanner' rather than 'Bill', which is what he calls him in the books. Moneypenny returns, albeit played by the aptly named Samantha Bond, and Q does his usual walk-on-and-steal-the-show routine. Britain, which has a male PM, now has its own surveillance satellites.

When Bond's Aston Martin DB5 drives up to the Monte Carlo casino, the man driving it is (according to one magazine) the real owner of the car – Jeremy Clarkson (one of the presenters of BBC's *Top Gear* motoring programme).

Paulina Porizkova was offered the role as Bond's leading lady, but turned it down. One of the reasons that Sean Bean was cast as 006 was that he had also been considered for the role of Bond.

Joe Don Baker, who plays the Felix Leiter replacement Jack Wade, previously played the villainous Brad Whitaker in *The Living Daylights*. Billy J. Mitchell, who plays the ill-fated Admiral Chuck Farrell, commanded the US nuclear submarine tracking the *Flying Saucer*, Largo's Ship, in *Never Say Never Again*. Co-producer Michael G. Wilson is sitting at the conference table in St Petersburg when Mishkin is confronting Ouromov. Wilson is the man with the moustache sitting to Ouromov's left. Both Elizabeth Hurley and Elle MacPherson were considered as potential Bond girls.

All the Bond films up to this point have used either elements from Fleming's Bond stories or at least their titles. It has been argued that this is the first film that has no elements at all, but there are distinct similarities between *GoldenEye* and the novel of *Moonraker*: the villain is taking revenge on Britain for actions committed during World War Two and said revenge uses a nuclear device obtained from the Russians.

Goldeneye had previously been used as the title of an American TV movie about Ian Fleming's life, starring Charles Dance as the author. It was the name of Fleming's house in Jamaica.

The reasons for the huge gap between *Licence to Kill* and *GoldenEye* are many and curious, but stem partly from the fact that *Licence to Kill* was almost the most unpopular Bond film of all time, only narrowly beating *The Man With the Golden Gun* in its takings. Critical reaction was dismissive. Clearly, something was wrong. Things went even more wrong when, in 1990, Albert Broccoli took legal action against MGM/UA (the studio that had backed Bond since *Dr No*) and Pathe (with whom they were about to merge), claiming that the companies were about to license the showing of the James Bond films on international television on disadvantageous conditions.

The legal wrangling was concluded in 1993, but in the intervening period a complete shake-up had taken place in the Bond hierarchy. Control of Eon passed from Albert Broccoli to Michael G. Wilson and Broccoli's daughter, Barbara, and rumours circulated concerning new directors, new writers and even new Bonds. Roger Spottiswoode (later to direct *Tomorrow Never Dies*) has said that he was approached to direct a film around 1991, although at that stage they did not have a script. Given that Timothy Dalton stated in 1993, following the conclusion of the legal problems, that Michael France was going to start work on a story, it is possible that the film Spottiswoode was asked to direct was the one that was to become *GoldenEye*.

By the time that a script was ready, Timothy Dalton had decided that he did not want to continue as 007, and the search for a new James Bond began once more. This time Pierce Brosnan, who had previously been cast as Bond for *The Living Daylights* but was unable to take up the role because of his commitment to NBC's *Remington Steele*, was successful.

John Gardner's novelisation states that it is based on a screenplay by Michael France and Jeffrey Caine. The actual film credits the script to Jeffrey Caine and Bruce Feirstein, based on a story by Michael France. In point of fact, Michael France wrote the first draft of the screenplay. Jeffrey Caine wrote a fresh draft based on France's ideas. An American playwright, Kevin Wade, was brought in to do a rewrite, and finally Bruce Feirstein was asked to do a final rewrite before filming. Feirstein was involved during the shooting as well, redrafting scenes almost on the hoof.

The novelisation has to go to slightly schizophrenic lengths in order to tie the events of the film in with Gardner's own ongoing book series. For a start, as already noted, Gardner's Bond is a captain, but he has to refer to Bond as a commander all the way through the novelisation. In addition, Gardner's Bond uses an ASP 9 mm, whereas the film Bond still uses a Walther PPK. Unwilling to compromise on this one, Gardner changes Zukovsky's line (see **Lines to Rewind For** later) to 'I know only three men who have used that particular brand of firearm, and I've personally killed two of them.' Unhappy with some of the dialogue he has been asked to include, Gardner also has his Bond think, 'Don't be so bloody melodramatic,' when another character says something Gardner doesn't like.

Around twelve minutes of material were cut from the film before release. Nine minutes of this was trimming of existing scenes – including one of the Tiger helicopter looping the loop after it had been stolen – but two whole scenes were removed, one of which concerned the arms dealer Vladimir Zukovsky (Robbie Coltrane). Xenia Onatopp's head-butt of Natalya in Cuba was removed by the British censor.

At the Monte Carlo casino, watch the cards carefully. Xenia's first hand when Bond arrives is two blanks and a 7 – 007. Bond's later winning hand is two picture cards and a 6 – in baccarat terms, 006.

Locations: Arkangel, Severnaya and St Petersburg in Russia, the French Riviera, London briefly and Cuba.

James Bond, Fashion Victim: Bond is wearing a cravat during the race at the beginning of the film. In anyone's book, a cravat is a definite fashion no-no.

Bond's Past Life: Bond has encountered Zukovsky previously, wounding him so that he walks with a limp.

Toys for the Boys: Bond has a digital camera that can be linked directly to a printer in his car while simultaneously sending pictures back to London for checking. Q demonstrates a plaster cast with rocket-firing device, an X-ray tray, a phone box with an airbag and what appears to be an ejector seat for the office. Later in the film, Bond uses a watch with laser and a pen with a grenade built in, but all he gets to do in the car with the radar screen, Stinger missiles behind the headlights and self-destruct mechanism is drive it (the BMW deal was finalised late in the making of the film, and the script had to be rewritten to incorporate the car).

Goodbye, Mr Bond: None, but we do get one 'Good morning, Mr Bond,' from Miskin.

Single Entendres: 'One rises to meet a challenge,' Bond tells Onatopp in the casino. Later, when he buys her a drink, he asks, 'How do you take it?' 'Straight up,' she replies, 'with a twist' – and we're prepared to believe her on that one.

'Did you check her out?' Wade asks Bond, talking about Natalya Simonova. 'Head to toe,' Bond confirms.

Lines to Rewind For: Zukovsky hears the click of Bond's gun cocking and, without turning, says, 'Walther PPK, seven point six five millimetre. Only three men I know use such a gun: I believe I've killed two of them.' He mispronounces 'Walther', by the way – it's actually supposed to be 'Valter'.

Trevalyan: 'England is about to learn the cost of betrayal – inflation adjusted for 1945.'

It's Only a Movie: 'Trust no one,' Boris tells Natalya. As he is a computer nerd, this is probably a reference to the famous *X-Files* motto.

Mistakes Can Be Fatal: When we see the chemical weapons facility in long shot at the end of the pre-title sequence, it's on top of a mountain range. However, earlier on, Bond has to bungee-jump from the top to the bottom of a dam to get into it. Aren't dams usually at the *bottom* of mountain ranges, not at the top?

Trevalyan and Ouromov have presumably set up the sequence in which Ouromov apparently kills Trevalyan in order to fool Bond into thinking he is dead. Why did they do that if their intention was to kill Bond anyway? Why didn't Trevalyan kill Bond when he had a gun pointed at him earlier? Also, was it really necessary for Trevalyan to gun down so many Russian soldiers to convince Bond? How does Ouromov feel about this? Or was the whole Janus charade discussed and arranged between Trevalyan and Ouromov in those few seconds while Ouromov had a gun at Trevalyan's head? Whatever way you look at it, it doesn't make any sense.

Bond's ticket to St Petersburg is in his own name. Isn't the SIS worried that the KGB might cotton on to his presence?

Ouromov removes the bullets from Bond's magazine after killing Miskin and throws the gun to Bond in order to place the blame at his door, but the gun is an automatic and Ouromov does not remove the bullet that's already been loaded into the gun itself following the firing of the previous bullet. Bond, however, fails to take advantage of this.

When Bond is watching Xenia's Ferrari through a monocular in Monte Carlo harbour, the monocular switches from his left eye to his right eye between shots.

James Bond Will Return In . . . He'll just return.

TOMORROW NEVER DIES (1997)

Starring: Pierce Brosnan as the hero – James Bond
Jonathan Pryce as the villain – Elliot Carver
Teri Hatcher and Michelle Yeoh as the love
    interests, Paris Carver and Wai Lin

Written By: Bruce Feirstein (but see **Observations** below)

Directed By: Roger Spottiswoode

Tag Line: None.

Relevance of Pre-Title Sequence? Quite a lot. It introduces Gupta and the GPS tracker, as well as the antipathy between Admiral Roebuck and M.

Title Song: Sheryl Crow (opening); k. d. lang (closing) – but see **Observations** below.

Cringe-Worthy Title Sequence: It's a mess. There are the requisite women, someone loading and firing a gun, a naked woman whose skin is formed of microcircuits which can occasionally be seen as flesh when a TV screen moves over it, and a diamond necklace that presumably becomes a ring of satellites. What it has to do with any of the plot, even loosely, is anyone's guess! (We're not keen on it.)

Plot: When a British ship, the *Devonshire*, is fired on by the Chinese and sunk, apparently in international waters, the only clue is a signal sent out secretly on the Global Positioning

Satellite (GPS) frequency from a satellite belonging to the Carver Media Group Network. Its head, Elliot Carver, is obsessed with gaining prime position in broadcasting, and the only place on Earth his stations cannot be received is China. Since Bond had had a relationship with the woman who is now Carver's wife, Paris, M assigns him to try to pump her for information. Carver is responsible for the fake GPS signal, thanks to a device controlled by a techno-terrorist, Gupta. Bond goes to the launch of Carver's new network in Hamburg, and meets Paris, who is not overjoyed to see him. Carver is suspicious of Bond, and has him 'made uncomfortable'. Bond escapes, and is surprised when Paris shows up at his door. She tells Bond about a secret installation in Carver's printing works. Carver, meanwhile, has discovered her treachery.

Bond breaks into the printers, and finds the GPS tracker. Wai Lin, a Chinese woman whom Bond had encountered at Carver's launch party, has also broken in, and attracted attention, although she gets away easily. Bond fights his way out and is driving back to his hotel when Carver rings, telling him he knows Bond has the tracker and Paris. Bond finds Paris dead, and her killer, Dr Kaufman, waiting for him. Bond turns the tables on Kaufman, kills him, and evades his henchmen.

Bond flies out to the South China Sea, where, with Jack Wade's assistance, he makes a HALO (High Altitude, Low Opening) jump above the wreck of the *Devonshire*. Within the ship, he finds that a cruise missile has been taken – and Wai Lin also investigating. They are lucky to escape from the wreck, but then are captured by Carver's chief henchman, Stamper, and taken to Carver's Saigon headquarters, where they pass a Chinese general, Chang, whom Wai Lin recognises. The agents escape and, after a chase through the streets of Saigon, they eventually agree to team up. Wai Lin is investigating the theft of stealth materials, connected to General Chang, and they realise that Carver is using a stealth boat. They deduce where he is operating from, and manage to board the boat, with time running out before Carver manipulates a war during which he will fire the stolen cruise missile at Beijing.

In London, Bond and Wai Lin's signals have been received, and reluctantly Admiral Roebuck orders the fleet to look for the stealth boat, which now becomes visible as Wai Lin sabotages the engines. However, she's captured by Stamper. Bond kills Carver, and is about to defuse the missile when Stamper reappears, dropping a chained Wai Lin into the water. Bond and Stamper fight, with Bond escaping to rescue Wai Lin while Stamper is incinerated by the missile's abortive launch. War is averted.

Observations: Bond is seen to drink Smirnoff vodka when he is waiting for one of Carver's men to come to his hotel room – which was filmed at Stoke Poges Golf Club, the same place as the golf match in *Goldfinger*.

The licence plate for Bond's new BMW is BMT2144 – as near as could be got to the licence of the Aston Martin, BMT214A. He is still a commander in this film, and we see him in naval uniform for the third time.

The first time that he and Wai Lin kiss is when they are underwater, and Bond is breathing oxygen into her mouth (reminiscent of Chico Marx's line when he was caught with a chorus girl).

The relationship between M, Moneypenny and Bond has shifted since *GoldenEye*. Moneypenny is responsible for some of the worst double entendres of the entire series, and it is clear that Bond has confided in her about his and Paris's affair. Misogynistic dinosaur or not, Bond is clearly one of M's key agents, and he is given far more leeway here than in *GoldenEye*.

M's Chief of Staff, although never referred to by name on screen, is Charles Robinson, played by Colin Salmon (*Prime Suspect II*, *Space Island One*). Michael Kitchen, who played Bill Tanner in *GoldenEye,* was unavailable to reprise the role. There's a new Minister of Defence, played by Julian Fellowes, and Jack Wade (Joe Don Baker) plays a crucial role.

Sir Anthony Hopkins was approached to play Carver, but,

according to Brosnan, the script was not adequately prepared for him to be willing to come on board. In his place came Jonathan Pryce, star of the stage musical *Miss Saigon* and the film of *Evita*.

Michael G. Wilson gets some dialogue, as Carver's bureau chief ordered to 'slime' the President.

Bond and Wai Lin set out to explore the South China Sea from the same island that Scaramanga used as his base in *The Man With the Golden Gun*, properly called Ko Phing Kan, but known as 'James Bond Island'!

Bond 18 (as it was officially known) bears no resemblance to any of Ian Fleming's work. The original plot of *Tomorrow Never Dies* (then known as *Aquator*) concerned the handover of Hong Kong in July 1997 and the concurrent theft of gold bullion. An unused treatment was prepared by the novelist Donald E. Westlake in which Elliot Carver was surnamed Harmsway, and was a Hong Kong-born British media mogul. Until close to shooting, Wai Lin's name was Lin Pow – Pow means 'bun' in Chinese, and the actress Michelle Yeoh suggested the change. The arms bazaar seen in the pre-title sequence was originally going to feature in *The Living Daylights*.

Although Feirstein is credited as sole writer, the original idea came out of a meeting held between several Hollywood writers, including Feirstein, Nicholas Meyer (*Star Trek II* and *VI*), David Campbell Wilson and Daniel Petrie Jnr. The original shooting script was by Petrie, and was the basis for Raymond Benson's novelisation of the film. Feirstein was brought back on to the film during shooting, when it was clear that many scenes were not working properly, although the pre-credits sequence, and the interplay between Bond and Q at Hamburg Airport had already been filmed in between Pierce Brosnan's commitments on the publicity tour for *Dante's Peak*.

The original title appears to have been *Tomorrow Never Lies*, which makes reference to Carver's newspaper *Tomorrow*. However, the story goes that a fax with this title on was misread as 'Tomorrow Never Dies', and the title stuck. Pulp released their rejected theme for the film under this title as the B side of the single 'Help the Aged'.

Teri Hatcher's part as Paris Carver was originally larger, but this was apparently cut after test screenings. Spottiswoode revealed that about four minutes were cut, and three others reinstated. A deleted joke by Q about a new 'jaguar' for Bond explains the large cat prowling around the crate behind them in the airport sequence.

Raymond Benson inherited the mantle of Bond noveliser for this film, and turned in a very ... workmanlike novel. There is little suspense generated, which is a shame as we consider that, in many ways, the Petrie script it was based on was superior to the end result – the henchman does not die after the main villain, for a start. Benson adds scenes in China which take away any surprise about Wai Lin's appearance at Carver's launch party, and makes Elliot a sufferer of TMJ (temporo-mandibular joint syndrome – an ache in the jaw, accompanied by a clicking and grating sensation caused by stress and grinding one's teeth in one's sleep). He also makes mention of the movie of *You Only Live Twice*, referring to Bond's supposed First in Oriental languages at Cambridge, and states that this is Bond's first HALO jump (something the movie leaves ambiguous, although John Gardner mentions a previous one in his novelisation of *GoldenEye*). There is an oblique reference to *Zero Minus Ten* when Bond asks if he is returning to Hong Kong.

The opening credits read, 'Albert R. Broccoli's Eon productions present Pierce Brosnan as Ian Fleming's James Bond 007'. Does everyone belong to someone now?

It is dedicated in a closing caption, 'In Loving Memory of Albert R. "Cubby" Broccoli'.

Locations: The Khyber Pass, the South China Sea, London, Oxford, Hamburg, Saigon.

My Name Is . . . James Bond, banker.

James Bond, Fashion Victim: We always did like a man in naval uniform – as well as Man from C&A (or his shirts).

Bond's Past Life: Eight years previously, Bond was in a relationship with Paris Carver, who was at the time a world-famous model. He walked away without telling her because, she believes, she got too close.

Toys for the Boys: In the opening mission, Bond uses a Dunhill cigarette lighter which becomes a grenade.

Q supplies Bond with a new BMW, complete with voice-assisted navigation system, GPS tracking, a bulletproof body, rockets, metal spikes, self-inflating tyres, a defence system which delivers electric shocks, and a metal cutter hidden under the badge. In addition Bond gets a special phone, which not only allows him to drive the car by remote control, but also get key types, duplicate fingerprints and deliver 20,000 volts of electric shock – as well as make phone calls.

Wai Lin's office in Saigon seems to have been kitted out by the Chinese equivalent of Q Branch. There's a dragon that shoots fire, and a fan that sends a web of rope out, as well as a fully equipped armoury including Omega watches and the new Walther P99.

Patronising Lines: 'Very good,' Bond says, as Wai Lin knocks barrels in the way of their pursuers.

'Your government is being so predictably eager to save face,' Carver taunts Wai Lin. And let's not forget Carver's embarrassing display of martial arts.

Goodbye, Mr Bond: Sadly, none.

Villainous Foibles: Carver's henchman, Stamper, is a psychopath who enjoys murder and torture. He was a student of Dr Kaufman (before the latter's untimely execution by Bond) in the art of chakra torture. Sadly lost from the final screenplay was the revelation that Stamper's pain reflexes were the wrong way round, and increased pain gave him increased pleasure.

Sadism: There's a lot of it in *Tomorrow Never Dies*. Stamper machine guns seventeen British survivors from the HMS *Devonshire*, and films the massacre.

Bond is beaten up by three thugs at the launch party, and then gets in a fight with other thugs when he breaks into the printing works, pushing one of them into the presses.

Dr Kaufman is prepared to shoot Bond in cold blood, and, when Bond turns the table, he executes the assassin. ('I'm just a professional doing a job,' says Kaufman. 'Me too,' says Bond, and fires.)

Stamper relishes the prospect of using the chakra tools on Bond and Wai Lin, although it's Bond who gets to use them as weapons against him.

There is a vicious battle between Wai Lin and thugs working for General Chang, which shows off Michelle Yeoh's fighting skills.

Bond throws a couple of the stealth boat's sailors into the sea, and uses another one as a shield from Stamper's guns, allowing him to be hit, and fall into the water, apparently as 007.

Bond 'gives the people what they want' and holds Elliot Carver in front of the drilling machine, killing him.

Wai Lin is chained up and dropped from the stealth boat by Stamper, before the latter tries to get his revenge on Bond in a tough fight, which culminates in Bond dropping a cruise missile on his foot and the missile trying to take off.

Single Entendres: 'You always were a cunning linguist, James' – and most of Miss Moneypenny's other lines!

Lines to Rewind For: 'What the hell is he doing?' Admiral Roebuck demands. 'His job!' M says flatly.

And again: 'With all due respect, M, sometimes I don't think you've got the balls for this job.' 'Perhaps. But the advantage is I don't have to think with them all the time.'

'I could shoot you from Stuttgart and still create the proper effect,' boasts Dr Kaufman.

Carver: 'Oh and, Mr Stamper, would you please kill those bastards!'

It's Only a Movie: M instructs Moneypenny to give a story to the papers that is a deliberate nod to the original newspaper reports of Robert Maxwell's death.

Mistakes Can Be Fatal: Would a satellite really have a logo inscribed on its solar panels? Wouldn't that screw up the energy-collection process?

When the SIS contact Bond in Oxford, he's speaking to Charles Robinson. When he's put through, he's talking to Moneypenny – is she senior to Robinson?

Bond refers to 'time for station break' which is an Americanism.

Knowing that he is expecting one of Carver's men to try to finish the job, 007 sits down and puts away a good proportion of a bottle of vodka . . . Huh?

How does the video of Bond and Carver's talk rewind and play itself without either Gupta or Carver touching the controls?

Why would it take Bond four hours to get Paris out of Hamburg?

How does Carver get Bond's cellphone number?

Why does Kaufman trust Bond's instructions for the remote control for the car? Surely he would guess that Bond would take any possible avenue for escape?

Kaufman tells Bond he is to torture him if Bond doesn't give him the information – obviously he's divined this, since Stamper doesn't give him any such instructions, and anyway it's clear that Stamper is subordinate to Kaufman.

If the reading of the GPS satellite control is so pinpoint-accurate that it enables Bond to be HALO-jumped with such accuracy that he lands directly above the *Devonshire*, how come nobody noticed during the flight that they were going to be heading into Vietnamese waters?

There's a piece of dialogue between Bond and Wai Lin about the Omega that seems out of place.

How are Bond and Wai Lin able to approach the stealth boat so easily – if the boat could pick up the motion of the drill on its sensors, then surely the dinghy would be picked up?

Why is Carver more worried about Bond than Wai Lin? Or is he just being sexist?

Why would Carver want exclusive broadcast rights in China for one hundred years? He's not exactly a young man, and he's just had his wife killed.

James Bond Will Return . . . We certainly hope so!

File 003:
Television

CASINO ROYALE

Broadcast: 21 October 1954 8.30 p.m. EST

Starring: Barry Nelson as the hero – Card Sharp
           Jimmy Bond
           Peter Lorre as the villain – 'Le Chiffre'
           Linda Christian as the love interest –
           Valerie Mathis

Written By: Antony Ellis and Charles Bennet

Directed By: William H. Brown

Plot: As he arrives at the casino in Monte Carlo, American Combined Intelligence Agent Jimmy Bond is shot at, but he ducks behind a tree. In the casino, he meets his contact, Clarence Leiter of the British Secret Service, who tells him his mission is to beat Le Chiffre at the baccarat table the following night. Le Chiffre is the Soviet paymaster, and has been embezzling funds. He needs to make 80 million francs, or he is in serious trouble. Bond is also observed by a mysterious woman, who is with Le Chiffre, and has a history with Bond.

On Le Chiffre's instructions, the woman, Valerie Mathis, comes over to Bond, and they go back to his hotel, where she comes to his room. Bond is aware Le Chiffre sent her, and that his room is bugged. After playing music loudly to cover a private conversation with the woman, he allows her to say her piece – if he loves her, leave the hotel. When out of earshot of the bug, she tells Bond she is sure Le Chiffre will kill him if necessary. She then returns to Le Chiffre, who is not happy about the situation at all.

The following evening, one of Le Chiffre's men tries to steal Bond's gambling stake from Leiter but is foiled. Bond is preparing to play, when a call comes threatening Valerie's life. Bond ignores it, and proceeds against Le Chiffre, who, however, is on a winning streak. When all seems lost, an envelope arrives for Bond with money and a note: 'Here are

35 million francs. You have to win.' And he does, cleaning Le Chiffre out in two successive hands. Bond is delayed at the table by one of Le Chiffre's bodyguards, who carries a gun in his cane, but gets away from him. To his surprise, when he comes to change the money, he sees that the donation was from Valerie – who has vanished.

While Leiter searches, Bond goes back to his hotel, and hides the cheque behind the door number on his room. Valerie arrives, closely followed by Le Chiffre, who offers her life in exchange for the cheque. Valerie turns out to be an agent of the Deuxième Bureau.

Le Chiffre proceeds to torture Bond in the bathroom, attacking his toes with a pair of pliers. Eventually, Valerie can't take it, and says Bond was using a screwdriver when she came in. Le Chiffre leaves them alone while they search the room, accidentally leaving his cigarette case on the edge of the bath. Bond retrieves Le Chiffre's hidden razor blade from the cigarette case, frees himself and Valerie, and disposes of Le Chiffre's henchman when he comes to check. Le Chiffre finds the cheque but Bond shoots him. He staggers into the living room and it's revealed he's shot Bond as well. The two face each other, as Le Chiffre goes for his hat and the razor blade concealed in it . . .

Observations: This formed an entry in CBS's *Climax* series, and was hosted by William Lundigan, who took a few moments before the film began to explain what a baccarat shoe was. CBS had purchased the rights to Fleming's novel for $1,000. Unfortunately, the last minute or so of the film is lost (the whole thing was only discovered by accident in 1981), but we can presume that Bond survives and Le Chiffre doesn't!

As a part of the Bond canon, this is totally out of place, but *Casino Royale* itself is markedly different from the other Bond novels. We have a sneaking fondness for this.

Relevance to Ian Fleming's Book: The basic plot of Fleming's novel is adhered to closely, even if the nationalities of the characters have been changed. As a sop to the sensibilities of the times, the beating of Bond's genitals became the plier-ing of his toes!

Location: Monte Carlo.

My Name Is . . . Card Sense Jimmy Bond (really!).

James Bond, Fashion Victim: If you want to get an idea of what a Bond with an American haircut would look like (as in *Live and Let Die*), then Barry Nelson provides the answer . . .

Bond's Past Life: He gained the nickname 'Card Sense Jimmy Bond' when playing against a maharajah at Deauville.

Villainous Foibles: Le Chiffre has a 'toadlike' face. He adopted the name because after the war he was simply a number (hello, number six!). He is a ruthless fanatic whose only weakness is gambling. He carries three razor blades with him: in his hat, the heel of his shoe, and his cigarette case. He is always surrounded by three armed guards.

Sadism: Although nothing compared with the book's conjunction of carpet beater and flesh, the gritty reality of the bathroom torture scene is much stronger than would be allowed in a pre-watershed drama now. Le Chiffre has no reservations about hitting a woman, either.

Lines to Rewind For: 'Are you the fellow that was shot?' Bond is asked. 'No,' he replies. 'I'm the fellow that was missed.'

Claiming Le Chiffre loves torture, the villain's simple response is, 'How did you find out?'

Mistakes Can Be Fatal: How did Le Chiffre know that Leiter would be bringing money to finance Bond?

JAMES BOND JUNIOR

The initial US TV run of this crudely animated series was aired from September 1991 onward. Bearing no resemblance whatsoever to the *James Bond Junior* novel of 1967, the basic set-up of the series is as follows: Warfield Academy is a high-security school in England (on the South Coast) which has been specially designed to accommodate the relatives of Secret Service employees from around the world. James Bond's nephew is there, as is Felix Leiter's son and Q's grandson. The kids are supposed to be schooled safely there, but James Bond Jnr and his friends continually come across the evil schemes of Saboteurs and Criminals United in Mayhem (SCUM), an evil organisation resembling SPECTRE in many ways. SCUM employs such well-known villains as Goldfinger and Doctor No, as well as new ones such as Doctor Derange and Baron von Skarin.

The series consisted of 65 episodes and, sad to say, we can find nothing within the continuity of the films to deny the possibility that Bond could have a nephew. Ian Fleming's books certainly indicate he has no family, although John Pearson's *James Bond: The Authorised Biography* does mention a brother. However, the odds of Felix Leiter producing a Californian beach boy as a son and Q having an eccentric genius as his grandson are rather higher.

The presence of Bond producer Michael G. Wilson as one of the creators (and no, we can't find a secret cameo by him in any of the episodes) means that the visual continuity to the films is quite tight.

Alas, most of the episodes appear to be lost to reviewers on a tight timescale. All we have been able to obtain are the handful that we discuss below – some of which are based on prerecorded video releases, some on comic adaptations and some on the novelisations.

As a final note, the video releases (US NTSC format) say in large letters 'Not Rated' on the back cover. Well, they're certainly not rated by us.

1. THE BEGINNING

Starring: The hero – James Bond Jnr
The villain – SCUM Lord and Jaws
The love interest – Tracy Millbanks

Written By: Francis Moss and Ted Pedersen

Plot: On his way to enrol at Warfield Academy, 007's nephew, also named James, is driving his uncle's Aston Martin when he is attacked by the forces of SCUM, under the control of the evil SCUM Lord. Escaping by using the flight convertor, Bond lands at Warfield, where he meets his classmates, including Felix Leiter's son, Gordo; and Q's grandson, Horace Boothroyd (nicknamed IQ). SCUM Lord is after Bond Snr's car since he believes it contains a top-secret High Powered Electromagnetic Pulse Generator, which he can use to erase computer data within a fifty-mile radius, and neutralise the economic and defence computers of the UK.

The car is stolen by Jaws, with Tracy stuck inside, and James goes to the rescue. He saves the girl, but the car is destroyed – and the device was never in it in the first place. In its stead, Uncle James gives young Bond a sports car.

Observations: Well, Jaws is back on the side of evil, acting as henchman to SCUM Lord. He still makes buildings collapse when he lands on them, though. It looks as if the Aston Martin has had its last outing, even if it has had a flight converter added to it. (Maybe that's why the Aston Martin seen from *GoldenEye* onwards has a different registration plate.)

This episode was adapted for the first issue of the *James Bond Junior* comic book by Cal Hamilton, drawn by Mario Capaldi. In the adaptation, SCUM Lord's dog gets its own parachute. How caring of him! It also was novelised as *A View to a Thrill* by John Vincent, where some of the inconsistencies of the screenplay are ironed out.

Locations: Somewhere in the United Kingdom.

Bond's Past Life: Well, this opens up a whole new life for him ... Seriously, we are not privy to the film Bond's childhood, except for the line from *GoldenEye* about the death of his parents, which of course came after these had been made.

Bond's teacher Mr Mitchell was in the FBI before coming to Warfield, and worked with Bond Snr.

Toys for the Boys: The Aston Martin seems as equipped as ever, complete, as noted above, with flight conversion. IQ provides James with a watch which includes a buzz saw and a laser.

Goodbye, Young Bond: Yes, the junior version comes from SCUM Lord.

Villainous Foibles: SCUM Lord has a vicious dog, Scuzzbucket, and wears his dark glasses and coat whatever the weather. Jaws has had his whole jaw, rather than just the inside, replaced with metal.

Sadism: Are you kidding?

Mistakes Can Be Fatal: The position on the gearshift for reverse switches from shot to shot. The Aston Martin doesn't have a registration plate (OK, now we're being fussy!).

2. EARTH-CRACKER

Starring: The hero – James Bond Jnr
                 The villains – Goldfinger and Oddjob

Written By: Unknown

Directed By: Unknown

Plot: While out walking in the woods around Warfield Academy, Bond and his friends are attacked by Oddjob in a tank. Oddjob kidnaps a student named Lotta Dinaro, takes her to a nearby airfield and loads her into a SCUM cargo aircraft heading for Puerto Rico. Lotta's father is a rich eccentric who has spent his life searching for the lost Inca city of El Dorado, supposedly located near Puerto Rico, so Bond and friends travel there in the hope of finding him and his daughter together.

Soon after they arrive, they discover that Goldfinger is threatening to kill Lotta in an attempt to force her father to reveal the location of El Dorado – the city of gold. Dinaro tells Goldfinger what he wants to know, and the villain uses an ultrasonic weapon to excavate the city and start melting the gold of which El Dorado is composed. Bond gains control of the ultrasonic weapon and uses it to cause an earthquake, burying El Dorado, Goldfinger and Oddjob.

Observations: A rich foreign student at Warfield Academy named Lotta Dinaro? Oh yes, very funny.

Bond calls his Peruvian mule 'Moneypenny'.

This entry is based on the comic book adaptation for issue 3 by Cal Hamilton, drawn by Mario Capaldi.

Locations: England, Peru.

Toys for the Boys: A watch that can fire a climbing rope, a gold-detector hidden inside a camcorder, grenades disguised as batteries and a homing device.

3. THE CHAMELEON

4. SHIFTING SANDS

5. PLUNDER DOWN UNDER

Starring: The hero – James Bond Jnr
               The Villains – Captain Walker D. Plank and
               Jaws

Written By: Unknown

Directed By: Unknown

Plot: Bond and friends are on a school trip to Greece when Tracy Millbanks's uncle – the captain of an oil tanker – is lost along with his ship, the apparent victims of a sea monster. It's not the first ship to vanish. Finding Jaws nearby, and suspecting he has something to do with the loss of the ship, they follow him out to sea and, when he dives beneath the waves, they give chase in scuba gear.

On the sea bottom they discover a giant telescopic metal claw – the device that's been taking the ships. Swallowed by a submarine disguised as a great white shark, they are taken to an underwater city full of lost ships and controlled by the evil Captain Walker D. Plank. He intends using the ships, under remote control, to somehow take over the world.

Following their discovery of Tracy's uncle, and their imprisonment by Plank, IQ builds a device out of Gordo Leiter's computer game that allows them to take control of the ships and cause them to open fire on each other, sinking the entire fleet and holing the undersea base.

Observations: This entry is based on the comic book adaptation for issue 4 by Cal Hamilton, drawn by Mario Capaldi.

Locations: Greece. Underwater off the coast of Greece.

Toys for the Boys: A watch that turns into an electromagnet (curiously familiar), a ring that's got a laser inside, and IQ's amazing redesign of Gordo Leiter's computer game.

Villainous Foibles: Captain Walker D. Plank is such a piratical cove that even his parrot has an eye patch and a wooden leg.

Lines to Fast-Forward Past: The unamusingly named Captain Walker D. Plank: 'Yo ho ho and a sub fulla SCUM!'

6. A CHILLING AFFAIR

Starring: The hero – James Bond Jnr
                   The villain – Doctor No

Written By: Mark Jones

Directed By: Bill Hutten and Tony Love

Plot: SCUM thugs under the direction of Doctor No steal a cryogenic cylinder from a hi-tech storage unit. It contains the frozen body of a master criminal whose plan was to sleep for a hundred years. He's been out for forty years now, but Doctor No is aware that he hid $40 million in stolen platinum, and No intends reviving him and getting from him the location of the hidden cache.

Meanwhile, on a trip out, Bond Jnr and friends go to the aid of a Professor Ivan Frost – a scientist who is being kidnapped. He's an expert in cryogenics ('the science of freezing living organisms'). One of the kidnappers leaves a matchbook behind which leads Bond to a sushi bar in the East End of London. From there they trace Doctor No to a hidden base near Maidstone, where No is using the knowledge of Professor Frost to defrost the criminal. Bond rescues Frost and disguises IQ as the master criminal. They lure Doctor No out of his base and dump him where the police will find him.

Observations: Bond and his friends make it back to Warfield Academy with 007 seconds to spare before their exams start.

Locations: London and Doctor No's base near Maidstone in Kent.

Toys for the Boys: IQ has installed a new heat beam in James Bond Jnr's watch, and he's also been working on a hand-held device that will control any electrical device he attaches it to.

Villainous Foibles: Doctor No's taste in clothes has altered radically – whereas before he preferred plain white smocks, now he goes for purple jumpsuits with red trimmings and big shoulders. Then again, his skin is now green and he sports a Fu Manchu moustache.

7. NOTHING TO PLAY WITH

8. LOCATION DANGER

9. THE EIFFEL MISSILE

Starring: The hero – James Bond Jnr
Tthe villain – Dr Derange and Skullcap
The love interest – Marcie Beaucoup

Written By: Doug Molitor

Directed By: Bill Hutten and Tony Love

Plot: James Bond Jnr spots Skullcap – agent of SCUM – heading through the airport. He tries to intercept him, but Skullcap escapes, leaving behind plans for the Achilles missile. Reports indicate that terrorists have smuggled a nuclear warhead into Paris, and Bond is convinced there is a connection.

Bond and friends sneak out of Warfield Academy and head for Paris, but are attacked by Skullcap along the way. In Paris, Bond is attacked by Dr Derange but escapes. Bond realises that the Eiffel Tower would form the perfect gantry for the missile, and discovers Dr Derange and his missile in the sewers beneath.

Derange intends firing the missile at Moscow and allowing the blame to fall on the French, thus destroying *perestroika* for some unexplained reason. Bond and his companion – Marcie Beaucoup – are captured and strapped to the missile, but Bond uses the acetylene torch in his watch to break their chains and then alters the missile's guidance system so that it fires harmlessly into space. Derange and Skullcap escape, of course.

Observations: The novelisation by John Vincent is different from the transmitted episode in many respects, some minor and some major. Derange's plan in the book is to use the chaos created by the missile firing to loot the Louvre and steal the *Mona Lisa*. Or something.

Somebody obviously thought this was a good episode. It also appeared as the second issue of the comic book, adapted by Cal Hamilton, drawn by Mario Capaldi. They manage to include a passenger aircraft with an ejector seat – we think not!

Locations: Somewhere in Britain, and Paris, France.

Toys for the Boys: IQ builds a digital signal generator that can disable the electronic security systems on the Warfield Academy gates. He later tries to fob Bond off with a sword disguised as a loaf of French bread and a landmine disguised as a beret. Oh, and a watch with a homing beacon and an acetylene torch.

Mistakes Can Be Fatal: The Achilles missile requires a gantry to be fired from, which is what leads our heroes towards the Eiffel Tower, but Derange has placed the missile in a deep pit *below* the Eiffel Tower without a gantry.

10. A WORM IN THE APPLE

11. VALLEY OF THE HUNGRY DUNES

12. POMPEII AND CIRCUMSTANCE

13. NEVER GIVE A VILLAIN A FAIR SHAKE

14. CITY OF GOLD

15. NEVER LOSE HOPE

16. NO SUCH LOCH

17. APPOINTMENT IN MACAU

18. LAMP OF DARKNESS

19. HOSTILE TAKEOVER

20. CRUISE TO OBLIVION

21. A RACE AGAINST DISASTER

Starring: The hero – James Bond Jnr
               The villain – Dr Derange

Written By: Jeffrey Scott

Directed By: Unknown

Plot: Bond, IQ, Gordo Leiter and arch-twit Trevor Nose-worthy IV win the Warfield lottery for a trip to the Le Mans Grand Prix. When they get there, Bond discovers that the evil Dr Derange of SCUM has kidnapped the British driver Miles Prower and has stolen his car for nefarious purposes unknown. Bond enters the race as Miles Prower, using Prower's spare car in order to tail Derange and determine what he is up to. Derange forces Bond off the track, then drives to a nearby nuclear power station, where he transfers a quantity of liquid plutonium into the tanks of his car (this will somehow allow him to build his own nuclear power station for reasons that remain maddeningly unclear).

Bond follows Derange's mechanics to the disused winery where Miles Prower is being held captive. Bond renders the mechanics harmless and releases Prower, who has overheard Derange's plan. Bond drives to the nuclear plant, but Derange escapes. Bond chases him (in a lorry that has been 'souped up' with liquid plutonium) and manages to catch him before he can escape.

Observations: Bond tips his lorry up on one side so that a homing missile can pass beneath. Reminiscent of the end of *Licence to Kill*, released in 1989.

Locations: Warfield Academy, somewhere in the UK, and near Le Mans in France.

Toys for the Boys: Bond already has a watch with an acetylene torch inside, and in a spare five minutes IQ soups the spare Grand Prix car up with retractable wings (which fall off the first time they are used) and jet propulsion. He also installs an inflatable lining in Bond's coveralls. Derange, by comparison, has a car that can deploy oil slicks, infrared homing missiles, tyre shredders, smoke grenades and gas.

Villainous Foibles: Dr Derange has the worst French accent since Inspector Clouseau.

Sadism: Well, we had to watch it.

Mistakes Can Be Fatal: Why does Dr Derange actually enter the Le Mans Grand Prix if all he wants to use the car for is to make a fast getaway after stealing the liquid plutonium? Having stolen the liquid plutonium, why does he then re-enter the race? How can James Bond Jnr win the race when he completed only the first and last laps, and was using two different vehicles? Why do we even bother picking these things up?

22. THE INHUMAN RACE

23. LIVE AND LET'S DANCE

24. THE SWORD OF POWER

Starring: The hero – James Bond Jnr
The Villain – Dr No

Written By: Unknown

Directed By: Unknown

Plot: During a trip to the British Museum, Bond Jnr and his friends stumble across the audacious theft of an ancient Japanese sword by a group of Ninjas. Tracy Millbanks is kidnapped when she tries to interfere, and the Ninja make their escape in a helicopter. IQ manages to trace the helicopter's registration number, and he, Bond and Gordo Leiter manage to infiltrate the Ninjas' base near Dover. There they discover that the evil Dr No has stolen the sword, although he does not tell them why. Dr No and his Ninjas escape with Tracy, but Bond Jnr realises they are heading for Japan. He and his friends give chase, and track Dr No to Tokyo. There the evil doctor also kidnaps a Japanese historian, Professor Tanaka.

Dr No has discovered that the material of which the sword is composed – refined from a meteorite that fell on Japan many hundreds of years before – can intensify the beam of a laser manyfold. The clue to finding the meteorite is hidden in the hilt of the sword, and Dr No forces Professor Tanaka to decode it for him. Bond and Tanaka's daughter, Cherri, follow Dr No to the cave where the meteorite is hidden. Bond is discovered, but in his attempts to kill the young meddler Dr No triggers a rockfall. He and his Ninjas retreat, and Professor Tanaka takes control of the meteorite.

Observations: This entry is based on the John Vincent novelisation of the episode. Strangely, the book claims that this is the first meeting between Bond Jnr and Dr No, when it patently isn't.

Locations: London, the South Coast and Japan.

Toys for the Boys: IQ provides Bond Jnr with various devices, including a watch with a built-in laser and missiles, a rebreather (similar to the one Bond Jnr's uncle uses in *Thunderball*), a gun which fires a climbing rope and a crossbow which fulfils much the same function. He also gives Tracy Millbanks a pair of earrings with biological sensors in them to monitor her life signs, and he carries a flower with a camera concealed within it.

Mistakes Can Be Fatal: It takes the same time for Bond Jnr and friends to fly from England to Tokyo as it does for Trevor Noseworthy to run an eight-mile cross-country. Actually, perhaps this isn't a mistake.

25. IT'S ALL IN THE TIMING

26. DANCE OF THE TOREADORS

Starring: The hero – James Bond Jnr
                   The villain – Baron von Skarin

Written By: Alan Templeton and Mary Crawford

Directed By: Bill Hutten and Tony Love

Plot: A research institute near Warfield Academy is broken into, and some experimental memory chips are stolen. Baron von Skarin threatens to hack into the Sandhill nuclear reactor in Britain and cause a nuclear meltdown unless the British Government pays SCUM one million pounds (in gold bullion), but he can't actually carry out his threat without those experimental memory chips. The SCUM agent who stole them has woven them into the sequined lining of a dress belonging to Dulce – a Spanish dancer – while she is performing at Warfield Academy.

Dulce's troupe returns to Pamploma, but IQ has fallen in love with her, and the Bond Jnr crew decide to take IQ to see her. Before they can get to see her, Dulce is kidnapped by von Skarin (who has double-crossed his agent and is taking the memory chips without having to pay for them). Von Skarin sets off the meltdown but Bond lures a bull into crashing head first into von Skarin's computer, thus cutting his control and averting the disaster.

Observations: Major Boothroyd (Q) writes books. At least, that forms the basis of IQ's excuse to get to Spain.

Mr Millbank's first name is Bradford.

The café in which von Skarin kidnaps Dulce has a rotating table, just like the one in *Live and Let Die*.

This episode was adapted for issue 5 of the comic book by Dan Abnett, drawn by Mario Capaldi and Bambos Georgiou.

Locations: Somewhere in Britain, and Pamploma in Spain.

Toys for the Boys: IQ has developed a high-tensile fishing line and fishing lures with homing devices in.

Single Entendres: Von Skarin's agent is called Miss Tiara Hotstones. Sorry?

Lines to Fast-Forward Past: Baron von Skarin: 'I vill be . . . in touch!'

Gordo Leiter: 'Is that a traffic helicopter?' James Bond Jnr: 'No – that's Baron von Skarin's chopper!'

27. FOUNTAIN OF TERROR

28. THE EMERALD KEY

29. SHIP OF TERROR

30. DEADLY RECALL

31. RED STAR RISING

Starring: The hero – James Bond Jnr
               The villains – Dr Derange and the Chameleon

Written By: Jeffrey Scott

Directed By: Bill Hutten and Tony Love

Plot: In Russia, Dr Derange and the Chameleon steal some top-secret Soviet laser satellite guidance codes and replace them with altered versions so that SCUM can aim the Soviet satellite laser from space and slice open the walls of the Soviet Treasury bunker. Meanwhile, Warfield Academy have arranged an exchange programme with a Soviet school, and Bond, Gordo Leiter and Phoebe Farragut are sent on a trip to Moscow.

During a visit to the Moscow Space Centre to see the latest launch, Bond discovers the Chameleon but fails to stop the codes being launched to the laser space station. Bond tracks Derange and the Chameleon to the Treasury bunker, where Derange uses the space-based laser to cut his way into the diamond reserve. IQ breaks Derange's control of the laser and Bond traps Derange in the bunker by melting the area around the hole Derange made, and sealing him in.

Locations: Somewhere in England, and somewhere near Moscow.

Toys for the Boys: IQ gives Bond an umbrella satellite dish and some gloves with vibrational amplifiers that will amplify his touch.

Lines to Rewind For: Russian student: 'A talking umbrella? You Westerners have such strange toys.'

32. SCOTTISH MIST

33. THE ART OF EVIL

34. THE HEARTBREAK CAPER

35. MINDFIELD

36. LEONARDO DA VINCI'S VAULT

37. FAR OUT WEST

38. AVALANCHE RUN

39. QUEEN'S RANSOM

40. BARBELLA'S BIG ATTRACTION

41. THERE FOR MS. FORTUNE

42. INVADERS FROM S.C.U.M.

43. GOING FOR THE GOLD

44. A DERANGE MIND

45. CATCHING THE WAVE

46. LAST OF THE TOOBOOS

47. S.C.U.M. ON THE WATER

48. GOLDIE'S GOLD SCAM

Starring: The hero – James Bond Jnr
            The villain – Goldfinger, his daughter
               Goldiefinger (!) and Oddjob
            The love interest – Tracy Millbanks

Written By: J.R. Morton

Directed By: Bill Hutten and Tony Love

Plot: During a Warfield Academy field trip to Africa, Bond discovers a remote-control device attached to a rhinoceros, then another one attached to an insect. In fact, the animals are being controlled by Goldfinger, who has a base in a nearby gold mine. Goldfinger intends eventually that remote-controlled animals will mine gold for him (no doubt the insects will be especially useful – perhaps he has the gold bug), but in the short term his plan is to contaminate all the gold mines in Africa with 'fake' radioactivity, and take control of them when their owners abandon them.

Bond, meanwhile, tracks the signals that are controlling the animals and locates Goldfinger's base. He infiltrates the base but is taken prisoner and fitted with a controlling device. Bond begins working for Goldfinger, but IQ, Gordo Leiter and the rest rescue him. Bond sets off the alarm in Goldfinger's base, making him think that there is a *real* plutonium leak, and, when Goldfinger and Goldiefinger escape, Bond causes their helicopter to crash into a waterfall.

Observations: Goldiefinger?!

File 004:
The Comic Strips

A Brief History of the Comics

The first comic strips involving James Bond were published by the British *Daily Express* newspaper from mid-1958 onward. For slightly over ten years the newspaper faithfully serialised Ian Fleming's work (with a rather abrupt curtailment to the *Thunderball* adaptation). The credits for these adaptations are as follows:

Casino Royale (Jul. 1958–Dec. 1958; writer: Anthony Hearne; artist: John McLusky)

Live and Let Die (Dec. 1958–Mar. 1959; writer: Henry Gammidge; artist: John McLusky)

Moonraker (Mar. 1959–Aug. 1959; writer: Henry Gammidge; artist: John McLusky)

Diamonds Are Forever (Aug. 1959–Jan. 1960; writer: Henry Gammidge; artist: John McLusky)

From Russia With Love (Jan. 1960–May 1960; writer: Henry Gammidge; artist: John McLusky)

Doctor No (May 1960–Oct. 1960; writer: Henry Gammidge; artist: John McLusky)

Goldfinger (Oct. 1960–Apr. 1961; writer: Peter O'Donnell – creator of *Modesty Blaise*; artist: John McLusky)

'Risico' (Apr. 1961–Jun. 1961; writer: Henry Gammidge; artist: John McLusky)

'From a View to a Kill' (Jun. 1961–Sep. 1961; writer: Henry Gammidge; artist: John McLusky)

'For Your Eyes Only' (Sep. 1961–Dec. 1961; writer: Henry Gammidge; artist: John McLusky)

Thunderball (Dec. 1961–Feb. 1962; writer: Henry Gammidge; artist: John McLusky)

On Her Majesty's Secret Service (Jun. 1964–May 1965; writer: Henry Gammidge; artist: John McLusky)

You Only Live Twice (May 1965–Jan. 1966; writer: Henry Gammidge; artist: John McLusky)

'The Living Daylights' (Sep. 1966–Nov. 1966)

Towards the end of their adaptations of Fleming's material, when they were left with the last few short stories and the rather inadequate novel *The Spy Who Loved Me*, there was a distinct change in their output. Original material was integrated into the Fleming adaptations to extend the short stories to novel length and to 'pep up' the weakest novel, and then entirely original stories were written in order to continue a highly successful part of the newspaper's appeal. Some of these original stories appeared in the *Daily Express*, one in the *Sunday Express*, some in the *Daily Star* and some in newspapers in other countries. In all, 33 new James Bond adventures were published – far more than in any other medium, and often closer in tone to Fleming's creation (Kingsley Amis's *Colonel Sun* was also adapted). The last of these comic strips – *Polestar* – was curtailed even more abruptly than *Thunderball*. For the first time in any James Bond reference work, the plots of these 'new' Bond adventures are described below, along with descriptions of the continuity they display with Fleming's own novels and any odd points of interest along the way.

These strips were undoubtedly popular in Scandinavia, and at least 25 further adventures followed. As far as we can tell, these tales appeared only in these countries, bringing the curtailed *Polestar* to a close, and sending 007 on new missions around the world. Writers included Jack Sutter, better known for his work on Disney Comics. Brief details of these non-English-language adventures are also appended below.

In 1989 more original James Bond comic strips started to appear in English – this time as widely distributed mini-series published by American comics publishers. Full entries for these comics close the section.

A short-lived comic series tied in with the *James Bond Jnr* animated TV series was also published between 1992 and 1993. The first five of the twelve issues were adaptations of the TV episodes; the remaining seven were original stories. Much against our better judgement, and only because we felt obliged to cover the TV series, we also cover the comics here.

It's worth noting that a fifth category of James Bond comics has been published: adaptations of some of the films. These comprise: *Doctor No* (1963), by Norman Nodel; *For Your Eyes Only* (1981), written by Larry Hama and drawn by Howard Chaykin; *Octopussy* (1983), with a script by Marvel UK's Steve Moore and drawn by Paul Neary; *The Living Daylights* (1987), adapted by Jack Sutter and drawn by Sarompas (which was reprinted in Finnish in 1992); *Licence to Kill* (1989), written by Mike Grell and Richard Ashford and drawn by Grell; and *GoldenEye* (1996), of which only one part of Don McGregor and Claude St Aubin's adaptation appeared.

THE MAN WITH THE GOLDEN GUN

Published In: The *Daily Express* from January 1966

Written By: Jim Lawrence

Drawn By: Yaroslav Horak

Plot: Almost identical to that of Ian Fleming's book, with one interesting variation. M ensures that a recuperating Bond becomes personally involved with the assassination attempt on Scaramanga by sending one of Scaramanga's victims to the same nursing home as Bond, knowing that Bond will see him (Bond is recuperating from his brainwashing at the hands of the Soviet Union, of course). The victim, an SIS agent and former friend of Bond named Philip Margesson, has been sadistically crippled by Scaramanga and is refusing to say what happened. Bond gets him to talk, and discovers that the nurse attending Margesson is a Soviet agent.

OCTOPUSSY

Published In: The *Daily Express* from November 1966

Written By: Jim Lawrence

Drawn By: Yaroslav Horak

Plot: Much the same as Ian Fleming's short story, but expanded by the addition of Hans Oberhauser's daughter Trudi, who tells Bond that her father's body has been discovered, and two Chinese businessmen named Yat Foo and Kim Foo who are smuggling Major Dexter Smythe's gold to Hong Kong for him in coffins supposedly containing Chinese bodies. During a confrontation in Smythe's house, Bond knocks out one of the Foo brothers, kills the other one, and confronts Smythe underwater, where events return to those described by Ian Fleming.

Observations: SIS Station J covers Jamaica.

Mary Goodnight appears in a brief sequence – she's stationed in Jamaica in Ian Fleming's book *The Man With the Golden Gun*.

My Name Is . . . Mark Hazard, a detective from the Ministry of Defence.

Patronising Lines: Tailed by a Chinese man in a car, Bond pulls him out into the road saying, 'All right, Confucius – outside!' He adds, 'Forgive barbarian tactics, but humble servant object most strongly to being tailed.' Later, when he discovers gold in a coffin that's meant to hold a Chinese body, he says, 'At least something in the coffin is yellow!' Yes, all very politically correct.

THE HILDEBRAND RARITY

Published In: The *Daily Express* from May 1967

Written By: Jim Lawrence

Drawn By: Yaroslav Horak

Plot: The events of Ian Fleming's short story are prefaced by an extended sequence in which Milton Krest steals a top-secret remote-controlled submarine code-named Sea Slave during its test voyage. He's working with a woman named Nyla Larsen, who becomes interested in James Bond when he arrives under instructions to help locate the Sea Slave. Larsen invites Bond to join her, Milton Krest and Krest's wife Liz on their cruise so that she can keep an eye on him, but (during Krest's sideline hunt for the Hildebrand Rarity) Bond soon discovers Krest's real plan. As in the short story, Krest is killed when someone stuffs the Hildebrand Rarity into his mouth: Bond doesn't know whether Liz Krest or Nyla Larsen did it.

THE SPY WHO LOVED ME

Published In: The *Daily Express* from December 1967

Written By: Jim Lawrence

Drawn By: Yaroslav Horak

Plots: The events of Ian Fleming's novel – which has Bond arriving unexpectedly at a US motel and preventing a woman being raped by criminals – are here prefaced by the case Bond was working on before he started his drive through the USA. In Canada Mike Farrar – a test pilot involved in the trials of a new stealth aircraft code-named the Ghosthawk – is being blackmailed by a man named Horst Uhlmann. Farrar tells the Mounties, and they transmit the information to the

British Secret Intelligence Service. Uhlmann is a former member of SPECTRE, and if he is still working then that organisation might still be in operation. Bond is sent to Canada, where he impersonates Farrar in an attempt to get close to SPECTRE. Alas, he ends up killing Uhlmann and losing any chance he had of finding out more about the regenerated SPECTRE. From there he decides to drive to Washington, DC, to make his report, and ends up taking part in the events detailed in Ian Fleming's *The Spy Who Loved Me*.

Observations: The new head of SPECTRE – code-named Spectra — is a woman who wears a fright-mask to avoid being identified. Their headquarters are still in Paris.

The mission that Bond has been on in Canada is not the same as described in the original novel.

Bond recalls the events of *You Only Live Twice*, where he saw Ernst Stavro Blofeld die.

Locations: London and Toronto, leading into somewhere in backwoods America.

My Name Is ... Wing Commander Jeremy Boone; Mike Farrar.

THE HARPIES

Published In: The *Daily Express* from 4 October 1968

Starring: The hero – James Bond
The villains – Simon Nero and the Harpies
(sounds like a sixties pop group!)
The love interest – Helen Nero

Written By: Jim Lawrence

Drawn By: Yaroslav Horak

Plot: A top scientist, Dr John Phineus, has invented the Q-Ray, which is debating handing over to the Government.

Before he can do so, he is kidnapped by the Harpies, an all-female gang who use hang-gliders and rocket packs, and are responsible for assorted crimes in America. Bond discovers that Phineus's main rival in both his business and private lives is Simon Nero, head of Aerotech Security. Bond gains the trust of Aerotech's Chief of Security, Reece Mulyan, and persuades him to give him a glowing reference; he then arranges for Mulyan's kidnapping, and supposed death. Posing as a corrupt police inspector, Bond is appointed as Mulyan's successor and infiltrates Aerotech, where, with the help of Nero's daughter Helen, he finds Phineus. Helen Nero is killed during their escape.

Observations: Bond maintains a flat in Earl's Court under his then current alias, Mark Hazard (as in *The Man With the Golden Gun*). Bond is offered a knighthood for the second time, which he refuses again.

M, Bill Tanner (who turns out to have been a classics scholar) and Moneypenny all appear. Reece Mulyan is kept prisoner at the Park, the 'nursing home' in Kent at which Bond was de-brainwashed. The Harpies are a rival to both SPECTRE, who get a name check, and the Mafia.

The plot falls down slightly. The Harpies in Virgil's *Aeneid* are led by someone whose name, like Nero's, means black. Their chief victim is the blind king, Phineus. Did Nero therefore decide to call his gang 'The Harpies' simply because he was going to use them against Phineus, and then think up the bright idea of their using hang-gliders and rocket packs?

Locations: England – London, Cambridge and Derbyshire.

My Name Is . . . Mike Hazard, corrupt police inspector.

Toys for the Boys: Bond uses 'a suitcase transceiver G-4 type, with the mike and speaker built into the latch, and the microcircuitry in the leather wall'.

Sadism: The fight between Bond and one of the Aerotech security guards is brutal, and stretches over a number of days' entries.

Lines to Flick Past: 'Ah yes, those rocket-clad young women who kidnapped me, like the Harpies in Virgil's *Aeneid* who attacked the blind king Phineus!' As opposed to any other rocket-clad young women who were around, presumably . . .

'When a lady starts to bite, the game's over!'

Mistakes Can Be Fatal: Why does Mulyan give 'Hazard' such a glowing reference to his boss on the basis of one simple phone call that he hasn't even corroborated yet? And, come to that, when does he get a chance to talk with him?

Why would Nero give the plum job of Chief of Security to someone he's only just met? (Although, as we've seen, this is something that all Bond villains tend to make a habit of . . .)

RIVER OF DEATH

Published In: The *Daily Express* from 24 June 1969

Starring: The hero – James Bond
               The villain – Dr Cat
               The love interest – Kitty Redwing

Written By: Jim Lawrence

Drawn By: Yaroslav Horak

Plot: When a Chinese defector is killed in a SIS safe house by poison gas delivered by a howler monkey, it is the fourth such mysterious death involving animals in five months. Bond discovers that the monkeys are imported by L.T. Grey and Co. in the East End. After he visits the shop, he is followed by one of the shopkeepers, who tries to kill him. News arrives from Brazil that Dr Cat, chief torturer and inquisitor for the Red Chinese, has possibly resurfaced undercover at a river hospital up the Amazon. Another 00 agent, York, is missing presumed dead. Bond flies out and encounters Kitty Redwing, a Native American CIA agent. He meets Fernando Gomez, a businessman who owns both the hospital and L.T. Grey. An unsuccessful attempt is made on his life with a vampire bat, and York's headless body is delivered to the SIS before Bond goes to a party, where he is introduced to Joao Onca, the doctor in charge of the hospital – really Dr Cat. Kitty reveals she is a CIA agent on Onca's trail, since he is threatening to create a pan-Indian movement.

Bond investigates L.T. Grey, and realises that it is another pun on 'cat' (El Tigre). Bond and Kitty are kidnapped and taken to the hospital, where Onca/Cat reveals he knows 007's identity. His fate is to be injected with an extract of insect venom which will make his skin ultra-sensitive, and then become a heart-transplant donor for Gomez's benefit, while Kitty will become Onca's concubine. They escape, and release Onca's nerve gas into the atmosphere. Gomez is captured when he flies in for the operation, and Bond and Kitty leave, after shooting Cat.

Observations: Bond is back using his Beretta (he used a Walther 7·65mm in *The Harpies*). Major Boothroyd wouldn't be pleased! Kitty Redwing worked with Felix Leiter in the CIA.

Station S covers Rio de Janeiro (as opposed to VH in *Moonraker*). Another 00 agent bites the dust – although we find out only his name, York, not his number.

M, Bill Tanner and Moneypenny all appear. Moneypenny files Bond's report away as 'River of Death File 127'.

Dr Cat physically resembles Joseph Wiseman as Dr No, and is equally in debt to Dr Fu Manchu for his ideas.

Locations: The Alps (briefly), London, Rio de Janeiro and the upper reaches of the Amazon.

My Name Is ... Mike Hazard, journalist; a Canadian Mohawk Indian.

Sadism: Bond is attacked by a vampire bat, and threatened with a red-hot poker. Kitty is tortured, but off-panel.

Lines to Flick Past: Dr Cat leaves Bond 'in the redoubtable embrace of his little Red Indian Squaw from the CIA'.

Mistakes Can Be Fatal: Kitty never introduces herself to Bond – he divines her name from the caption box!

COLONEL SUN

Published In: The *Daily Express* from 1 December 1969

Starring: The hero – James Bond
The villain – Colonel Sun
The love interest – Ariadne Alexandrou

Adapted By: James D. Lawrence from the novel by
Robert Markham (Kingsley Amis)

Drawn By: Yaroslav Horak

THE GOLDEN GHOST

Published In: The *Daily Express* from 21 August 1970

Starring: The hero – James Bond
The villain – Felix Ignace Bruhl
The love interest – Velvet Lee

Written By: 'From an original story by J.D. Lawrence'

Drawn By: Yaroslav Horak

Plot: Madam Spectra, the head of the revived SPECTRE, offers £1 million worth of information to the SIS, and sends a £25,000 diamond as proof of her bona fides. They want to hold Bond as their hostage until it's paid. Bond agrees, and goes to Cannes, where he is contacted by Kapski, a SPECTRE operative, but another group attack them. Before Kapski succumbs to his fatal wounds he draws a crescent shape and says, 'Br . . . br . . .'

Bridget Penwyn, a witch, is predicting disaster for the new technological miracle, the Golden Ghost, a nuclear-powered airship made in England, due to go on its maiden flight. Bond thinks Kapski might have been trying to draw the airship and say 'Bridget', so visits her. Before she can say much, she is killed by an explosion. Bond, however, finds a lighter with the Golden Ghost insignia on it, so joins the maiden flight.

Meanwhile the airship pilot's fingerprints are found at Bridget's cottage, and a check on the manufacturing company reveals that one of its members, Felix Ignace Bruhl, was a member of SPECTRE. Bond engineers an introduction to Bruhl via one of the stewardesses, Velvet Lee, but then gets on his wrong side when he stops Bruhl behaving like a pig with Velvet. At the lunch table, they are all drugged and wake up on a small South Atlantic Island.

Bruhl is holding the passengers and the dirigible hostage for £10 million each. The passengers are encouraged to write letters exhorting their loved ones to pay up – and Bond is fed to the sharks as an example to them. Using a switchblade in his buckle, Bond frees himself, and proceeds to deal with Bruhl's men. Bond and the woman escape in the airship, but Bruhl has got on board, and there is a final battle which ends with Bruhl falling to his death.

Observations: Former SPECTRE chief Blofeld owned a Marseilles Import Firm between 1961 and 1963, Dutourd Freres et Cie. M, Moneypenny and Bill Tanner all appear, as does Spectra in the opening panel.

Whoever wrote this story didn't know the way James Bond speaks. His dialogue includes such classics as 'me old luv' (Moneypenny), 'Blimey! I feel downright naked without that friendly little Beretta under my arm!' and 'Sorry, mate' to the owner of a house. The story holds up well enough – the idea that SPECTRE will warn the Secret Service about someone else's plots and try to benefit from that is neat – but it's a struggle to get through when the lead is so badly portrayed.

Locations: England, the Golden Ghost, and an island in the South Atlantic.

My Name Is . . . Mark Hazard, of Transworld News Service.

Toys for the Boys: Bond has a switchblade in his buckle, and carries a knife strapped to his leg.

Sadism: The final fight between Bond and Bruhl takes place in a kitchen and is up there beside *Never Say Never Again* and *The Living Daylights* in its unfriendly use of kitchenware.

Lines to Flick Past: 'The lubberly fools' from M, and the aforementioned Beretta quote.

Mistakes Can Be Fatal: Letting whoever wrote this do the dialogue!

FEAR FACE

Published In: The *Daily Express* from January 1971

Starring: The hero – James Bond
                      The villain – Ferenc Kress
                      The love interest – Briony Thorne

Written By: James D. Lawrence

Drawn By: Yaroslav Horak

Plot: Briony Thorne, formerly agent 0013, arrives back in Britain, and is hunted by the Security Services since they believe she had been turned by the Chinese Communists. The only person she can trust is her former lover 007, and she tells him that she was framed, and that the man responsible, Ferenc Kress, is involved with something to do with Magnus Mining and Lambert. Magnus Mining is run, although not owned, by Sir William Magnus and has just made major ore strikes. The only Lambert that MI6 files throws up is Ivor Lambert, who works for an engineering firm. The only mark against him is his involvement in the death of a young stripper, whose demise, a drunk alleged, was caused by a man with no face.

As Bond discovers that Lambert was involved with tele-factoring – robotics – a bearded man gains access to Magnus's office, shooting people along the way, opens the safe with the plans, then blows himself up. Bill Tanner tries to take Briony in, but 007 knocks him out, and he and Briony go to Lambert's office, where they find Kress waiting. Sir William, he and Lambert have concocted the scheme so Magnus will profit from the finds directly, using Lambert's robot to examine and transmit the details. Kress, however, has got greedy and wants to sell the plans abroad. Bond takes advantage of the thieves falling out to gain the upper hand, and clears Briony's name.

Observations: Bond is willing to bet on Briony based on the tossing of a coin. We're not sure that we would really want this country's security to be that easily decided!

Agent 0013 was Briony Thorne, before she was framed. It's implied that she's reinstated at the end of this story. M, Moneypenny, Bill Tanner and a room of MI6 agents (all male – M says: 'I want her, gentlemen!') are seen.

The plot is reminiscent of the Cybernauts, seen in the sixties series *The Avengers*.

Location: London.

Bond's Past Life: Bond and Briony were lovers before her 'defection'.

Lines to Flick Past: 'The whole thing is utterly impossible, except in science fiction yarns.' We would tend to agree with Inspector Craig.

DOUBLE JEOPARDY

Published In: The *Daily Express* from April 1971

Starring: The hero – James Bond
The villain – Fritz Kumara
The love interest – Lalla Sadab

Written By: James D. Lawrence

Drawn By: Yaroslav Horak

Plot: After paintings are stolen from the Manhattan Museum of Art – apparently by its director, who's then found dead – Lady Cynthia Winter, the wife of a top Ministry of Defence official, is blackmailed with a photo of a lookalike engaging in sexual antics. In France, Aristide Brizaud, the head of Brizaud Chemicals, seems to steal his own new industrial enzyme processes, and is then killed. However, when the killer tries to sell the process, he is caught by 007, who suspects that SPECTRE is involved. Lady Cynthia's husband, Sir John, is suspected of spying and, after she tells him that she was blackmailed into acting as a spy, he shoots himself, claiming the blame.

Bond investigates the death, and prevents Lady Cynthia from killing herself. She uses the Identikit to create a picture of her blackmailer, whom Bill Tanner recognises as Pujar, an agent of SPECTRE. M meanwhile sends Bond on the trail of Fritz Kumara, who is Red China's top gun. He's holed up in Morocco with a Romanian called Tatianu, and his Arab girlfriend Lalla Sadab.

Bond gets to know Lalla, as the CIA and Interpol identify Tatianu as a plastic surgeon, and Lalla as a nurse. Pujar is also there, and Bond discovers that SPECTRE is replacing people with surgically altered duplicates. Their next target is Martin Lewis, the US Secretary of Defence, who is attending a peace conference in Berlin. Thanks to Lalla changing sides, Bond manages to warn London that Lewis is a duplicate, and the peace conference is saved.

Observations: Bond's favourite poet is Robert Louis Stevenson.

Locations: New York, London, France, Morocco, Berlin.

My Name Is ... Jeremy Blade of the London Ornithological Society.

Toys for the Boys: Bond uses a briefcase that fires bullets, and a hang-glider.

Sadism: Bond is tortured with electrodes.

Lines to Flick Past: Bond describes Lady Cynthia as a 'bonny bird'!

Mistakes Can Be Fatal: After Sir John's suicide, would any self-respecting butler have allowed Lady Cynthia to still have access to a gun?

STAR FIRE

Published In: The *Daily Express* from August 1971

Starring: The hero – James Bond
                     The villain – Luke Quantrill
                     The love interest – None

Written By: James D. Lawrence

Drawn By: Yaroslav Horak

Plot: Sir Robert Wullam rescues his daughter from the hippy cult run by 'Lord Astro'; a few days later he is delivered a pendant which apparently belongs to her, although he doesn't recognise it, by Luke Quantrill, a man who bears a number of grudges. Sir Robert is then killed by a fireball which comes out of nowhere. Astro is pleased, claiming that starfire has dealt with Sir Robert as retribution.

Another of Quantrill's enemies, McGrath, writes to a newspaper denouncing Astro – and he too is killed by a fireball. Professor Corbett, a senior scientist working on a new Alpha Wing design, also denounces Astro and is killed, although his briefcase's contents are stolen. Vic Strawn, boss of Rex Industries, is interviewed about Astro, rubbishes him – and is killed. His chauffeur was previously given a watch by an 'advertising agency' which is found in the wreckage.

Since McGrath was a CIA agent, MI6 is called in to investigate and, although Astro is the obvious suspect, the clues point to Quantrill. When Bond visits his electronics firm, he finds a safecracker mid-job, but all they find is a pen in the safe. Joining forces with CIA agent Perelli,

Bond discovers that Quantrill had sold classified data to the Russians six years earlier in 1965, and was persona non grata in the industry. Bond follows his trail to Paris where he had worked for a model-plane manufacturer, Dutard et Cie, which is the cover for an underworld operation – where Bond spots Roche, a SPECTRE agent.

A trap is laid for Bond by SPECTRE which he turns to his advantage, and discovers that Madam Spectra is annoyed at Quantrill for getting greedy. Quantrill, meanwhile, is visiting his brother and sister-in-law, who originally was his girl-friend. Returning to London, Bond warns Perelli away from Quantrill, although Perelli reveals that all the deaths were linked to Quantrill in the past. Perelli ambushes Quantrill, but the latter kills him, and heads down to his brother's birthday party, with the pen – which is the homing device for the fireball – as a deadly gift. Bond arrives in time to lure Quantrill outside and ensure that he has the pen on him as the fireball arrives.

Observations: This is a much more straightforward espionage tale than hitherto; there's no love interest for Bond at all, and really nothing to characterise it as an 007 tale. M, Bill Tanner and Moneypenny all play a small part, while Madam Spectra gets a brief namecheck.

Locations: London, Paris, Devon.

My Name Is . . . Mark Hazard.

Toys for the Boys: SPECTRE have developed a nerve-gas gun.

Mistakes Can Be Fatal: Why does Bond go to Paris on Quantrill's trail? Why not just call Interpol (as he has done on numerous previous occasions in the comic strips)?

TROUBLE SPOT

Published In: The *Daily Express* from December 1971

Starring: The hero – James Bond
                   The villain – Baron Sharck
                   The love interest – Gretta

Written By: James D. Lawrence

Drawn By: Yaroslav Horak

Plot: Bond's claim to be Mike Channing is seen through by Channing's girlfriend, Gretta, when he is posing as the dead man on the French Riviera. Bond is trying to discover where 'the Box' is, and finds that he is only one of the parties on its trail. Baron Sharck, a Russian commissar known as Commissar Sharkface, is also seeking it, and kidnaps Bond and Gretta, believing they have it. They manage to escape, and Bond discovers a note with the name 'Belluna' on it. Gretta thinks that Channing's wife, Folly Wilde, may have the box and she and Bond head for California, where Folly lives. On the way, Gretta reveals that Folly is blind, and since Bond can imitate Channing's voice, she will believe Bond is Channing!

Belluna turns out to be the California small town where Folly is staying at a nudist colony – which is lucky, as Bond can recognise her only by a birthmark on her backside. Incredibly, Folly does believe that Bond is Channing, and takes him to where she has hidden the box. Although Bond has left her behind, Gretta follows, as do Sharck and his men. When Bond has recovered the box, Gretta shows her true colours, and tries to take it from him. Unfortunately, Sharck is close behind, and he shoots her. Bond and Folly manage to escape from the trap Sharck sets, killing him along the way. The box contains the skull of a Russian who had turned double agent – the skull is the proof that he is definitely dead.

Observations: Another espionage tale which doesn't really need to have 007 at its centre. A rare occasion on which M is not seen or referred to, although both Bill Tanner and Moneypenny make very brief appearances. The plot itself, based on the unlikely event that any wife, whether blind or not, will totally mistake a stranger's voice for her husband's, and that she will be at a nudist colony allowing Bond to identify her, strains the credulity more than a little!

This was reprinted as 'The Mystery of Box' by Diamond Comics in New Delhi.

Locations: French Riviera, California.

My Name Is . . . Mike Channing.

Toys for the Boys: Bond's car is equipped with a sub-machine-gun in the wing.

Patronising Lines: 'A little faster with those knots, Olga dear – or would a few strokes on the flank with your own whip help you undo them more deftly?' Bond enquires.

'If you can make her accept your voice as her husband's, what's to stop her accepting all of you?' Gretta demands, she thinks totally reasonably.

'It's a hard world, Folly,' is Bond's epitaph on Gretta. 'Can't blame a woman for wanting to survive. She'd no man to look after her.'

ISLE OF CONDORS

Published In: The *Daily Express* from June 1972

Starring: The hero – James Bond
                    The villain – Signor Uccelli
                    The love interest – Crystal Kelly

Written By: James D. Lawrence

Drawn By: Yaroslav Horak

Plot: Bond is in Italy, following the trail of Ghislaine Perault, a Belgian woman who stole memos from her Foreign Office boyfriend, and was then found dead. Near a palazzo belonging to the Gallews, he is stopped by a naked young woman on horseback, Thyrza Holt. She claims to have been held prisoner by the Gallews, but Bond returns her there. The

Gallews proceed to drug Bond, and find a miniature showing Ghislaine. Panicked, they go to 'the Island' and are brought before Signor Uccelli, who feeds them to his condors. Bond awakes to find a black woman going through his clothes. Crystal Kelly is a Private Investigator looking for Thyrza. She and Bond compare notes before they are attacked by Rafaele Barbaro, one of Uccelli's men. Bond shoots him and they leave him there.

The trail leads to the 'Isle of Condors' – Uccelli's island – and 'Mark Hazard' swims there, claiming that his boat has been sunk by a jealous husband. He discovers that Uccelli is running a training school for female spies, who carry out their tasks – as Ghislaine did – but are eventually fed to the condors. Bond finds Thyrza but they are captured by Uccelli, who plans to let his birds loose on them – but Crystal arrives in the nick of time. In the ensuing fight, Bond sprays Uccelli with the spymaster's own homing scent for the birds – but is merciful and throws him a gun to shoot himself before the birds can finish the job.

Observations: Crystal very heavily resembles Rosie Carver from *Live and Let Die*, which was being filmed when this appeared. It's not outside the realms of possibility that the idea of allowing Bond to have a romance with a black woman was created for the strip to see what, if any, feedback might surround the film's dealing with the same subject.

M is once again conspicuous by his absence, and Bill Tanner and Moneypenny don't arrive until the last page.

My Name Is . . . Mark Hazard.

THE LEAGUE OF VAMPIRES

Published In: The *Daily Express* from October 1972
Starring: The hero – James Bond
              The villain – Xerxes Xerophanos (The Big
                Double Cross)
              The love interest – Margo Xerophanos

Written By: James D. Lawrence

Drawn By: Yaroslav Horak

Plot: A vampire cult is growing across Europe, with young people attracted to the wild parties. Journalist Dolly Haret is investigating, but has got too close. She is saved from an attack by 007 but Bond is knocked out and a 'vampire' kills Dolly. The cult appears to be responsible for a number of deaths, and Bond is ordered to return to London – reluctantly leaving behind Bridget, an MI6 operative, who is also killed.

An MP has been the most recent target, and MI6 have been alerted by shipping industrialist Xerxes Xerophanos that his wife Margo may have been seduced into the cult. Bond infiltrates a cult ceremony, where Margo is to be the victim.

Xerophanos is behind the cult: his wife is an heiress in her own right, and he wants to get her money. His plan is to kill her father using a tactical nuclear missile when he is opening a new plant in Norfolk, then produce Margo's body and inherit. Bond and Margo are captured by Xerophanos, and taken on board the ship from where he will fire his missile. Bond, however, threatens to explode Xerophanos's backup missile and the crew mutinies.

Observations: M and Bill Tanner brief Bond, but there's no sign of Moneypenny. There's a passing reference to the Union Corse, claiming it's the Sicilian Mafia, but not linking it to 007 (cf. *OHMSS*).

Locations: Corsica, London, Home Counties, Norfolk.

My Name Is ... Mark Hazard (which Dolly sees through straightaway).

Bond's Past Life: 007 helped 'Zarkov defect in Vienna' – a story Dolly covered.

DIE WITH MY BOOTS ON

Published In: The *Daily Express* from March 1973

Starring: The hero – James Bond
                      The villain – Benny the Barber Pignelli
                      The love interest – Voyle

Written By: James D. Lawrence

Drawn By: Yaroslav Horak

Plot: A new chemical, Nopane, has been developed in Britain as a sedative, but it gets used as a recreational drug. The secret has fallen into the hands of the American Mafia, who are fighting between themselves to get it. Bond is sent to find Posy Gee, the niece of the scientist who invented the drug, and with the assistance of a former Royal Navy sailor, Smoky Turpin, rescues Posy from Benny Pignelli. Bond uses a zip gun hidden in his shoes to shoot Pignelli and deals with his moll, Voyle, who has been stringing Bond along through the story.

Observations: There's a nicely executed sequence at the start, where Bond is carried on a girder suspended from a crane to the outside of one of the gangster's apartments. Otherwise it's a rather boring story. It's rather like a *Doctor Who* tale, in that Bond gets caught, escapes, runs around, gets caught, escapes and so on. There's no sign of any of the London-based MI6 staff.

Nopane is a neat idea: the user becomes impervious to pain, but, as with so many of the other inventions featured in the comic strip, it never reappears.

Locations: New York City and State.

Toys for the Boys: Bond uses Harlem hotshot shoes (containing a zip gun), a laser concealed in his wristwatch and image-intensifying glasses.

Lines to Flick Past: Bond describes Nopane: 'It can groove

291

you out of this world on absolutely cosmic highs.' Yes, *Bond* says that.

THE GIRL MACHINE

Published In: The *Daily Express* from June 1973

Starring: The hero – James Bond
                   The villain – the Regent of Hajar
                   The love interest – Zebeide Rashid

Written By: James D. Lawrence

Drawn By: Yaroslav Horak

Plot: Bond is trying to restore Emir Nasreddin of Hajar to his throne, displacing his uncle, or Britain will lose critical oil rights to the country. The only clue he has is Abu Rashid, who is in Las Palmas. Unfortunately, Rashid is killed before 007 can get information from him, so he has to see if Rashid's sister, Zebeide, can help. She is one of the wives of the Regent – who is holding Nasreddin in his palace. Bond is smuggled into Hajar in a 'feminorama' – a machine that contains videos of women, scents and drinks, as well as a space for someone to hide. This is a bribe for the Regent, which he refuses.

Bond makes contact with Zebeide, but falls foul of Rimel, the Regent's henchman who was responsible for Rashid's death. Escaping from a panther, Bond, Zebeide and the freed Emir have a harrowing journey to the border, but, despite everything that the Regent throws at them, they escape.

Observations: This is the most visually orientated of the strips to date: there's a nicely drawn fight scene between Rimel and Bond in Las Palmas, and the escape to the border – which took over a month of strips to portray – would work extremely well as the climax of a cinematic 007 adventure.

We don't see M, but Bill Tanner and Moneypenny (masquerading as Miss Cashilling) both assist Bond, with Penny receiving her first visual change, oddly making her resemble Caroline Bliss from *The Living Daylights* fourteen years later! The Prime Minister is informed of Bond's success – the same person as in *Golden Ghost*, so we presume Ted Heath. We're a little uneasy about his foreign policy though: bribing a foreign ruler with videos of women!

Locations: Las Palmas, London, Hajar.

My Name Is . . . Seamus O'Seven; Mohammed J. Bond.

Toys for the Boys: Bond uses a minisensor supplied by Q Branch which registers movement.

Patronising Lines: To Zebeide after she's had virtually every different form of ammunition fired at her: 'Dammit, don't faint on me now!'

Lines to Flick Past: 'Just caution, luv . . . I never did dig that Light Brigade jive!' Yes, James Bond – ex-Eton, Fettes and possibly Cambridge scholar – strikes again.

BEWARE OF BUTTERFLIES

Published In: The *Daily Express* from December 1973

Starring: The hero – James Bond
The villain – Attila
The love interest – Suzi Kew

Written By: James D. Lawrence

Drawn By: Yaroslav Horak

Plot: Bond and a new 00 agent, Suzi Kew, are assigned to kill Orsk, involved with the Butterfly Eastern European spy network, in Paris. This they do, and on leave in Jamaica afterwards Bond is kidnapped by Attila, the head of the network, who wants him to help save the life of Mehmet Istvan, an Albanian scientist whom Bond helped to defect. Bond's gear is found, and he's believed dead.

Bond is hypnotised, and sent to Hong Kong, where he

persuades Istvan to ditch his bodyguard, so he can be kidnapped by Attila's men. Suzi Kew is sent after Bond by MI6, and finds him in Jamaica with no memory of the preceding month. Sir James Molony gives him neuroshock treatment, which restores his memory, and Bond then infiltrates Attila's network by claiming he has been let down by the Secret Service, supposedly killing Suzi and kidnapping Istvan's assistant, Kirsten Landvag. Attila isn't taken in, and is going to sell Bond to the Russians: Bond appeals to Attila's greed with five precious butterflies which he'll trade for his life, and manages to kill Attila, freeing Kirsten and Istvan.

Observations: Suzi Kew, who turns up regularly as Bond's occasional lover and assistant, makes her first appearance here, apparently as a newly qualified 00 agent, although we never learn her number, and later she is based in Paris. Continuity references to *The Man With the Golden Gun* slide in with Sir James Molony's appearance, while M, Tanner and Moneypenny all play their requisite parts.

Locations: Paris, Jamaica, London, Hong Kong.

Bond's Past Life: 007 helped Mehmet Istvan defect from Albania.

Toys for the Boys: Bond uses a detonator in a signet ring to explode the butterfly case, has a watch radio (hello, Dick Tracy), and a smoke cartridge in the heel of his shoe.

THE NEVSKY NUDE

Published In: The *Daily Express* from May 1974

Starring: The hero – James Bond
The villain – Sir Ulric Herne
The love interest – Susan

Written By: James D. Lawrence

Drawn By: Yaroslav Horak

Plot: MI6 has received a tip-off regarding Operation Nevsky along with a map of Sussex. SMERSH agent Ludmilla sky-dives naked from a plane from which renegade aristocrat Sir Ulric Herne sends a transmission claiming to be from King Arthur's ghost urging Britain to rise in glory again. Bond ambushes Ludmilla and her contact, but both end up dead.

Bond searches the contact's flat in Camden, finding a camera which has pictures of the Cornish coastline. Mysterious ghostly knights have been seen in that area, and when Bond investigates he finds a group of students, including Susan and Dirk, who have kidnapped Lord Melrose, the Secretary of State for Defence, and are intending to frighten him with an apparition of King Arthur. Their plan has been hijacked by SMERSH, via Dirk's cousin, Sir Ulric, and they intend smuggling Melrose out by submarine. Bond prevents the submarine from diving, and then goes after Sir Ulric.

Observations: A plotline referring to 'the Golden Elixir of Life' is begun in the opening panels, but never followed through. This is the first time that SMERSH has appeared in the Bond world since the film of *From Russia With Love*, eleven years earlier. Tanner, Moneypenny and M go out with Bond to Sussex for the start of Operation Nevsky.

Locations: Sussex, Cornwall.

THE PHOENIX PROJECT

Published In: The *Daily Express* from September 1974

Starring: The hero – James Bond
                    The villain – Kazim
                    The love interest – none

Written By: James D. Lawrence

Drawn By: Yaroslav Horak

Plot: Margo Arden, a secretary in charge of sorting out

clearances for Project Phoenix, has been hypnotised while on holiday in Istanbul into adding a name to the list. When Phoenix – the code name for a suit of armour formed of bonded boron elements which renders the wearer impenetrable to bullets, grenades and fire – is demonstrated, the interloper has altered it so that the wearer dies. He then kills Margo.

Bond is ordered to interrogate the tour guide who led the trip to Istanbul, but he is killed before he can talk. Bond travels to Turkey, where he pursues the trail of arms dealer Kazim with the aid of British agent Hafford. Bond inveigles his way into Kazim's circle, and is instructed to forcibly collect a young American couple, who have been bugging Kazim.

The woman, Jenny Starbuck, wants Kazim to admit that he framed her father for the theft of a space tracking device, which he does, knowing she won't be leaving.

Bond's cover is blown but he manages to escape using a working copy of the Phoenix suit that Kazim was intending to sell.

Locations: England, Istanbul.

Observations: There's a change in feel present in this strip. For the first time we have a 'splash page' – i.e. a 'cover' for the story – and 007 doesn't appear for over a month's worth of strips. The relationship between Bond and M is clearer cut: Bond doesn't want to blackmail the courier but M says, 'I'm not asking you, 007 – I'm telling you! So spare me your sentimental drivel.' Bond has some pidgin Turkish, and recognises a Texan twang from years of listening to Felix Leiter. Bill Tanner and Moneypenny are briefly seen. Oddly, there's no mention of Kerim Bey or his family.

THE BLACK RUBY CAPER

Published In: The *Daily Express* from February 1975

Starring: The hero – James Bond
The villain – Mr Ruby
The love interest – Damara Carver

Written By: James D. Lawrence

Drawn By: Yaroslav Horak

Plot: Bond's latest target is Herr Rubin, known as Mr Ruby, responsible for an explosion in a black area. With Suzi Kew's help, he antagonises Ruby by breaking into his Swiss chalet, and frames Ruby's girlfriend, Roanne Dreux, so that the gangster believes that she was helping Bond.

In Ghana, Ruby is using Roscoe Carver, a black sculptor whom he spirited out of America when Carver was being sought by the FBI in connection with the Black Brotherhood of Freedom, to create a statue inside which he is going to plant a bomb. Carver's daughter, Harlem model Damara, teams up with Bond to defeat Rubin, who follows a planted trail in order to catch Bond but is killed when Bond pours molten metal on him.

Observations: Suzi Kew, Moneypenny and Tanner are all of assistance, while the MI6 agent in Ghana is Jack Nguvin.

Locations: Switzerland, London, Ghana.

My Name Is . . . Mark Hazard.

Toys for the Boys: Bond has been equipped with a flipstick – a vaulting pole formed of telescopic aluminium sections.

TILL DEATH US DO PART

Published In: The *Daily Express* from July 1975

Starring: The hero – James Bond
The villain – Stefan Radomir
The love interest – Ardra Petrich

Written By: James D. Lawrence

Drawn By: Yaroslav Horak

Plot: Ardra Petrich's father worked for the East European section of MI6, and her married lover, Stefan Radomir, believes that she knows what her father knew. She flees to Austria to Radomir, trying to get away from MI6, but Bond pursues her and kidnaps her. Ardra believes that Bond has been sent to seduce her and bring her back to Britain – which does appear to have been M's plan – but he is so annoyed at this, and the way that Ardra behaves, that he won't go along.

Bond eventually manages to persuade her that Radomir does not have her best interests at heart when she overhears him offering to sell her to the KGB for $25,000, which rather takes the shine off the affair.

Observations: For once we see the repercussions of Bond's actions: when he kidnaps Ardra, Radomir reports it to the Austrian police, who make a formal complaint, and M is carpeted by the Prime Minister, as he informs Tanner and Moneypenny.

Locations: Austria, London.

Toys for the Boys: Bond makes good use of an all-terrain vehicle equipped with a hot-air balloon, as well as a gas-firing gun secreted in his car.

THE TORCH-TIME AFFAIR

Published In: The *Daily Express* from October 1975

Starring: The hero – James Bond
                 The villain – Carmen Perez
                 The love interest – Suzi Kew

Written By: James D. Lawrence

Drawn By: Yaroslav Horak

Plot: Bond is trying to find Tim Hurst, an agent who had been offered Torch-Time, the communist schedule for Latin-American subversion. A note brings him to a deserted beach in Acapulco at midnight, where he discovers Carmen Perez buried up to her neck. Escaping an ambush, Bond rescues the woman, who says she was lured by a message from Hurst. Clues point to Ricardo Auza, a gigolo who preys on American women, who is a SMERSH assassin probably responsible for Hurst's death.

Suzi Kew has been sent to help Bond, and they find Tim's body in Mexico City, along with a tape recorder, without tape. Bond realises that Carmen is an enemy agent after the information, and there is the proverbial Mexican standoff between Carmen, Auza, Bond and Carmen's fellow agents. This is resolved by 007, who takes Carmen's dress in which she had secreted the tape, removes it, and then acts as a decoy while Suzi gets the tape away.

Observations: Regular partner Suzi Kew is the only other MI6 agent to appear.

Locations: Acapulco, Mexico City.

HOT SHOT

Published In: The *Daily Express* from January 1976

Starring: The hero – James Bond
            The villain – Doctor No (yes, really!)
            The love interest – Fatima Khalid

Written By: James D. Lawrence

Drawn By: Yaroslav Horak

Plot: Chaos is being caused by Eblis terrorists, leading to an unlikely alliance between 007 and Fatima Khalid, a Palestinian freedom fighter. The man believed to be in charge of the terrorists, Ibn Awad, is found dead with tiger claw marks on him. Indian Intelligence tell them that a note found near the body with the name Huliraya on it refers to a businessman who loves tigers. Very little is known of the man, but a rare photo shows he is light-skinned and wears black gloves and Chinese Mandarin gowns.

Bond checks out his yacht, which was near one of the aircrashes caused by the Eblis, but is thrown off. Fatima follows Huliraya to Kuwait, while Bond posits the theory to M and Bill Tanner that Doctor No has returned. Fatima calls Bond from Morocco to where she has pursued Huliraya, but she is captured. Bond teams up with two PLO agents to rescue her.

An optical physicist has also disappeared in Morocco, and he has been used by Doctor No to create a weapon called the Hotshot, which reflects and magnifies the sun's rays. Doctor No intends to use this to destroy a plane carrying Secretary of State Henry Kissinger to a Middle East peace conference. Bond gets aboard Doctor No's oil-tanker base, and prevents the weapon from being fired, before blowing up the oil tanker.

Observations: Henry Kissinger knows Bond well enough that 007 needs to sign a radio message as simply 'James'. Bill Tanner gets a trip away from the office to brief Bond in Gibraltar. The Service is still using Transworld Consortium as its cover.

A gun that magnifies the sun's rays and is used to destroy planes. Truly, Doctor No is another 'man with the golden gun'.

This is the Doctor No of Ian Fleming's novel, rather than the film: Bond makes reference to the fact that No has been shot before and survived, although no real attempt is made to explain how he got out from under the pile of bird mess at the end of his eponymous novel.

Locations: Bombay, Santa Cruz, London, Kuwait, Morocco, Gibraltar, the Atlantic Ocean.

My Name Is . . . Mark Hazard (again, it doesn't fool the bad guys).

Toys for the Boys: Bond swoops down to rescue a damsel in distress using a backpack with rotor blades.

NIGHTBIRD

Published In: The *Daily Express* from June 1976

Starring: The hero – James Bond
The villain – Ferdinand Polgar
The love interest – Ilka Hallett

Written By: James D. Lawrence

Drawn By: Yaroslav Horak

Plot: Lisa Farrar, an actress whom Bond used to date, is kidnapped by an unusual VTOL plane which resembles a giant bird, from which weird creatures sporting antennae and robotic masks emerge. A ransom is demanded, but not paid, and she is found dead. Bond is in Paris when an old contact tries to pass him information, but is killed before he can talk.

Both cases seem to be simply for Interpol, but Bond doesn't let it rest. Industrialist André Brissac, a German biologist and Yugoslavian Stepan Zvoruk are all kidnapped by the 'Martians', and when Brissac is released he claims he was on an artificial moon. Clues point to Ferdinand Polgar, a film producer in whose flat Bond finds a drawing of the Martians. A make-up artist, Claude Jarnac, has also vanished.

Bond befriends Polgar's girlfriend, Ilka Hallett, and gains access to Polgar's Sardinian villa, where he discovers the place where the kidnapees had been held. It turns out that Polgar was formerly a small-time crook who got terrible acid burns in a raid on Hallett Labs (run by Ilka's father) that went wrong. Jarnac had been making masks for Polgar so had to be silenced. Polgar wants to kill both Hallett and his daughter in a fire, but changes his mind and takes them to his yacht. With help from Smoky Turpin, Bond rescues them and kills Polgar.

Observations: The MI6 London staff all make brief showings, as do Suzi Kew and Smoky Turpin (from *Die With My Boots On*). There's a passing reference to the 'departmental

Scrooge' in MI6 accounts – Captain Troop's successor, no doubt.

Locations: An Aegean island, Paris, assorted locations around Europe, Sardinia, New York.

Toys for the Boys: A grappling-iron gun helps Bond to break into Polgar's villa.

Mistakes Can Be Fatal: When Bond discovers the kidnappees' hiding place, he says that it is as Lisa mentioned. Since she was killed, as no ransom was paid, how does he know?

APE OF DIAMONDS

Published In: The *Daily Express* from November 1976

Starring: The hero – James Bond
                  The villain – Hartley Rameses
                  The love interest – Cleo Fahmi (sort of)

Written By: James D. Lawrence

Drawn By: Yaroslav Horak

Plot: A film is sent to MI6 showing a giant gorilla attacking a girl, identified as Gazila Fahmi from Cairo, along with a playing card showing the 'Ape' of Diamonds. Said ape then kidnaps an Arab dignitary, leaving another card, and Bond goes to Cairo to follow the one lead: Gazila.

He visits Bianco, who now owns the game park where Gazila worked. He says he's never heard of her, but has a letter from her sister on his desk. Bond finds a lighter with hieroglyphics which phonetically spell Rameses and Gazila. Bond goes to the palace owned by Hartley Rameses, who Colonel Fuad of Egyptian Intelligence warns him is a very dangerous man. He is about to break in . . . when Gazila's sister Cleo comes out, tells him she used the trained gorilla to kill Rameses, and Bond offers her a job.

Observations: This was the last strip to appear in the *Daily Express*, and it is very, very obviously rushed at the end. However, at least this time we get an ending. The coincidence of the remake of *King Kong* featuring in cinemas earlier in the year has not gone unnoticed!

Locations: London, Cairo.

My Name Is ... Mark Hazard, potential purchaser of a trained gorilla. As one is.

WHEN THE WIZARD WAKES

Published In: The *Sunday Express* from January 1977

Starring: The hero – James Bond
The villain – Attila Toth
The love interest – Lilla Kerenyi

Written By: James D. Lawrence

Drawn By: Yaroslav Horak

Plot: Proof is required that Zoltan Toth, a traitor to the Hungarian resistance, definitely died in 1956. When Bond and agent Lilla Kerenyi open the tomb in which he was walled up, the body moves – before a bomb destroys the place. A massive scam is taking place: the Mafia, led by Attila Toth, are trying to get $10 million from the Hungarian Government by claiming that Zoltan Toth is not dead and has smuggled the real Crown of St Stephen out of Hungary. This is not true: the real crown is in Fort Knox, but the CIA can't tell the Hungarians this because SPECTRE has threatened to give the Russians a list of CIA agents in Hungary if they do.

Alongside this, the Russians are after Lazlo Frekete, who has created a missile targeting system, and are holding his brother in exchange. With assistance from Lilla and Vienna agent Harry Winkler, 007 foils both plans.

Observations: The strip now appears as three rows of three panels, allowing slightly more development in each issue; however, the potential is wasted here as this complex plot of double-crosses just confuses. M, Tanner and Moneypenny get one-panel appearances.

Locations: Hungary, London, Vienna.

Toys for the Boys: Bond arrives at Toth's castle using a powered hang-glider.

Patronising Lines: 'Just in time, girlie!' Bond greets Lilla.

SEA DRAGON

Written By: James D. Lawrence

Drawn By: Yaroslav Horak

Plot: Alas, we have been unable to locate a copy of this strip.

DEATH WING

Starring: The hero – James Bond
The villain – Matteo Mortellito
The love interest – Jessabel Kane

Written By: James D. Lawrence

Drawn By: Yaroslav Horak

Plot: Miss Brewer, a spy, is caught by Bond trying to interfere with RAF tests. Bond tries to locate her employers, which leads him to investigate Worldwing Air Freight Ltd. This is run by the Godfather, Matteo Mortellito. Bond does his usual getting into the villain's good books and discovers that Mortellito has created Deathwing flying sleds – effectively a movable shell around the aviator. With the help of Mortellito's assistant, Jessabel Kane, Bond prevents Mortellito from using them.

Observations: This entry is based on the edited version which appeared in *James Bond Agent 007* number 5 (1992) in Scandinavia.

Bond gets taken in by the beautiful Miss Brewer twice before he gets into his stride. M, Penny, Tanner and Suzi Kew all assist.

Locations: England, Mexico, Las Vegas, New York.

THE XANADU CONNECTION

Starring: The hero – James Bond
                  The villains – Kubla Khan and Tekla Brent
                  The love interest – Ylang

Written By: James D. Lawrence

Drawn By: Yaroslav Horak

Plot: Bond rescues Heidi Frans from a castle in East Germany, and they make their escape using a device that burrows through the ground, similar to the Mole in *Thunderbirds*. Heidi has information about code name Marco Polo – British archaeologist Ivor Brent – who is missing. Bond has to work with Brent's wife, Tekla, who seems overfriendly. The hunt leads them to Mongolia, where they find Brent. However, a local villain, Kubla Khan, has other plans – and Tekla has been working with him all along. With the assistance of a Mongolian girl, Ylang, Bond and Brent escape.

Observations: This entry is based on the edited version which appeared in *Agent 007 James Bond* number 1 (1984) in Norway.

M, Moneypenny and Tanner are involved with Bill at the controls of the 'Mole'.

Locations: East Germany, London, Mongolia.

Toys for the Boys: The 'Mole'.

SHARK BAIT

Starring: The hero – James Bond
The villain – Yurogin
The love interest – Katya Orlova

Written By: James D. Lawrence

Drawn By: Yaroslav Horak

Plot: Bond is working with KGB agent Katya Orlova against a renegade Red Navy plot involving sharks.

Observations: This entry is based on the version of the strip that appeared in Scandinavia in *James Bond Agent 007* number 4 (1992); but unfortunately it is one of the most dialogue-heavy stories, with the pictures being of little help!

Locations: UK, Australia.

THE SCENT OF DANGER

Written By: James D. Lawrence

Drawn By: Yaroslav Horak

Plot: Again, we could find no version of this strip while we were researching this book.

SNAKE GODDESS

Starring: The hero – James Bond
The villain – Vidyala
The love interest – Freya

Written By: James D. Lawrence

Drawn By: John McLusky

Plot: Moneypenny is attacked at home by a giant snake. There is a connection with Freya, a girl who claims to be the reincarnation of the Norse goddess of the same name. A gigantic snake attacks a Cornwall village, and Bond gets closer to Freya, who is in fact being used by a Sri Lankan villain, Vidyala, who runs his own Global Engineering company. Bond discovers that the gigantic snake is in fact Vidyala's control centre and he intends attacking the Navy. Bond has to battle Vidyala's servants, the Siamese twins Kim and Chang, before he can rescue Freya and prevent Vidyala's plan.

Observations: This is based on the edited version which appeared in *James Bond Agent 007* number 8 (1985) in Scandinavia as *Operation Ragnarokk*. For once, Bond doesn't try to claim he wants to join the villain's side. We get to see Moneypenny and M at home – Moneypenny has only a single bed.

Locations: London, Cornwall.

DOUBLE EAGLE

Starring: The hero – James Bond
               The villain – Wulf Ehrnt
               The love interest – Helga

Written By: James D. Lawrence

Drawn By: Yaroslav Horak

Plot: After a former Gestapo torturer is killed by a large eagle before Bond's eyes, Bond and Moneypenny are assigned to work with Leslie Aird trying to prevent Operation Double Eagle from taking place. With the help of turncoat Helga, Bond uncovers Wulf Ehrnt's plan and prevents an assassination taking place at the Berlin Wall.

Observations: This entry is based on the edited version

which appeared in *James Bond Agent 007* number 5 (1986) in Scandinavia. Nice to see Moneypenny out in the field for once.

Locations: Lisbon, Berlin (both East and West).

DOOMCRACK

Published In: The *Daily Star* from 2 February 1981

Starring: The hero – James Bond
The villain – Madam Spectra and SPECTRE
The love interest – Liliane Miklos

Written By: James D. Lawrence

Drawn By: Harry North

Plot: Bond is escorting Liliane Miklos from Egypt back to London. She is acting as representative of Dr Vlad Sinescu, who has invented a weapon called Doomcrack. When a KGB agent tries to hijack the plane, Bond is convinced it's because the KGB want to prevent Doomcrack falling into British hands. Sinescu wants £5 million for Doomcrack, and demonstrates its potential by killing a Russian agent, and shooting down a drone gunship.

Bond pays the fee in cash, and Sinescu hands over the weapon, but they are ambushed, with Sinescu and the weapon being kidnapped. Buildings all over the world are threatened by the sonic maser powers of Doomcrack, and ransoms of different amounts are demanded from world governments. Both French President Valery Giscard d'Estaing and US President Ronald Reagan capitulate after the Eiffel Tower and the Statue of Liberty are threatened.

Bond believes that SPECTRE is back in operation, and when he learns that Dessau, the KGB agent, didn't even know who Liliane was, he realises that Liliane was a SPECTRE agent and the whole demonstration was a charade. The real

Liliane Miklos is found dead in Egypt. Bond is framed for taking information from MI6, and is taken by Liliane to SPECTRE's submarine headquarters, where he comes face to face with Madam Spectra. She decides to trust him because Esmerelda (her Persian cat) takes a liking to Bond. Liliane changes side when she realises that she means nothing to Madam Spectra, and helps Bond to escape, bringing Sinescu with them. Bond then uses Sinescu's new improved Doomcrack 2 to blow up the submarine and put an end to Madam Spectra once and for all.

Observations: A new artist means new interpretations, and Harry North makes Bill Tanner and Moneypenny both much younger than previously. M is based on Bernard Lee, while Q is definitely Desmond Llewellyn. Bond has also now got a very swish penthouse flat.

It is not unreasonable to assume that Lawrence was asked to tidy up his version of SPECTRE before John Gardner reintroduced the organisation in his novel *For Special Services*, which would then be in the planning stages. We finally learn what has been happening there: 'Blofeld's death left a power vacuum, and the ensuing struggle for leadership wrecked the organisation,' Bill Tanner theorises, to which James responds, 'So we've assumed – but no one knows for sure what happened to Madam Spectra.' Madam Spectra herself is an elderly woman who wears a turban and pets her white cat. She's a bit of a prat, though – believing in Bond's change of side because her cat likes him . . .? No wonder the organisation is wrecked!

The strip was reintroduced to British audiences with a three-line opening day (as the *Sunday Express* strip had been printed), but it then reverted to Monday–Saturday one-line format.

Toys for the Boys: Q sprays Liliane with a scent that Bond can follow wearing a fake moustache. (Well, it would have fitted into *Moonraker*!) He also provides Bond with a cigarette laced with a hypnotic drug that renders the smoker open to persuasion.

THE PARADISE PLOT

Published In: The *Daily Star* from 20 August 1981

Starring: The hero – James Bond
                    The villain – Father Star
                    The love interest – Suzi Kew (briefly)

Written By: James D. Lawrence

Drawn By: John McLusky

Plot: Industrialist Basil Arden is kidnapped after being visited by the angelic form of his deceased daughter – witnessed by 007, who finds that her angel's wings are faked. However, he's knocked out. Arden's main competitor, Max Hoch, recently visited Arden, and was in a car smash on the way back. In hospital an electrode was discovered in the pleasure centre of his brain.

Both Arden and Hoch lost children recently, but in neither case was a clearly identifiable body found. In fact, both are working for Father Star, alias Gabriel Starovsky, a mesmeric speaker who founded a hippy cult which has matured into a powerful organisation. Hoch is one of his converts, and he is holding Arden.

The trail leads to Project Polestar based on Estrellita Island in the Caribbean. Bond plays his usual card of having left MI6, and is accepted into Star's organisation. Star uses his Starship – a nuclear-powered dirigible – to make stealth attacks on the enemies of his converts. He also controls the Sky Spook, a radar-blind USAF plane, along with its pilot, Major Calvin Shaw. Arden is brainwashed, returned to his home – from where he makes a donation to Star's cult – and his enemy, Draax, is attacked.

Bond gains Star's confidence by preventing a Russian Army officer from taking over an army that Star is training in Africa, and is trusted with the next raid – kidnapping a cabinet minister from HMS *Intrepid* on its way to America. Bond does so, but then attacks Star, collects the minister, and steals Star's jet hydrofoil. Although Shaw and Star attempt to follow him in the Sky Spook, Bond uses one of Star's own gadgets to screw up the electronics, and returns to Earth.

Observations: When Bond returns to London, he has to attend a special honours ceremony, with Moneypenny telling him: 'Twice a knight, and after all you've been through!', implying that he has been knighted. The Scandinavian translation is even more explicit, finishing with Moneypenny greeting him as Sir James.

M now resembles the film actor Ronald Coleman, and wears a bow tie; Bill Tanner could be Rik van Nutter's brother. The most interesting introduction though is Q'ute – Ann Reilly, although she's not named as such here – John Gardner's addition to Q Branch. She's pretty much exactly as we imagined her. Suzi Kew also takes a brief turn, nearly killing a girl whom she thinks has killed Bond. She seems to be based in Paris now, rather than being a 00 agent.

The strip started its downward appearance trend here, featuring only from Monday to Friday. The adventures of 'Checkout Girl', 'The Incredible Hulk' and 'Judge Dredd' entertained Saturday readers.

Locations: Scotland, London, Paris, Estrellita Island, the Atlantic.

Toys for the Boys: Bond follows Arden's daughter wearing his backpack copter once again.

Sadism: Bond is dying from a lethal vapour he's inhaled when checking a lead in Paris, but still has time to grab the woman who did it, twist her arm behind her back and say, 'Must we hurry things, luv? I'm rather enjoying this.'

DEATHMASK

Published In: The *Daily Star* from 7 June 1982

Starring: The hero – James Bond

The villain – Ivor Nyborg
The love interests – Suzie Kew,
        Hermione Hune, Zoe Livyenko

Written By: James D. Lawrence

Drawn By: John McCluksy

Plot: There is a spate of deaths, thanks to a fast-acting virus that leaves the face of the corpse severely swollen, and makes animals act as if they are rabid. A Greek deathmask is found clutched in a dead spy's hand in Tangiers, a lead Bond follows from Athens to Istanbul, where a dying enemy agent splutters the word 'Minos'. Another fatality has happened, this time in Crete, where a diver could say only 'Minotaur' before he died.

Bond investigates the cave near which the diver was found, and finds a vast cavern with a building with a mask displayed on it. The entrance, however, is blown up and he and Suzi Kew, who is helping him, only just escape. The mask is the sign of Minos Ltd, and financial journalist Hermione Hune briefs Bond about Ivor Nyborg, and recognises that the belly dancer for whom the deathmask was originally made is Nyborg's mistress, Zoe Livyenko. Bond gains Zoe's trust by saving her from an attack that he had in fact planned, and is taken to Nyborg.

Nyborg has genetically engineered a virus which he is intending to release around the world from his new automatic plane, the Global Ghost. Bond succeeds in preventing the plane's robotic pilot from releasing the virus, and crashes the plane on to Nyborg's headquarters.

Observations: M, Tanner, Moneypenny, Q'ute and Suzi Kew are all present and correct.

Locations: Tangiers, Athens, Istanbul, London, South of France.

My Name Is . . . James Macbeth, ex-Royal Marine Commandos, ex-SAS and ex-African mercenary.

312

Villainous Foibles: Nyborg suffers from acromegaly (a hormonal condition that causes abnormal growth of the hands, feet and face), and wants everyone to look like him – or worse.

Mistakes Can Be Fatal: Suzi says she was flown in from Kuwait – but, both before and after this story, she's clearly based in Paris.

FLITTERMOUSE

Published In: The *Daily Star* from 9 February 1983

Starring: The hero – James Bond
                   The villain – Doctor Cat
                   The love interest – Suzi Kew

Written By: James D. Lawrence

Drawn By: John McClusky

Plot: More mysterious deaths are taking place: an Argentine actress, Isabella Garcia, wants to sell a South American intelligence report to MI6, but she dies under Bond's nose. All Q'ute can find is a small wound on her left buttock. Bond is disturbed when he finds his housekeeper May screaming – a seemingly dead cat, sent in a shoebox, came back to life in her hands.

Meanwhile, in Paris, Aguirre, a freelance agent, wants to sell the same intel report, and Bond and Suzi Kew arrange a meeting which is interrupted by a hit man, Scheldt. Bond distracts him, and finds a lighter on him – odd for an ascetic man who neither drank nor smoked. Aguirre also dies, and Q'ute determines it's from a vampire bat: the lighter was used to spray a scent on Aguirre which lured the bat.

Bond realises that Doctor Cat is back (*River of Death*), and he and Suzi walk into an ambush at Cat's new headquarters in a castle on the Rhine. Cat orders Bond to strip – so he can tell him a few 'facts of death' – but Bond manages to use a gun in his medallion to shoot Cat, then sprays him with the lure and leaves him to the vampire bats.

Observations: We only saw Cat being shot in *River of Death*, so it's feasible he could have survived. He's certainly had plastic surgery, because he looks *nothing* like he did before (which really is cheating). 'Flittermice', by the way, is Cat's fancy way of talking about his bats.

Locations: Spain, London, Paris, Germany.

Toys for the Boys: Bond has a gun secreted in his medallion (now there's a neat trick).

POLESTAR

Published In: The *Daily Star* from May 1983 to July 1983

Starring: The hero – James Bond
                     The villain – Robert Ayr
                     The love interest – Red Doe

Written By: James D. Lawrence

Drawn By: John McClusky

Plot: In Arctic Canada, 007 finds the body of his contact, Lorna Kirk, as a frozen ice statue. She was looking into Robert Ayr, boss of Polestar Petroleum, near whose base Bond is. Bond is saved from a rabid timberwolf by Red Doe, a Cree Indian, whose mother was killed in the same way. Meanwhile, missiles fired at the USA are being intercepted from the North Pole, but no launch site can be found.

M and Tanner decide that Bond will try to infiltrate Polestar as renegade rocket scientist Jack Boyd, who sold secrets to the Russians and is on the run. This attracts Ayr's attention and his men hear the shots Bond is forced to fire to save him and Red Doe from the wolves. They arrive at the camp but . . . '007 reacts fast!' . . .

Observations: And that was that, as far as readers of the *Daily Star* were concerned. The strip simply disappeared, without any further explanation. However, the adventure was completed for the Scandinavian audience.

Plot (continued): Bond and Red Doe are taken into Polestar but they are confused that they are looking for an American scientist, but have found an Englishman. They torture him, but are eventually convinced that he is Boyd. He starts working for them, but has to break his cover when Ayr tries to rape Red Doe, and manages to get himself, the girl and Ayr away.

Locations: Arctic Canada, London.

My Name Is . . . Jack Boyd, rocket engineer.

CODENAME: NEMESIS

Published In: *Agent 007 James Bond* number 7, 1983 (Scandinavia)

Written By: Jack Sutter

Drawn By: Josep Gual

Plot: James Bond survives being thrown off a train in Eastern Europe on his way back from a mission, and works with agent Amanda Pinkerton investigating three men, one of whom is a traitor. Along the way, he discovers a resurgent neo-Nazi movement, and finds himself on the wrong side of Felix Leiter . . .

Locations: Eastern Europe, Belgrade, London, Geneva, Marseilles (France).

Toys for the Boys: A cigarette lighter with a gun, and a rocket-fired grappling hook, both provided by Q.

OPERATION: LITTLE

Published In: *Agent 007 James Bond* number 4, 1984
(Scandinavia)

Written By: Jack Sutter

Drawn By: Sarompas

Plot: Bond teams up with a mysterious 'Little', Felix Leiter and KGB agent Sergei Kailiagin against Wolff, a lunatic genetic manipulator based at the South Pole.

Locations: Russia, Florida, the South Pole.

Toys for the Boys: We see Q in his laboratory giving Bond his 'utility belt'.

THE MAD EMPEROR

Published In: *Agent 007 James Bond* number 6, 1984
(Scandinavia)

Written By: Peter Sparring

Drawn By: Josep Gual

Plot: Bond is set loose from MI6 after he incurs heavy gambling debts, although he was drugged when doing so. He comes up against the self-styled Emperor Henry Christophe of Haiti, who wants control over the West Indies, but the power behind the throne is Argentine General Juan Diaz de Solis, who wants revenge for the Falklands War. Bond's lover, Miriam, is killed during the climatic battle between US troops and those of de Solis.

Locations: Atlanta (Georgia), Nassau, Haiti.

OPERATION: UFO

Published In: *James Bond* number 1, 1985 (Scandinavia)

Written By: Jack Sutter

Drawn By: Josep Gual

Plot: Key scientists are kidnapped by a flying saucer. Bond poses as Professor Bond and wakes on board a ship from Deokas with a woman called Ilia where scientists are trying to solve Deokas's problems . . .

Locations: The Alps, South America, London, America.

OPERATION: BLUCHER

Published In: *James Bond* number 4, 1985 (Scandinavia)

Written By: Sverre Arnes

Drawn By: Josep Gual

Plot: With the help of Juliet Galant, 007 battles a resurgence of neo-Nazis in Norway. They are led by Blegman, connected to a group in Brighton, England, and masterminded by junior Foreign Office minister Sir Ernest Gotheringham.

Observations: Bond is using Universal Exports as MI6's cover.

Locations: London, Brighton, Oslo.

CODENAME: ROMEO

Published In: *James Bond* number 5, 1985 (Scandinavia)

Written By: Sverre Arnes

Drawn By: Josep Gual

Plot: Bond is on the trail of Walter Junghans, who uses bombs code-named Romeo and Juliet as assassination weapons, with the help of an in-house boffin, Byrnes, and the CIA.

Locations: Zurich, London, Paris and West Berlin.

DATA TERROR

Published In: *James Bond* number 6, 1986 (Scandinavia)

Written By: Sverre Arnes

Drawn By: Sarompas

Plot: Bank computers are wiped clean, causing economic chaos. Bond investigates Silvia Hall of Essex Micro Technics but her jealous boyfriend Billy Braxton knows who Bond is, and kills Silvia. Another woman calls Bond but Billy gets there first. He follows a third woman, Loni Brown, to Braxton's hideout and captures him.

My Name Is . . . Grapefruit.

Mistakes Can Be Fatal: Apart from cars being drawn with left-hand drive, Arnes has his standard British police armed.

EXPERIMENT Z

Published In: *James Bond* number 8, 1986 (Scandinavia)

Written By: Bill Harrington

Drawn By: Manuel Carmona

Plot: Renowned war correspondent Dalia Levy is also a Mossad agent. She's after a Nazi, Carl von Borkman. Bond encounters Dalia in London but is sent on the trail of Experiment Z in Rio de Janeiro. He meets Gerda, Erich von Borkman's girlfriend, and ends up going up the Amazon with them. Bond stops von Borkman Snr's work and Dalia comes to his rescue.

Locations: Tel Aviv, London, Rio de Janeiro, the Amazon basin.

SPY TRAPS

Published In: *James Bond Agent 007* number 2, 1987 (Scandinavia)

Written By: Jack Sutter

Drawn By: Sarompas

Plot: After a mild holiday romance, Bond returns to business in Greece, and is sent (via videotape) by M to retrieve a vital film. The trail leads him on a motorbike chase through Athens, and through the Greek countryside pursuing a Russian agent – whose control is Bond's brief girlfriend!

Observations: There's a lovely line where Bond is on a pushbike, and mutters, 'If only Q could see me now – all his fine technology, and I end up on a bike!'

Location: Greece.

My Name Is . . . James Blade.

DEADLY DOUBLE

Published In: *James Bond* number 4, 1987 (Scandinavia)

Written By: Jack Sutter

Drawn By: Sarompas

Plot: Agent 009 dies getting film of genetic mutations in the Amazon jungle. Bond parachutes in and sees dinosaurs, and a tribe of beautiful bald women, one of whom, Artemis, leads him to Dr Klaus, who seems eccentric but harmless. However, his twin brother, Willi, is working for the villainous August. Bond foils an attempt to destroy New York, with Felix Leiter's assistance, then returns to the Amazon to capture Faust.

Observations: M flies out to Rio to brief Bond; Felix Leiter gets a complete change of appearance.

Locations: London, the Amazon, Rio de Janeiro, New York.

GREEK IDOL

Published In: *James Bond* number 5, 1987 (Scandinavia)

Written By: Bill Harrington

Drawn By: Manuel Carmona

Plot: Greek shipping millionaire Dimitri Kimopolous decides to frame James Bond for the murder of his rival, who has been attacking his shipyards. However, he doesn't count on his daughter falling in love with Bond . . .

Observations: M's travelling the world again, this time to Athens.

Locations: Athens, Greece, Istanbul.

CUBA COMMANDOS

Published In: *James Bond Agent 007* number 1, 1988
(Scandinavia)

Written By: Jack Sutter

Drawn By: Sarompas

Plot: Bond is diverted from his Caribbean holiday by CIA agent Melody Hopper to help track three rogue US soldiers in Cuba. Their mission seems straightforward until they encounter three mischievous schoolboys who have run away to Cuba and constantly get in their way . . .

Observations: We see a US President, who just might be Ronald Reagan (at a pinch).

Locations: The Caribbean, USA, Cuba.

Toys for the Boys: Bond and Melody use jetpacks.

THE AMAZONS

Published In: *James Bond* number 1, 1988 (Scandinavia)

Written By: Bill Harrington

Drawn By: Josep Gual

Plot: Concern is raised that the Soviets have infiltrated the female protesters outside a USAF base in Britain. It's a terrible hardship for Bond to sort out which of these beautiful women are working for the opposition!

Locations: England, Scotland.

LETHAL DOSE

Published In: *James Bond Agent 007* number 2, 1988 (Scandinavia)

Written By: Sverre Arnes

Drawn By: Josep Gual

Plot: After the deaths of a number of retired agents, Bond visits the Steiner Clinic and despite being framed for the murder of a nurse succeeds in stopping Helena Steiner and Julius from implanting a device in the heart of Major Simmons, another retiring agent . . .

Observation: Bond doesn't like rats.

Location: England.

DEADLY DESERT

Published In: *James Bond* number 3, 1988 (Scandinavia)

Written By: Bill Harrington

Drawn By: Sarompas

Plot: Bond is sent to Tunisia to try to find Dalton Carter, agent Z17. With the help of Misty Morel and the dubious assistance of her friend Chantal, Bond locates him – or does he?

Locations: London, Tunisia.

TERROR TIME

Published In: *James Bond* number 5, 1988 (Scandinavia)

Written By: Bill Harrington

Drawn By: Manuel Carmona

Plot: A terrorist group kills the Carnovian Ambassador at a first night. It's linked to an international ring of art forgers which Bond learns about from Fenella O'Flynn. Fenella turns out to be one of the terrorist leaders, who are financing their operation using the fakes.

Observations: We see Blades Club – with a Soho-esque front to it!

Locations: London, Provence.

THE VANISHING JUDGES

Published In: *James Bond* number 7, 1988 (Scandinavia)

Written By: Bill Harrington

Drawn By: Josep Gual

Plot: Old Bailey Judge Shears is kidnapped after sentencing a vicious killer, just one of many judges who have disappeared worldwide. Bond becomes involved with Pamela Shears and Melody Savage on a trail that leads to mastermind Harvey Creed.

Locations: London, Florida.

FLIGHTS FROM VIETNAM

Published In: *James Bond* number 8, 1988 (Scandinavia)

Written By: Bill Harrington

Drawn By: Manuel Carmona

Plot: Bond is sent on assignment to Singapore and gets caught up with Vietnamese boat people as he seeks Nam Rang – alias missing agent Jerry Hoyt.

Observations: M plays battleships in the bath!

Locations: London, Windsor (M's house), Singapore, South China Sea.

THE UNDEAD

Published In: *James Bond* number 1, 1989 (Scandinavia)

Written By: Bill Harrington

Drawn By: Martin Salvador

Plot: Bond goes to Paris, where Professor Marcel Debucourt is meeting his Eastern counterpart, Tallin, to discuss mind-power research. Bond gets caught in a fantastic tale of extrasensory projects and ageing elixirs . . .

Locations: London, Paris.

ISTANBUL INTRIGUE

Published In: *James Bond* number 2, 1989 (Scandinavia)

Written By: Bill Harrington

Drawn By: Manuel Carmona

Plot: Bond is assigned to Istanbul, where he tries to obtain information from Brogan – only to find that there are others on the trail as well . . .

Locations: London, Istanbul.

WITH DEATH IN SIGHT

Published In: *James Bond* number 6, 1989 (Scandinavia)

Written By: Bill Harrington

Drawn By: Manuel Carmona

Plot: In one long chase sequence, Bond is trying to get back to London with secret Soviet plans but is ambushed consistently along the way . . .

Locations: Norway, Scotland and down through England.

DANSE MACABRE

Published In: *James Bond* number 7, 1989 (Scandinavia)

Written By: Bill Harrington

Drawn By: Josep Gual

Plot: Bond has to look after ballerina Daniella Heim, a Groznian refugee who attracts the attention of millionaire Niko Kolyanis.

Observations: Bond is a champion rower at Henley Regatta.

Locations: London, Berlin, Venice.

It's Only a Comic Strip: Bond's licence plate is 007 1B.

Mistakes Can Be Fatal: In the poster for Daniella's first appearance, her name is given as Nadia.

OPERATION UBOKI

Published In: *James Bond* number 8, 1989 (Scandinavia)

Written By: Bill Harrington

Drawn By: Josep Gual

Plot: In a Central African state, Bond and M become involved in political intrigue, and the machinations of the Leopard Women of the Ubokis . . .

Observations: Bond receives a medal from the Ubokis.

Locations: A mythical African state.

THE LIVING DEAD

Published In: *James Bond* number 7, 1990 (Scandinavia)

Written By: Jack Sutter

Drawn By: Sarompas

Plot: In Thailand, Bond is destroying a drugs operation when he finds Tanya, a fellow spy whom he thought had been killed in West Berlin, and stumbles on a plot to replace the President of the USA, to foil which he needs help from old friend Felix Leiter . . .

Locations: Thailand, Washington, London.

Toys for the Boys: Q really equips 007 on this mission. Backpack, snake-charming reed, explosives.

CODENAME: MR BLUE

Published In: *James Bond* number 9, 1990 (Scandinavia)

Written By: Jack Sutter

Drawn By: Sarompas

Plot: Bond has to defeat the plans of Mr Blue, who intends to hold the world to ransom with his gases which affect human behaviour . . .

Observations: Q's inventions are critical to this tale.

Locations: South of France, London, Istanbul.

GOODBYE, MR BOND

Published In: *James Bond* number 1, 1991 (Scandinavia)

Written By: Bill Harrington

Drawn By: Sarompas

Plot: Bond is injured during a mission. While convalescing at an agents' rest home, Hevening Court, he becomes embroiled in the plans of Doktor Saviz, a robotics expert who intends to replace all of the world's top agents with his robots. As you do.

Locations: Asia, then England.

OPERATION YAKUZA

Published In: *James Bond* number 5, 1991 (Scandinavia)

Written By: Ian Mennell

Drawn By: Sarompas

Plot: Bond is sent to Japan to look for missing agent Suzi Chi and finds he is caught in a madman's revenge . . .

Locations: London, Hong Kong and Japan.

PERMISSION TO DIE

Published By: Dark Horse Comics in 1989 and 1991 in three parts

Starring: The hero – James Bond
                  The villains – Doctor Erik Wiziadio
                  The love interests – Edaine Gayla and
                      Luludi Bey

Written And Drawn By: Mike Grell

Plot: Erik Wiziadio, a rocket scientist refugee from behind the Iron Curtain, is offering Britain his new technology if his niece, Edaine, is rescued from Hungary. Bond is assigned to the task, and uses a tribe of gypsies, including Kerim Bey's daughter, Luludi, to attack the convoy on which she is being transported. Getting Edaine across the border into Austria,

Bond takes her to Idaho, where Wiziadio has an underground complex.

Through a combination of oxygen and methane, Wiziadio has created a new form of rocket propulsion – but plans to use it to cause a nuclear explosion in Victoria, British Columbia, which will persuade governments not to use nuclear weapons any more. Edaine, who is merely Wiziadio's student, knows that the scientist will be pilloried for this and arranges for his lair to explode after he has launched the rocket, which Bond has already sabotaged. Bond and a local hunting guide, Mary Carver, escape.

Observations: Bond's drinking habits are known far and wide – Wiziadio says it's too early for Martinis and offers champagne instead. The story, set in 1989 (44 years after Hiroshima), sees Bond being given an ASP 9mm in place of his Walther PPK by Major Boothroyd – in line with the Gardner novels. Grell doesn't seem to make his mind up whether he is following the continuity from the books or the films. His M is clearly Bernard Lee, his Moneypenny Lois Maxwell, the DB5 has the number plate from the films, Bond uses the breathing device from *Thunderball* and the visual references are to the Kerim Bey of the movie of *From Russia With Love*. However, Bond uses his Boldman alias from the Gardner novels, smokes triple-ringed cigarettes and has May as his housekeeper.

Certainly this is one of the better amalgamations of the two continuities. Bill Tanner and Felix Leiter (with hook) turn up; and May gets a name check.

Wiziadio and Edaine were responsible for Three Mile Island and Chernobyl.

The final third of this story seems incredibly rushed, after the steady pace of the first two chapters. We meet Wiziadio, hear his plan, and see his comeuppance in just 46 pages.

Locations: United Kingdom, Hungary, United States (Idaho).

My Name Is . . . Boldman.

James Bond, Fashion Victim: The dinner dress complete

with kilt in the opening sequence is OK – it's a formal meal at Lady Graymalkin's, after all; but formal dress in the middle of a gypsy encampment in the wilds of Hungary, albeit with trousers rather than kilt . . . We think not.

Toys for the Boys: Bond uses anti-surveillance devices, has a two-seat version of *Little Nellie* from *You Only Live Twice* delivered to him, and uses the breathing device from *Thunderball*.

Patronising Lines: When Mary rescues Bond from being burnt to death by the rocket exhaust, he says, 'Well thank God for feminine curiosity.' She gets her own back quickly, though.

Villainous Foibles: Wiziadio has a scarred face as a result of an interrogation before he escaped from the East. He has a huge organ on which he plays Bach's 'Toccata and Fugue' – which is a neat trick if you can do it (but see **Mistakes Can Be Fatal** below).

It's Only a Comic: Wiziadio's lair (complete with chandelier) and mask are clearly modelled on *The Phantom of the Opera* (Andrew Lloyd Webber version).

Mistakes Can Be Fatal: Although Wiziadio is clearly playing Bach's 'Toccata and Fugue' in D Minor on the organ, the music score printed is from the piano reduction.

JAMES BOND JUNIOR 6: THE GILT COMPLEX (1992)

Published By: Marvel Comics in 1992

Starring: The hero – James Bond Jnr
The villains – Goldfinger and Oddjob

Written By: Dan Abnett

Drawn By: Mario Capaldi

Plot: IQ's eccentric Uncle Max sends him a mysterious pendant and two tickets for the Orient Express, with instructions to join him in Venice as soon as possible. IQ and Bond set out, but while passing through France they are attacked by Oddjob. While defeating him, they accidentally discover that the stone in the pendant has the power to turn things to gold – Uncle Max has discovered the philosopher's stone!

Arriving in Venice they discover that Uncle Max has gone missing – then they too are taken captive by the evil Goldfinger in his lion-headed submarine. Bond and IQ use the philosopher's stone to turn the submarine into gold: too heavy for its ballast tanks, it sinks to the bottom of the Venice Lagoon while they make their escape.

Observations: The first five issues of the comic book adapted episodes of the TV show. This is the first original story.

IQ has an Uncle Max who is an eccentric (no! really!) chemist: Q's son, we would guess, implying that Q has at least two children.

The noise the Orient Express makes while passing through France is 'radakachek'. Thought you'd like to know.

Locations: England, the South of France (as seen from the roof of a train) and Venice.

Mistakes Can Be Fatal: Maybe we weren't paying attention, but why did Uncle Max send for IQ?

JAMES BOND JUNIOR 7:
SURE AS EGGS IS EGGS!

Published By: Marvel Comics in 1992

Starring: The hero – James Bond Jnr
The villain – SCUM Lord and Jaws

Written By: Dan Abnett

Drawn By: Mario Capaldi

Plot: Bond saves the life of Kalinka Rubels, daughter of Russian Special Envoy Maxim Rubels, when her horse bolts. Maxim Rubels is in England to arrange an exhibition of priceless Fabergé eggs, and invites Bond and friends to a private viewing of the eggs as thanks for saving his daughter.

Bond recognises SCUM agent Tiara Hotstones at the viewing, and tails her to a meeting with SCUM Lord himself. SCUM Lord intends stealing the eggs in order to destroy the fragile Anglo-Russian detente. Bond and IQ try to prevent the robbery, but fail. Maxim Rubels gives them 24 hours to recover them, after which he will go public.

Bond and IQ go to ask Kalinka for help, but find her being kidnapped by Jaws. They give chase, but are kidnapped as well. However, Tiara Hotstones double-crosses SCUM Lord, allows Bond and friends to escape and returns the eggs.

Observations: Much as it pains us to notice continuity in this farrago of nonsense, Tiara Hotstones previously appeared in the *James Bond Junior* animated TV series episode 'Dance of the Toreadors'.

Locations: England.

Toys for the Boys: IQ's electro-binoculars.

JAMES BOND JUNIOR 8:
WAVE GOODBYE TO THE USA!

Published By: Marvel Comics in 1992

Starring: The hero – James Bond Jnr
                  The villains – Goldfinger, Walker D. Plank,
                      Oddjob

Written By: Dan Abnett

Drawn By: Mario Capaldi

Plot: Walker D. Plank has located the wreckage of a Spanish treasure armada full of gold on the ocean floor, but it's too deep for his submarine to reach. Conveniently, Goldfinger has developed a device that can shift tectonic plates, causing geological upheavals. Together, they intend raising the section of ocean floor with the armada and splitting the booty. The resulting tidal wave will destroy the Eastern seaboard of the USA, alas, but that's the way the cookie crumbles.

Holidaying on a nearby CIA 'safe' island, Bond, IQ, Gordo Leiter and Tracy Millbanks notice a lot of activity around a supposedly deserted island. Investigating, they spot Goldfinger's tectonic machine but are taken captive. Escaping, Bond and Leiter gain access to Plank's submarine just as he and Goldfinger start the tectonic upheavals. Bond manages to reverse the settings on the machine, sinking the island. Goldfinger and Plank blame each other, and in the confusion Goldfinger scuttles Plank's submarine.

Location: The Caribbean.

JAMES BOND JUNIOR 9: ABSOLUTE ZERO!

Published By: Marvel Comics in 1992

Starring: The hero – James Bond Jnr
                 The villain – Dr No

Written By: Dan Abnett

Drawn By: Mario Capaldi

Plot: The Fifth Annual Inter-Collegiate Sports Championships are taking place in Switzerland, and Bond is skiing for Warfield. Meanwhile, nearby, Dr No is using a machine that can make glaciers. His plan is to hold the Swiss to ransom: if they do not turn the contents of their Swiss Banks over to him, he will bury Zürich, Geneva, Berne and Lucerne beneath tons of ice.

Bond and his friends stumble across Dr No's glacier machine. He causes an avalanche in an attempt to kill them, but fails. He orders his troops – cunningly disguised as a Bermudan skiing team – to kill them, but they fail too. IQ cunningly reverses the controls on Dr No's glacier machine, forcing the glaciers back up the mountain and swamping his control centre with ice.

Location: Switzerland.

Toys for the Boys: IQ has a Swiss Army knife with . . . a laser!

JAMES BOND JUNIOR 10: FRIENDS LIKE THESE!

Published By: Marvel Comics in 1992

Starring: The hero – James Bond Jnr

Written By: Dan Abnett

Drawn By: Mario Capaldi

Plot: Uncertain

JAMES BOND JUNIOR 11: INDIAN SUMMER!

Published By: Marvel Comics in 1992

Starring: The hero – James Bond Jnr
              The villains – Ms Fortune and Baron von Skarin

Written By: Dan Abnett

Drawn By: Mario Capaldi

Plot: It's the end of the Warfield school year, and the pupils are preparing to leave. Phoebe Farragut is distressed when Vishna Bhuti, the friend in India with whom she was going to stay, writes telling her not to come, as her village is suffering 'the curse of Humarabad'. Bond, IQ and Tracy Millbanks accompany Phoebe to India to help her friend, and discover that Vishna's father is an archaeologist who recently started excavating a ruined temple in the jungle. Ever since, the local people have been claiming that ghosts and monsters have been stalking the land.

Meanwhile, SCUM agents Ms Fortune and Baron von Skarin are both in the vicinity, having separately discovered from SCUM files that the fabled Star of Kali – the largest diamond in the world – is supposed to be in the temple. They have been using holograms and robots to frighten the locals off so that they can take the diamond for themselves.

Bond and friends locate the diamond, but are confronted by the forces of SCUM. Bond uses IQ's personal electronic organiser to cause Ms Fortune's robot snake to attack Baron von Skarin's robot tiger. In the confusion the temple collapses and Bond and friends escape with the diamond.

Observations: One of the SCUM agents wants the diamond to form the heart of his new super laser. The other one wants to set it in a brooch. Guess which is which.

Locations: Humarabad, India.

Toys for the Boys: IQ modifies his electronic organiser so it controls Ms Fortune's robot snake.

JAMES BOND JUNIOR 12: HOMEWARD BOUND!

Published By: Marvel Comics in 1992

Starring: The hero – James Bond Jnr
                  The villains – SCUM Lord, Nick Nack,
                  Skullcap, Walker D. Plank, Ms Fortune,
                  Oddjob, Goldfinger, Baron von Skarin,
                  Dr Derange, Dr No and Jaws

Written By: Dan Abnett

Drawn By: Mario Capaldi

Plot: Returning to Warfield Academy after the winter break, Bond is attacked by various minions of SCUM after SCUM Lord places a bounty on his head. They all fail, he gets back to school, and presumably all the villains go home.

Locations: England, France and what looks like Switzerland.

Toys for the Boys: Young Bond carries with him a device invented by IQ that can disrupt the telemetry of incoming missiles. He also appears to wear a mini-parachute just in case it's needed.

SERPENT'S TOOTH (1992–3)

Published By: Dark Horse Comics in 1992 and 1993 in three parts: untitled, 'Blooded in Eden' and 'Mass Extinction'

Starring: The hero – James Bond
The villain – Indigo
The love interest – Sunny Vasquez

Written By: Doug Moench

Drawn By: Paul Gulacy

Plot: Six years ago, a string of biogeneticists and nuclear scientists were kidnapped from Britain. Five years ago, a British nuclear submarine was attacked beneath the Arctic ice and its cargo of missiles stolen. Now, Bond is sent to Peru to discover what happened to agent 009, who had a lead on the vanished missiles. The agent was investigating Paradiso Industries, a company headed by the reptilian Indigo.

Investigating Indigo's operations, Bond discovers that he is holding the kidnapped scientists. Aware of Bond's interest, Indigo relocates to a hidden base in the Peruvian jungle, where he has been kidnapping young girls from the local villages for many years. Bond infiltrates Indigo's base, and discovers that the man intends detonating his nuclear weapons at strategic points along the undersea fault lines, causing tidal waves that will sweep across the world. Indigo's calculations suggest that 83 per cent of the world's population will be killed – and he will rule the rest. The kidnapped girls – now grown into women who serve him – will be the Eves with whom he will repopulate the world in his own twisted image. As if that wasn't enough, Indigo has been re-creating extinct species such as dinosaurs and dodos using genetic manipulation.

Indigo takes his base – hermetically sealed – underwater and starts the countdown. Bond confronts him and kills him in a fight, and manages to stop the bombs a few minutes before they are due to explode.

Observations: Agent 009 has gone missing in Peru – turned into a neanderthal creature by Indigo's genetic manipulation and then knifed by Indigo when he still remembers Bond. Poor 009 – an agent with the same number was killed in the film of *Octopussy*. M and Moneypenny both appear. Q goes on location in Peru with a ghastly Hawaiian shirt.

Let's run through that plot again – madman with a base hidden in a ruined temple in the South American jungle intends destroying the world and repopulating it with his own perfect people. Bond arrives in a souped-up boat provided by Q Branch and has a fight with an undersea creature. *Serpent's Tooth* is reminiscent of *Moonraker* with the serial numbers filed off, and with a jigger of *Jurassic Park* thrown in as well.

Locations: Switzerland and Peru.

My Name Is . . . Derek Pentecost, an expert in genetics.

James Bond, Fashion Victim: Well, for most of Parts Two and Three he's wearing a rather suspect black PVC wetsuit, cut tight around the crotch, with black half-gloves. He might almost be one of the Village People, dressed like that.

Bond's Past Life: Bond has a capped rear molar and once killed a KGB agent named Sergei Pavna.

Toys for the Boys: Q gives Bond a boat equipped with rocket launchers and a short-duration afterburner. He also provides a ring with a built-in ultrasonic mosquito repellent, a compass with a homing device and a false tooth packed with explosive.

Villainous Foibles: Indigo has a rare blood disorder which mimics cold-bloodedness. In an attempt to cure it, he has injected himself with reptilian DNA, which has caused changes to his body – scaly grey skin, claws and slitted eyes. Indigo's right- and left-hand men – Kane and Abel – are albinos and probably clones.

Single Entendres: 'Cocky man, aren't we?' says Sunny Vasquez to Bond, to which he replies, 'Care to verify?'

Mistakes Can Be Fatal: Expert scientists are referred to as 'biogeneticists', as if there's any other kind of geneticist.

A SILENT ARMAGEDDON

Published By: Dark Horse Comics in 1993 in two parts: 'DefCon 4' and 'DefCon 3'

Starring: The hero – James Bond
The villain – Cerberus
The love interest – Professor Jessica Penrose

Written By: Simon Jowett

Drawn By: John Burns

Plot: In 1982, a series of linked events occur. Firstly, an American missile base finds all its missile targets altered, although there have been no reported breaks in base security. The new targets are bizarre choices, including Torremolinos in Spain and Milton Keynes in England. Secondly, Bond is in

America and witnesses the first operation carried out by a new criminal organisation – Cerberus. The organisation has three branches – extortion, espionage and enforcement.

In an unspecified year around 1989, an American junkie computer hacker discovers a 'worm' program running free in a hospital database system. The worm can be programmed to search and retrieve information, such as bank-account details. The hacker sells the program to a small-time criminal, who makes a decent living out of computer fraud until he is killed by Cerberus in 1993. Cerberus want the program for their own purposes, but it is out on the information superhighway when they try to find it and they have to think of another way of retrieving it. Cerberus know that the program was written at a laboratory in Oxford, England – they had already attempted to kill the staff in the laboratory to prevent anyone discovering what they want to do with the program – but now they need the one remaining survivor in order to help them locate the program again. Her name is Terri Li, and she is a wheelchair-bound, thirteen-year-old computer genius.

After the attempt on her life, James Bond is assigned to guard Terri Li. Believing she knows more about the program than she is saying, Bond takes her to a high-powered computer facility in New York, but Cerberus attack the facility and kidnap Terri . . .

According to writer Simon Jowett, in the next two issues, a computer virus would have disrupted New York by affecting cashpoint machines, hospital equipment and prison cell locks. Bond would have discovered that Cerberus were responsible, and would have infiltrated their base beneath the streets of Hong Kong's Hidden City (where Terri was born). There he and Terri would have entered into a virtual-reality world in order to defeat Cerberus's plans, Terri having taken on the virtual appearance of a typical Bond girl, reflecting the crush she had on him.

Observations: The second (and so far last) issue climaxes with the appearance of a male villain named Erik Klebb. Judging by Bond's reaction to the name, he believes the man to be some relation to Rosa Klebb (who appeared in the Ian Fleming book *From Russia With Love*). Writer Simon Jowett has confirmed that Erik Klebb was Rosa Klebb's son, the result of a drunken liaison with a Russian soldier (Rosa Klebb having been shown in *From Russia With Love* to have been firmly of the lesbian persuasion).

The comic starts in 1982, and then moves to 1993. In 1982, Bond initially thinks that Cerberus's operations are the responsibility of SPECTRE (who first appeared in the book *Thunderball*). This is a supposition, based on Bond's line to Felix Leiter: 'It's very unlike our ghostly competitors to be so careless . . .' Simon Jowett has stated that the initial proposal for this story involved SPECTRE as villains rather than Cerberus, but the copyright holders, Glidrose, insisted on the change.

Moneypenny definitely makes an appearance, but Bond's (and her) boss is a tall, thin civil servant with a moustache and a bowler hat. If it's meant to be M, he's gone through a major change in appearance. Q (or rather, Major Boothroyd) gets a name check. Felix Leiter appears in the 1982 section.

Only the first two of a projected four parts were published. There were problems with the delivery of the artwork for the last two issues: issue three arriving six months late and issue four not arriving at all. The disruption to the distributor's schedules resulted in the comic being abruptly halted, rather than a new artist being assigned.

Locations: In issues one and two, the locations were various places in America, Oxford, London and Hong Kong. Issue three would have taken Bond and Terri across Europe, while issue four would have returned to Hong Kong.

LIGHT OF MY DEATH

Published By: Dark Horse Comics in 1993 in four untitled parts

Starring: The hero – James Bond

The villain – a man named Amos, who may
have been Blofeld's predecessor as head of
SPECTRE

The love interest – Tatiana Romanova

Written By: Das Petrou

Drawn By: John Watkiss

Plot: A British agent meets with a Swiss banker in the French
Alps, but both are killed when the cable of the cable car in
which they are travelling is severed by a laser beam. Bond is
sent to investigate, and meets up with Tatiana Romanova. She
is investigating on behalf of the KGB, whose European
currency reserves were being handled by the banker.

The British agent had been investigating an agricultural
corporation based in Hong Kong who appear to be siphoning
money – with the aid of an American diplomat – from Western
aid directed at the Far East, and Bond suspects that Mr Amos,
the man in charge of the corporation, had him killed to disguise
his crimes. After Bond investigates the corporation in Hong
Kong, he travels on to Cairo, where a conference of Far Eastern
leaders will be debating the strange reduction in the aid they
are getting. The assassin with the laser tries to destroy the
helicopter the leaders are travelling in, but Q has substituted a
remote-controlled helicopter instead. Once Bond pinpoints the
position of the assassin (on top of the Sphinx) he confronts and
kills him. Mr Amos apparently escapes.

Observations: Mr Amos, the head of the Hong Kong corporation who are siphoning off Western foreign aid targeted
at the Far East, has a white cat on his lap. Is his organisation something that might evolve into SPECTRE? Tatiana
Romanova first appeared in Ian Fleming's novel *From Russia
With Love*. She now appears to be a double agent working for
M but still assigned to the KGB. M and Moneypenny both
turn up, although M is thinner than we're used to, and Major
Boothroyd (Q) is in Cairo with Bond but is never seen.

The entire story takes place in 1961.

Light of My Death was published as a running story in Dark Horse Comics issues 8, 9, 10 and 11.

Perhaps it's our imagination, but bits of this story appear to be missing. Bond goes from a position of almost no knowledge in Part Two to knowing the name and location of the villain in Part Three, with no obvious means of getting between the two states.

Locations: The French Alps, London, Lyon, Cairo, Hong Kong.

Toys for the Boys: Bond's Hong Kong contact has a sampan with secret rocket engines strapped beneath it. Q has a remote-controlled helicopter. Bond has an exploding hip flask.

SHATTERED HELIX

Published By: Dark Horse Comics in 1994

Part One: 'The Greenhouse Effect'

Part Two: 'A Cold Day in Hell'

Starring: The hero – James Bond
The villain – Mr Barclay
The love interest – Serena Mountjoy

Written By: Simon Jowett

Drawn By: David Lloyd

Plot: Scientist Philip Boyce is kidnapped by the international criminal organisation Cerberus from a sealed arcology in Arizona, right under Bond's nose. Boyce used to work for the CIA in a secret biological-warfare institute in the Antarctic, and Cerberus want him to lead them to it. The experiments Boyce was working on were to create a virus which could attack human DNA and could be programmed to create a range of diseases, from glaucoma to cancer. There was an accident – some of the virus escaped and two researchers died, one when his entire bloodstream suddenly clotted and

341

the other when the acid in his stomach suddenly started digesting his entire body. The base was sealed and abandoned, but there are still two flasks of virus inside.

Bond follows Cerberus to the Antarctic with the help of expert Serena Mountjoy and a group of marines. The Cerberus agent, Mr Barclay, captures them, but Boyce takes advantage of their distraction to release a canister of the virus. The automatic safety mechanisms seal the base off: Bond and Serena escape just in time. Bond operates the base's self-destruct mechanism, and explosives shatter the ice around it, sending it plunging into the icy waters of the Antarctic.

Observations: Bond makes a passing and veiled reference to his friend Terri Li (*A Silent Armageddon*). Bond is referred to as Commander Bond at one stage, but he's Captain Bond in the Gardner novels by now. M turns up.

Locations: Arizona and the Antarctic.

Bond's Past Life: Ian Mountjoy was an old friend of Bond's (probably in the Royal Navy) before he was killed in an Antarctic expedition. Serena Mountjoy is his daughter.

Villainous Foibles: Mr Barclay's right-hand man – Bullock – is a huge mountain of muscle with special body-armour implants beneath his skin.

MINUTE OF MIDNIGHT

Published By: Dark Horse Comics in 1994 in one part

Starring: The hero – James Bond
                      The villain – Lexis
                      The love interest – Shadow Breight

Written By: Doug Moench

Drawn By: Russ Heath

Plot: A cartel of terrorist organisations headed by the

saturnine Lexis plans to threaten to blow up a large number of nuclear reactors simultaneously around the world. They intend to present world leaders with a list of disparate demands which will have to be satisfied if a global holocaust is to be avoided. Bond discovers this plan while undercover, and is sent back to the UK with a tape of Lexis discussing his plans. Bond's CIA escort on the flight attacks him and attempts to steal the tape: Bond throws him out of the aircraft without a parachute. Back in the UK, Bond is instructed by M to assassinate Lexis. Reluctantly, he does so, but the terrorist threat is not ended. A penetration agent within the Secret Intelligence Service is planning to help the terrorists kidnap M.

Observations: M and Bill Tanner appear.

Minute of Midnight was published as a one-off in Dark Horse Comics Issue 25. It ran back to back with an *Aliens vs. Predator* strip.

Locations: Washington, DC; the mid-Atlantic; somewhere just outside London.

James Bond, Fashion Victim: Bond is disguised as a hobo in the first few pages of the comic. Later he manages to make love to Shadow Breight while still handcuffed to a briefcase (how did he get his shirt off?).

Single Entendres: When Bond tells her that he drinks his Martinis shaken, not stirred, Shadow Breight says, 'Kinky with your drinks too.'

THE QUASIMODO GAMBIT

Published By: Dark Horse Comics in 1995 in three untitled parts

Starring: The hero – James Bond
The villain – Maximillian ('Quasimodo')
Steele

The love interest – Nebula Valentine

Written By: Don McGregor

Drawn By: Gary Caldwell

Plot: An American televangelist named Hazelwood and a born-again Christian mercenary named Maximillian Steele buy explosives and guns from an arms dealer in Jamaica. Bond has been sent to put the arms dealer out of business, and interferes with the deal. The arms dealer dies, but Hazelwood and Steele escape with their weapons. Bond has become intrigued with discovering what they are planning, and follows them to the swamps of the deep South, where they hide the weapons in bales of marijuana.

After being captured and escaping in the swamp, Bond follows as they smuggle the weapons up to New York, and discovers that they plan to detonate the bombs in a skyscraper overlooking Times Square at Christmas, spreading napalm over the shoppers and sightseers below. The intention is to serve notice on the forces of Satan that God's chosen troops are fighting back. Or something. Bond confronts Steele in the skyscraper and kills him. Hazelwood is killed by accident as he tries to escape.

Observations: While in Jamaica, Bond remembers Quarrel (*Live and Let Die*). M, Moneypenny and Felix Leiter (complete with false arm) are part of the cast.

The Quasimodo Gambit was originally written around 1988–9, before the blowing up of the World Trade Center in Oklahoma and the confrontation between ATF troops and religious fundamentalists at Waco, Texas.

Writer Don McGregor has said in an article in his comic adaptation of *GoldenEye* that he was disappointed with the published version of *The Quasimodo Gambit*. It's hardly surprising – the artwork is completely lifeless. However, the script must take a lot of the blame – where other Bond comics contain a novel's worth of plot squeezed into three or four issues, this one contains a mere short story blown up to unwieldy proportions.

Locations: Jamaica, Georgia (USA) and New York.

Bond's Past Life: Bond killed his first man in New York. The victim was a double agent.

Villainous Foibles: Maximillian Steele has a hump and what appears to be a cataract over one eye.

Sadism: Steele ties Bond to a tree in the swamp and covers him with leeches – including two in his mouth.

File 005:
The Role-Playing Games

File 053:
The Role-Playing Games

JAMES BOND 007

Published In: 1983, with game supplements published in later years

Game Designed By: Gerard Christopher Klug

Observations: *James Bond 007* is a role-playing game. For those of you who are uncertain what that means, a role-playing game is one in which a group of players improvise their way, in character, through a series of adventures, guided by a 'Games Master' (or GM). The events that befall them are partly guided by a pre-scripted scenario, known only to the GM, and partly generated randomly by the roll of a die.

James Bond 007 allows the players to be one of a series of 00 agents (but not usually James Bond himself). As the characters and events of the scenarios are limitless, there is little one can say about them in a book such as this. However, three interesting points should be noted.

First, the game is based on a licence granted by Eon Productions, rather than Glidrose, and so James Bond is the Bond of the movies rather than the books. This is obvious from some of the descriptions – the listed plot of *Dr No* involves a tarantula rather than a centipede, and Hugo Drax is described as being handsome.

Secondly, although many of the scenarios provided with the game are based on Fleming's plots, their details have been changed and their locations altered to make them less obvious to the players. In the scenario entitled *The Island of Dr No*, for instance, Dr No's island is located near Tobruk in the Middle East, rather than near Jamaica.

Thirdly, probably because of the legal case fought by Kevin McClory and Jack Whittington over *Thunderball*, neither SPECTRE nor Ernst Stavro Blofeld is used in the role-playing game. Instead, a similar organisation named TAROT (Technological Accession, Revenge and Organised Terrorism) has been created, fronted by a villain named Karl Ferenc Skorpios.

349

Most of the later supplements to the game are based on existing films, and follow their plots quite slavishly (with the proviso that the Games Master can change the plot if they feel it is too familiar by altering the aims of the villain, the location of events or the motivation of the subsidiary characters). *A View to a Kill* is, for instance, almost identical to the film of the same title, although the plot of *Octopussy* has been changed in one fascinating and important respect (probably because the plot of the film makes very little sense) and both *Dr No* and *The Man With the Golden Gun* now involve TAROT. Some of the modules have, however, been issued with new plots, and it's worth quickly running through some of them here.

Goldfinger II – The Man With the Midas Touch involves someone (maybe even Auric Goldfinger himself) attempting to turn base metals into gold and thus destabilise the world gold market. Events take place in Mexico City, Mexico, and near Ankara (Turkey).

You Only Live Twice II has no obvious connection to *You Only Live Twice* apart from the presence of some Japanese people. It takes place primarily in Australia, and starts with the theft of a file from MI6 headquarters. It is mainly of interest because it was written by Raymond Benson, who now writes the official continuation novels. A portion of the module was adapted for part of his first novel, *Zero Minus Ten*.

FIND YOUR OWN FATE

Four 'Find Your Own Fate' books were published to tie in with the release of *A View to a Kill*, using scenes and characters from that film but also introducing new situations as well. The idea, for those of you who have never come across the phenomenon, is that the reader is led through a series of actions that 'they' (i.e. Bond) take, and are presented with a choice of paths. Which choice the reader makes determines which page and paragraph they are directed to read next. The plot (such as it is) is carefully controlled so that the possible paths the reader might follow are kept to a minimum, and keep intersecting.

The books were entitled *Win, Place or Die* (by R.L. Stine), *Strike it Deadly* (by Barbara and Scott Siegel), *Programmed for Danger* (by Jean M. Favors) and *Barracuda Run* (by Steven Otfinoski). They were numbered 11 to 14 of the series, previous books having involved the adventures of characters such as GI Joe, Indiana Jones and the Transformers.

COMPUTER AND BOARD GAMES

A number of computer games have been released with Bond as the hero, but, as they usually reflected scenes and events from a particular film, rather than having a distinct, developing plot of their own, we have ignored them here.

File 006:
The Lookalikes

SPOOFS, INFLUENCES AND REFERENCES

They say that imitation is the sincerest form of flattery. They also say that success breeds imitation. In the 45 years since the first James Bond novel appeared, many similar but subtly different secret agents have appeared, some called James Bond and some not, some serious and some not, but all riding on the coat tails of Ian Fleming's creation.

It's pointless and probably impossible to detail all the different books, films and TV series that Ian Fleming's work has influenced. Do we count an episode of *The Muppets Tonight!* in which Pierce Brosnan appeared, spoofing his Bond persona? Do we count an episode of the American teen comedy series *Sabrina the Teenage Witch* in which a bald man with a maniacal laugh enters his white Persian cat in a pet competition? If not, then what makes *Austin Powers: International Man of Mystery* different?

There's a good argument to be made that the action genre as we know it would not have come into being were it not for the increasing success and excess of the Bond films during the 1970s (ironic, considering the fact that the revived Bond franchise in the 1990s had to compete with the genre it had itself spawned). Should we then count Arnold Schwarzenegger's *True Lies* and *Eraser* as a part of the Bond phenomenon?

Perhaps it might help if some form of classification were introduced, so that Bond's legitimate and illegitimate children can be divided into groups, depending on the scale of the debt they owe to Fleming. It seems to us that these fictions can be divided into three types: those that try to duplicate (or in some instances deliberately contradict) the spirit of Bond; those that take some definite element from the Bond books or films and exaggerate it for comic or satirical effect; and those that actually make some attempt (however lame) to be a part of the Bond canon.

The first group primarily covers all those spy series in which a lone figure with a taste for the high life fights against international conspiracies whose aim is global domination or widespread devastation. It has to be said that Fleming himself didn't improve matters when he helped create the earliest and most obvious Bond competitor – the American TV series *The Man From UNCLE*. Since then, many authors have tried to cash in on what they saw as the Fleming formula. In the USA, for instance, James Mayo wrote a series of novels concerning the adventures of agent Charles Hood. His titles alone were indicative of his debt to Fleming: *Hammerhead* wouldn't look out of place on a bookshelf next to *Thunderball* and *Moonraker*, while *Shamelady* is a deliberate reference to the name of Ian Fleming's boat on Jamaica. In the UK, James Leasor's *Passport to . . .* series of novels featured a hero named Doctor Jason Love, who had much the same cosmopolitan, globetrotting attitude towards life that Ian Fleming made his own, while Philip McCutcheon's Commander Shaw followed in Bond's footsteps, complete with matching accessory evil opponents (and was almost as long-running – Shaw's exploits ran from the early 1960s to the mid-1980s). Adam Hall had his *Quiller* novels (made into a short-lived TV series) but Peter O'Donnell (who adapted Fleming's novel *Goldfinger* for the *Daily Express* strip) was, perhaps, the most inventive of the Fleming wannabes, aiming his *Modesty Blaise* comic strips and novels firmly at the Bond audience while giving his heroine a firm personality, character and background of her own.

In complete contrast, but just as influenced by Fleming, both Len Deighton and John Gardner created characters that were meant to be an antidote to Bond. Deighton's unnamed protagonist, called Harry Palmer in the movie series, was a seedy individual working for a bureaucratic Secret Service, whereas Gardner's Boysie Oakes was a misfit who was accidentally mistaken for an assassin and played along with it for several novels. Fleming enjoyed Deighton's books, and once suggested (perhaps not entirely in jest) that they coordinate their books so that Bond was disparaging about 'Palmer' and 'Palmer' returned the favour at more or less the same time. Deighton subsequently collaborated with Sean

Connery on an abortive James Bond film entitled *Warhead*, while Gardner ended up writing James Bond books himself, thus proving that rebels usually become what they are rebelling against at some stage.

It is intriguing to note, by the way, that almost all of the above writers saw at least one of their books made into a film during the heyday of Sean Connery's Bond, with the exception of Philip McCutcheon.

The second group covers those films and television programmes that take recognisable elements from Bond and use them to comic effect. It's a trick used by cartoonists – exaggerate a distinctive feature to the point of ludicrousness. In fiction, one of the earliest attempts was the series of four novels concerning the adventures of Jewish secret agent Israel Bond written by Sol Weinstein – *Loxfinger* (1965), *Matzohball* (1966), *On the Secret Service of His Majesty, The Queen* (1966) and *You Only Live Until You Die* (1968).

An Italian film named *Operation Kid Brother*, built around the unsubtle concept of Sean Connery's brother Neil playing the brother of agent 007, was released on an unsuspecting world in 1968. Not entirely unexpectedly there were some cast-related in-jokes, given that Bernard Lee ('M'), Lois Maxwell (Miss Moneypenny), Adolpho Celli (Largo in *Thunderball*), Daniela Bianchi (Tatiana Romanova in *From Russia With Love*) and Anthony Dawson (Professor Dent in *Dr No*) all took part for reasons that must have seemed very good at the time.

Austin Powers: International Man of Mystery (1997) takes the mickey out of Bond very well, what with its balding supervillain with a Nehru jacket and delusions of grandeur and its sybaritic hero with a neat line of sexual innuendo. The US animated comedy series *The Simpsons* also excelled with its 1996 episode 'You Only Move Twice'. Oafish husband Homer is offered a job by the Globex Corporation, not realising that its owner – surname the Flemingesque Scorpio, first name the highly un-Flemingesque Hank – wants to take over the world. An unwitting Homer just gets in the way when a black-clad secret agent with a Scottish accent tries to interfere with Scorpio's plans, and he ends up being responsible for the agent's death. The same year's spoof movie *Spy Hard* stars Leslie Neilson as tuxedo-wearing secret agent WD-40 and is based around a scattergun approach, firing off so many bad jokes in so many different directions that at least some of them will hit the targets they are aimed at. The theme song, however, written and sung by 'Weird' Al Yankovitch, is, perhaps, the most perfect spoof of the straight-faced excesses of the Bond films ever committed to celluloid. Earlier, *Star Trek: Deep Space Nine* attempted to pay its own homage to Bond with the episode 'Our Man Bashir'. Everything in the episode – the music, the sets, the costumes, the character names – is redolent of the entire sixties spy bandwagon, to the extent that, for legal reasons, the episode cannot be repeated in the United States (although it is available on video in the UK). The name of the villain, for example, is Dr Noah – the same as the villain in the film of *Casino Royale*.

The third group is the most interesting, given that it covers those items that tread along the edges of the Bond copyright, sometimes one side of the line, sometimes the other. Cyril Connolly's spoof 'Bond Strikes Camp', first published in 1963, was a barb aimed at Ian Fleming from the centre of his wife's literary circle, and comes closer to hitting Fleming's distinctive style than anyone has managed since. In it, a secretly homosexual M sends Bond undercover in women's clothing in an attempt to pick him up. As the literary fade-out occurs, it's obvious that Bond is succumbing to M's rather clumsy charms. *National Lampoon*'s 1962 *Alligator* (supposedly by I*n Fl*m*ng but actually by Michael K. Frith and Christopher B. Cerf) was a rather more lowbrow attempt to spoof the series in which supervillain Alligator steals the Houses of Parliament and floats them down the River Thames, chased by secret agent B*nd. The spy spoof movie *Our Man Flint* mentions SPECTRE as if they are a real evil organisation in Derek Flint's fictional world, while, in a case of things coming almost full circle, the 1983 TV movie *The Return of the Man From UNCLE* stars George Lazenby as an unnamed tuxedo-wearing secret agent who drives an Aston Martin DB5 with the licence plate JB 007 – and if he's not meant to be James Bond then who the hell is he?

Even the Soviet Union got in on the act. The 1962 book *Priklyucheniyata na Avakum Zakhov* (*The Adventures of Avakum Zakhov*, also sometimes listed as *Zakhov Mission*), by the well-known Bulgarian writer Andrei Stoyanov Gulyashi (or Gulyashki), told the story of Socialist agent Avakum Zakhov – apparently a Soviet equivalent of Bond. Gulyashi followed it up in 1969 with *Sreshtu 007* (*Versus 007*) – an adventure in which Zakhov engages in combat with Agent 007 of the decadent Imperialist West. An alternative title for the book (either due to translation difficulties or possibly because the book was published in Turkey as well as Russia) is *Avakum Sreshti 007* (*Avakum Versus 007*). It has been suggested, although never confirmed, that the KGB commissioned Gulyashi to write the book as an antidote to the increasing popularity of Ian Fleming's books among literate Soviet citizens.

The most extensive and expensive Bond spoof is, of course, *Casino Royale*. Based at least in part on Ian Fleming's novel, and as 'official' as, say, *You Only Live Twice*, given that the makers of the film had indeed purchased the film rights on that book, it was released in 1967. It's still a byword for cinematic stupidity and cupidity, and proves that the Bond name alone is not enough to ennoble a project.

We started off this section with two quotations. There's another one that applies generally to these strange, mis-begotten spin-offs from the world of James Bond, and in particular to *Casino Royale*: familiarity breeds contempt. Things haven't quite got that bad yet, but there have been times over the past 45 years when we almost had too much of a good thing.

CASINO ROYALE (1967)

Starring: David Niven as the hero – Sir James Bond
Orson Welles as the villain – Le Chiffre
Woody Allen as the villain – Dr Noah
(Jimmy Bond)

Written By: That's an interesting question. The credited
writers are Wolf Mankowicz, John Law and
Michael Sayers, but a whole list of other
people are said to have contributed to the
many versions of the script, including Ben
Hecht, Billy Wilder, Joseph Heller, Terry
Southern, Peter Sellers and Woody Allen, as
well as at least two of the directors (John
Huston and Val Guest)

Directed By: Joe McGrath (the sequences with Peter
Sellers and Ursula Andress and some of
the sequence with Peter Sellers and Orson
Welles)
Robert Parrish (the rest of the sequence
between Peter Sellers and Orson Welles)
John Huston (the sequences at Bond's home,
and at the Scottish castle)
Val Guest (the sequences with Woody Allen
and some additional David Niven
sequences)
Ken Hughes (the Berlin section)
Richard Talmadge (the Second Unit Director
responsible for the climactic fight
sequence in the casino)

Tag Line: Casino Royale is too much ... for one James
Bond.

Relevance of Pre-Title Sequence? A few seconds moved
from the middle of the film and of no significance apart from
the fact that it features Peter Sellers – nominally the star of

the film. Perhaps the producers wanted to remind people that Sellers would be turning up eventually.

Theme Song: No opening theme, but the jokey end theme is sung by an uncredited bloke. A song in the middle of the film is sung by Dusty Springfield.

Cringe-Worthy Title Sequence: The opening credits are animated by Richard Williams, who later went on to fame with *Who Framed Roger Rabbit?*

Plot: The British Secret Service has lost eleven agents in a fortnight. The CIA has lost eight. The KGB has lost sixteen. Something bad is happening, and the heads of all the main Secret Services of the world join together to call the *real* James Bond out of retirement to help them track down the killer. Bond refuses, so M has his house blown up in order to force his cooperation. M is accidentally killed in the explosion, and Bond travels to Scotland to inform his widow. He does not realise that everyone in M's ancestral castle has been replaced by members of SMERSH, an evil organisation controlled by the mysterious Dr Noah. Noah's orders are that they are to corrupt and foul Bond's reputation, or kill him if they fail. Bond passes the various trials they foist upon him, culminating in a grouse shoot where the grouse have been replaced with explosive robot birds designed to home in on a button sewn to Bond's cloak. Bond destroys the bird-firing mechanism by flinging the homing button into it using his braces as a catapult, and travels to London where he takes over as head of the British Secret Service. By this time, 21 British agents have been killed.

Realising that SMERSH seem to be using an inordinate number of female agents, Bond authorises the training of Cooper (one of Britain's most attractive male agents) to resist feminine charms. To confuse the enemy, he also has all the British agents renamed 'James Bond – 007'.

Bond travels to Thailand to recruit Mata Bond – his daughter. The only clue he has (given to him by the woman impersonating M's widow) points towards a SMERSH base in East Germany operating under the cover of International Mothers' Help – an organisation that supplies nannies and is based in a building straddling the Berlin Wall. Mata Bond infiltrates SMERSH and disrupts the auction of art treasures that SMERSH agent Le Chiffre has organised in order to pay off the money he has embezzled from SMERSH to fund his gambling habit.

In London, Bond secures the aid of Vesper Lynd, a former agent who is now a successful and rich businesswoman. Bond wants her to employ a professional gambler named Evelyn Tremble to go up against Le Chiffre. At Casino Royale in Monaco, Tremble wins the game. Le Chiffre is humiliated and then is killed by SMERSH when he cannot return the money he's embezzled.

Vesper Lynd is kidnapped by SMERSH at Casino Royale, and Tremble goes after her. In London, Mata Bond is kidnapped by a flying saucer and taken to Casino Royale. SMERSH appear to have most of Bond's agents captive. Bond travels to Casino Royale but is also taken captive. Dr Noah, Head of SMERSH, tells Bond that he has a thousand robot doubles of Bond, and intends releasing them into the world to cause devastation. He also has a bacillus that will render all women beautiful and kill all men over four foot six inches. And he intends killing all world leaders and replacing them with robot doubles so he can rule the world through them. And he has also developed a pill that can turn people into walking atomic bombs.

Bond forces Dr Noah to reveal his true identity as young Jimmy Bond, Sir James Bond's nephew. One of Bond's agents (known only as 'The Detainer') also fools Dr Noah into swallowing the pill that turns people into atomic bombs. Bond breaks out and rescues all of his agents. As they escape through Casino Royale, a fight breaks out. The presence of vaporised lysergic acid (LSD) in the atmosphere of the SMERSH HQ might explain the final sequences, in which cowboys, indians, seals, donkeys, chimpanzees, a dog with a collar reading '007', the Keystone Cops and at least one gangster fight in the midst of the casino. The whole farrago ends when Jimmy Bond blows up, killing everyone.

Observations: Hard to credit, perhaps, but *Casino Royale* was originally intended by producer Charles K. Feldman as a serious Bond film. He had obtained the film rights to Ian Fleming's first Bond novel from the widow of the man who had originally purchased them from Fleming (Gregory Ratoff), and approached Sean Connery to star as Bond. When Connery refused, Feldman began to realise that the only way to make the film was as a spoof of the entire Bond canon.

'Charles Feldman was . . . furious about the success of the Bond films,' writer Wolf Mankowicz recalled. 'He had bought *Casino Royale* ages before, and he just couldn't forgive himself that he hadn't done anything with it. So finally he decided what he was going to do was ruin the Bond business . . . It was total lunacy. After eighteen months I really couldn't take any more of it, and I withdrew.'

The film might actually have succeeded if filming hadn't been completely disrupted by the disappearance of Peter Sellers (notoriously unreliable at the time) and, shortly afterwards, by the walkout of initial director Joe McGrath. Various other directors were brought in to film a script which was mutating on a daily basis. Sellers returned, but left again when his contract finished without actually finishing his scenes (hence his sudden disappearance from the plot). Director Val Guest attempted to film some bridging material and pull the whole thing together, but it was an almost impossible job.

Recalling his experiences working with Charles Feldman, director Val Guest said, 'He would call me up at some ungodly hour and say, "Look, I've got George Raft . . . Bill Holden will do Tuesday . . ." All this had to be written in overnight.'

'I never saw a script,' director Ken Hughes recalled. 'I was given some pages, but they said, "We're not going to use them anyway." '

David Niven plays the *real* James Bond – the one played by Sean Connery was allegedly given the famous name and number when the real one retired so he could carry on the legend. Niven's Bond has little time for his successor, or for his 'Aston Martin, complete with lethal accessories'. Niven, you will recall, was one of Ian Fleming's choices to play Bond in *Dr No*.

Ironically, there's more of Ian Fleming's *Casino Royale* in this film than there is of his *You Only Live Twice* in the film of that name. M turns up (his real name is, apparently, McTarry) as does Moneypenny's daughter. Bond's friend Mathis (from the Deuxième Bureau) also appears (he was in the original novel of *Casino Royale*) and Bond drives his usual Bentley. The carpet beater used by Le Chiffre in Ian Fleming's book is attached to the back of the chair when Le Chiffre tortures Evelyn Tremble.

One can't help wondering whether the chimpanzee that appears at the end is Wolf Mankowicz's attempt to get his vision of Dr No on the screen.

Watch out for Valerie Leon as one of the female agents sent to test Agent Cooper. She's also in *The Spy Who Loved Me* and *Never Say Never Again*. John Hollis, who appears briefly as a priest in Mata Bond's temple, later played a bald-headed person with a white cat (who may or may not be Blofeld) in *For Your Eyes Only*. Vladek Sheybal, who plays the SMERSH auctioneer, previously appeared as Kronsteen in *From Russia With Love*. Bert Kwouk, head of the Chinese delegation in the SMERSH auction, appeared in *Goldfinger* as a Chinese liaison and in *You Only Live Twice* as a SPECTRE operative. Milton Reid, one of Mata Bond's Indian attendants, was one of *Dr No*'s guards.

The voice of Dr Noah is provided by Valentine Dyall.

Locations: England, Scotland, Thailand, East Berlin and Monaco.

James Bond, Fashion Victim: Well, after the nightshirt and nightcap, who's counting?

Bond's Past Life: Bond won a Victoria Cross at Mafeking and was a hero during the Ashanti Uprising. He retired after he had to lure Mata Hari across the Spanish frontier to France, where she was placed in front of a firing squad and killed. They had a daughter together.

Toys for the Boys: It's a spoof of the increasing ludicrousness of the Q scenes in the Connery films, and it's probably the funniest scene in the film (mostly due to the snappy dialogue). We get scuba divers with bows and arrows; a bowler hat with an integral weapon ('Yes, we're still working on that one'); a pen that fires a stream of poison gas; a watch with an integral video communication system; and infrared glasses for cheating at cards.

Goodbye, Mr Bond: A very casual one from Le Chiffre, but it's to Evelyn Tremble rather than to Bond.

Lines to Rewind For: 'I did not come here to be devoured by symbols of monarchy,' says the head of the KGB as the lions close in on his car.

Passing the dead M's wig on to his widow, Bond asks, 'Should it be given a Christian burial? Just how personal is a toupee?' 'It can only be regarded as a *heir*loom,' says the (fake) McTarry widow.

Bond: 'Be careful, that's my loose kneecap.'

Bond again, rather cuttingly: 'It's depressing that the words "secret agent" have become synonymous with "sex maniac".'

Q, handing Evelyn Tremble a form as he enters the laboratory: 'If you'd be good enough to sign here, sir. It's not for me, it's for the Official Secrets Act.'

Jimmy Bond to one of Bond's female agents whom he has secured in his base: 'I'll unlock you immediately and we'll run amok. If you're too tired, we'll walk amok.'

It's Only a Movie: As M's car, complete with lion sitting on the roof, approaches Bond's manor house we hear the theme from *Born Free* (by John Barry, of course).

When Cooper is trained to fight off female charms, some of the women sent to test him are dressed as Ursula Andress from *Dr No* and Honor Blackman from *Goldfinger*.

When Mata Hari is escaping from SMERSH headquarters

in Berlin, she pulls up a manhole cover. The strains of 'What's New, Pussycat?' waft out – from the previous film that Peter Sellers and Woody Allen were in. Peter O'Toole, also from that film, appears in Peter Sellers's dream sequence. 'Excuse me,' O'Toole asks, 'are you Richard Burton?' 'No,' Sellers replies, 'I'm Peter O'Toole.' 'Then you're the finest man that ever breathed,' O'Toole says before walking off.

When escaping from SMERSH's HQ beneath Casino Royale, Bond asks a passing Frankenstein monster for directions.

During the climactic fight sequences, you might notice that SMERSH seem to be paying a man to paint women gold.

Mistakes Can Be Fatal: Spotting mistakes in *Casino Royale* must rank as one of the most trivial and pointless exercises of all time, but here goes:

How does Bond know enough about Le Chiffre's connection to SMERSH to put Evelyn Tremble on his tail?

Q indicates that he is working for MI5, rather than MI6 (or the SIS). This contradicts both Ian Fleming and the Connery films.

SMERSH seems to be the organisation behind the killings of the various Secret Agents, but SMERSH is a Soviet organisation and sixteen KGB agents have died. In fact, SMERSH here is portrayed as an international organisation with no political ties (more like SPECTRE).

File 007:
The Unseen Bond

As well as the many novels, short stories and films that we have become familiar with over the years, there have also been a number of 'shadow' Bond adventures that have never received much public attention. Most of these have been early drafts of the films – the 1969 Gerry Anderson proposal for *Moonraker*, for instance, or the planned version of *A View to a Kill* in which Max Zorin was attempting to manipulate the course of Halley's Comet. All of these 'shadow' adventures are described in the entries on the books and the films that eventually took their places, but two planned Bond projects deserve a little more attention: the 'lost' Bond novel by Geoffrey Jenkins and the 'lost' Bond film *Warhead*.

TITLE UNKNOWN (1971)

Following Kingsley Amis's *Colonel Sun*, another original 007 novel was commissioned by Glidrose from the thriller writer Geoffrey Jenkins (author of, among other novels, *A River of Diamonds*) after he convinced the copyright holders that he had worked on a smuggling plot with Ian Fleming. However, when the manuscript was submitted for approval, Glidrose exercised their option not to proceed. There have been times when we wish they had been so diligent later.

WARHEAD (1977)

Under the terms of the contract between Kevin McClory and Eon Productions during the making of *Thunderball*, copyright in the script would revert to McClory ten years after the film was released in Britain and he was not allowed to make any other Bond films in the intervening time. Towards the end of the tenth year, McClory kicked off plans to revisit *Thunderball*. Having already sorted out funding on the project, he approached Sean Connery to see if the actor would be interested in reprising his role. Connery refused, but, given Connery's immense experience in what would work in a Bond film and what wouldn't, McClory asked him to advise on the script. The thriller writer Len Deighton was already on board the project, and Connery joined him and McClory in writing a script based around many of the ideas thrashed out by Ian Fleming and McClory back in 1957. That script was originally entitled *James Bond of the Secret Service*, but was soon renamed *Warhead*.

A full-page advertisement in the 12 May 1976 issue of *Variety* – the weekly newspaper of the film world – announced the official start of production. Filming was set to start in February 1977, implying that the film would have been released in late 1977 or early 1978. There can only be speculation over who would have played James Bond, but one has to wonder whether Sean Connery would have been able to resist for long.

The film would have started off with Bond at Shrublands – but not the health farm in the southeast of England that we have become used to from *Thunderball* and *Never Say Never Again*. No, *this* Shrublands is a scuba-training school used by intelligence agents, and Bond is brushing up on his technique (in more ways than one, judging by the massage that the gorgeous Justine Lovesitt is giving him). Bond is initially unaware that Ernst Stavros Blofeld, head of the evil SPECTRE, is nearby, and has sunk a Soviet submarine carrying atomic weapons. Blofeld intends recovering the weapons from the wreck and using them to blackmail the United Nations into handing control of the oceans over to SPECTRE (he's worried about the levels of pollution being pumped into the sea by the developing nations). To alert the UN to his plans, he kills their Secretary General. Blofeld's recovery plans require that he replace a CIA agent at Shrublands with a SPECTRE duplicate in order to then sabotage the US recovery operation on the Soviet submarine, providing him with the time he needs to nip in and get the warheads.

Bond becomes aware that something is going on at Shrublands and sneaks into Blofeld's base along with his ace buddy Felix Leiter. Both men are captured, but are rescued by Q (who is accompanying M as part of the British Secret

Service's attempt to track down SPECTRE). Bond realises that Blofeld intends exploding the first of his atomic weapons in New York if the UN does not sign control of the oceans over to him, and so he and Felix travel there. Blofeld smuggles the warhead into Manhatten inside a robot hammerhead shark, but Bond locates and neutralises it. Bond then tracks Blofeld down in his temporary SPECTRE headquarters in the Statue of Liberty, and kills him.

It's odd, given Sean Connery's close involvement, but the script for *Warhead* displays most of the traits that made him leave the series. There's an overreliance on gadgets and spectacle, and Bond just wanders through, reacting to events rather than initiating them. And, in a stunning lapse of security for an SIS agent, Bond's cleaning lady is a SPECTRE agent.

The Blofeld of *Warhead* is different from the one in either the films or, indeed, Ian Fleming's books. He's a well-known millionaire backgammon player with no known connection to SPECTRE – who are known to the world's intelligence agencies. His name is actually subtly different as well – Ernst *Stavros* Blofeld as opposed to Ernst *Stavro* Blofeld. Fatima Blush (later to appear in *Never Say Never Again*) and Domino (from *Thunderball* and *Never Say Never Again*) also both appear, but they are sisters. M and Q are as we have come to know and love them.

Connery's involvement in *Warhead* had always been conditional upon there being no legal problems with the project, but once McClory and his backers went public it became clear that there were fine problems of interpretation involved in just what it was McClory had copyright on. Was it *Thunderball* alone, or was it all the material he and Fleming had been working on? And how extensive was that material? Once the legal sharks started circling, Sean Connery walked away from the project, and without him it was far more difficult for it to continue. Everything went quiet.

File 008:
Bond and MI6

AGENTS AND STATIONS

In keeping with its status as a worldwide collector of intelligence, the Secret Intelligence Service has its agents all over the world, supported by an extensive network of local headquarters – or, at least, the one created by Ian Fleming does. Fleming used to drop occasional references to these agents and headquarters into his fiction, and the various creators of fresh Bond adventures have continued the tradition ever since.

The convention established by Fleming was to have each SIS branch – known as a 'Station' – referred to by a letter of the alphabet. This quickly led to problems, the alphabet being so limited in size and the world so large. Fleming's occasional lapses of memory when it came to details didn't help either. The writers who have followed in Fleming's wake have done their best to be consistent, but they have been rushed and Fleming was never that consistent to begin with, so mistakes have inevitably crept in.

The following list of all SIS Stations referred to in any Bond story has been assiduously compiled by reference back to the original novels, short stories, films and comic strips. The problems are immediately obvious: Finland is represented by Stations F and H; Germany is represented by Station D and Station M; Jamaica is represented by Stations C, J and K (obviously a busy part of the world); and Rio de Janeiro by Stations S and VH. Equally, there are three Stations A (Austria, Australia and the USA), two Stations C (Caribbean and Canada), two Stations F (Finland and France), two Stations H (Finland and Hong Kong), two Stations J (Japan and Jamaica) and two Stations S (the Soviet Union and Rio de Janeiro).

Far be it from us to suggest that many of these supposed 'Stations' exist to give agents like Bond somewhere to go for their holidays, but there seems to be a preponderance of Stations in sunny areas and a relative scarcity in cold ones (only one Station for the whole of the Soviet Union?). The new M has been described as 'an accountant – a bean-counter . . .' Well, if she's interested in saving money then we can suggest a few places to start.

Designation	Location	
A	The United States	(books/short stories)
A	Australia	(books/short stories)
A	Austria	(books/short stories)
B	West Germany (Berlin)	(books/short stories)
C	The Caribbean	(books/short stories)
C	Canada	(films)
D	Germany (Deutschland)	(books/short stories)
F	Finland	(books/short stories)
F	France	(books/short stories)
G	Greece	(books/short stories)
H	Finland (Helsinki)	(books/short stories)
H	Hong Kong	(books/short stories)
I	India	(films)
J	Japan (but run from the UK)	(books/short stories)
J	Jamaica	(comic strips)
K	Kingston (Jamaica)	(books/short stories)
M	Munich	(books/short stories)
N	Cyprus (Nicosia)	(books/short stories)
P	Paris	(books/short stories)
S	The Soviet Union	(books/short stories)
S	Rio de Janeiro	(comic strips)
T	Turkey	(films)
V	Vienna	(films)
VH	Rio de Janeiro	(films)
W	West Germany	(books/short stories)
WB	West Berlin	(books/short stories)
Z	Zürich	(books/short stories)

Similarly, Fleming occasionally used to mention Bond's fellow agents – primarily by number, occasionally by name as well – and give some little hint of what was happening in their lives. Presumably, while Bond was off saving the world they were doing their bit as well, fighting other lunatic criminals and defeating other globe-spanning evil fraternities. Since Fleming's death, the other Bond writers have kept us filled in on Bond's office mates.

The size of the 00 section has varied over the years, from three in the novel *Moonraker* to what appears to be a healthy nine in the film *Thunderball*. Mentions of a 0013 take it even higher. Here's a list of the various other 00 agents and a little bit about them:

002 – (1) was rescued by 007 from a Portuguese police headquarters in Macao in 1954, according to the novel *James Bond: The Authorised Biography*. He could be the same as . . .
(2) Bill Fairbanks, who was shot by Scaramanga in Beirut in 1969, according to the film *The Man With the Golden Gun*.

003 – (1) was badly injured in 1951, according to the novel *James Bond: The Authorised Biography*;
(2) dies while trying to get out of Siberia in the film *A View to a Kill*.

004 – (1) is killed in Gibraltar in the film *The Living Daylights*;
(2) is based in Britain during *The Facts of Death*.

005 – used to be Stuart Thomas before he retired from field duty. He was missing, presumed dead while Head of Station G, according to the novel *Colonel Sun*, although he is apparently still Head of Station during *The Facts of Death*.

006 – (1) is an ex-Royal Marine Commando according to the novel *On Her Majesty's Secret Service*. He could be the same as . . .
(2) Alec Trevalyan, who appeared to die in 1986 but actually faked his own death and set himself up as a criminal gang boss in Russia in the film *GoldenEye*.

008 – (1) died in 1951, according to the novel *James Bond: The Authorised Biography*;

(2) is named Bill, and is rescued from Berlin in the novel *Moonraker* – he is junior to Bond;

(3) is based in Hong Kong in the film *The Living Daylights*.

009 – (1) died in 1955 in Hungary, according to the novel *James Bond: The Authorised Biography*;

(2) is next in seniority after Bond, according to the novel *Thunderball*;

(3) is killed by General Orlov's assassins in the film *Octopussy*;

(4) is found dead in the Amazon jungle in the Deadly Double comic;

(5) is turned into a neanderthal creature by genetic manipulation and then knifed to death in Peru in the comic *Serpent's Tooth*.

0011 – (1) died in 1951, according to the novel *James Bond: The Authorised Biography*;

(2) has been 'lost' in Singapore, according to the novel *Moonraker*.

0013 – is named Briony Thorne and was apparently turned by the Chinese, according to the comic strip *Fear Face*.

00? – was named Captain Norman Nash, and was killed by 'Red' Grant in the film *From Russia With Love*.

00? – is named Suzi Kew, and assists Bond in a number of the comic-strip stories, beginning with *Beware of Butterflies*.

00? – is named York, according to the comic strip *River of Death*.

Perhaps the only lessons that can be learnt from this, albeit truncated, list are that 001 is so secret that nobody mentions his name, and that 009 is not a lucky number to be.

'M' AS IN 'MI6'

Despite M's claim in the film *Dr No* that he's in charge of something called MI7, it's become increasingly clear over the course of the James Bond books and films that the organisation Bond actually works for is the Secret Intelligence Service, more familiarly known as MI6.

For those who don't spend their lives reading John Le Carré and Nigel West, the UK has two primary intelligence services. The Security Service (MI5) was born in 1916 out of a wartime counterespionage department. Its Director reports to the Home Secretary and its primary function until recently has been to locate and neutralise foreign spies operating in the United Kingdom, although its remit has recently been broadened to cover other criminal activities such as drug smuggling and distribution. The Secret Intelligence Service (MI6) was born out of a department known as MI1c around 1919, reports to the Foreign Secretary and, by contrast, operates exclusively outside the UK, collecting information of military or political significance that other countries wish to keep secret.

In the earlier Bond books Ian Fleming displays a marked reluctance to be specific, stating only that Bond is a Government agent operating from a building overlooking Regent's Park and that he occasionally claims to be working for the Ministry of Defence, but by the time of *Thunderball* Fleming acknowledges that Bond is employed by the SIS. John Gardner makes it even more explicit, mentioning both the SIS and the real building they occupied until the mid-1990s: Century House in Lambeth. Raymond Benson, current holder of the Bond literary baton, brings the references bang up to date by ensuring that M's office is based in the new SIS building at Vauxhall Cross (without going so far as to point out that the *real* head of the SIS is known as C, rather than M).

The films have also travelled the same path from ambiguity to certainty. The MI7 reference in *Dr No* apart, there was little in the Connery, Lazenby or Moore films to make it clear where Bond kept his blotter and desk diary. All we see in *Dr No* is a generic shot of the Whitehall skyline, but by the time of *A View to a Kill* we're shown a specific building whenever M is seen in his office. It's the Old War Office in Whitehall, just down from Trafalgar Square and just up from the entrance to Downing Street, but it's owned by the Ministry of Defence rather than the SIS or their masters in the Foreign Office. In *GoldenEye* the connection is made explicit, as the new M has a new office in what we know, in reality, to be the new SIS building in Vauxhall.

As far as anyone who doesn't work for them can tell, the real SIS has never had its headquarters in a building overlooking Regent's Park (although it might have had outstations there). Originally based in Whitehall Court, the SIS moved first to Melbury Road in Kensington, then to Broadway Buildings, overlooking St James's Park tube station in 1925, and then on to Century House in Lambeth in the early 1960s. The building shown in *GoldenEye* became its base in the mid-1990s.

The books and the films also diverge from reality, and from each other, in how many heads the SIS has had during Bond's time. Admiral Sir Miles Messervy is the M to whom Bond reports in every book from *Casino Royale* through to *Cold*, during which Barbara Mawdsley takes over. In the films, the M played by Bernard Lee is succeeded by an M played by Robert Brown (who may be the same character), before a female M – Judi Dench – appears. In reality, however, there have been nine heads of the SIS during Bond's time in the job. They are:

1953–1956	Major-General Sir John Sinclair
1956–1968	Sir Richard Goldsmith White
1968–1973	Sir John Rennie
1973–1978	Sir Maurice Oldfield
1979–1982	Sir Arthur Temple Franks
1982–1985	Sir Colin Figures
1985–1989	Sir Christopher Curwen

| 1989–1994 | Sir Colin Hugh Verel McColl |
| 1994–present | Mr David Spedding |

As time goes on, perhaps we can expect more correspondences between the fictional world of James Bond and the true (albeit rather odd) world inhabited by the operatives of the Secret Intelligence Service. It's clear, however, that the SIS for which Bond works is a parallel one to ours, with different Directors and working out of different HQs. But then, we already knew that. If Sir Hugo Drax had built and launched a nuclear missile from Kent it just might have attracted some attention, and a global media empire run by a certifiable lunatic named Elliott Carver is not the kind of thing one fails to notice when one pops down to the newsagent or turns on the cable TV.

And do we really believe that the *real* SIS has a cadre of trained assassins on call, 24 hours a day? Of course we don't.

BOND'S ORAL SKILLS

We all know that James Bond is superhuman, of course, but it's instructive to examine just how superhuman he is. We know that he can fly almost any type of aircraft, ride a horse and fire a gun as well as being an expert marksman. We know that he's an expert on fine wines and good food. But what about his mental acuity? How smart is Bond?

If the various books and films are all taken at face value, here's a list of the languages Bond speaks fluently:

Arabic
Cantonese Chinese
French
German
Italian
Russian
Spanish

He also has a smattering of the following:

- Afghan
- Greek
- Japanese
- Mandarin Chinese
- Turkish

And, of course, he's learning Swedish in *Tomorrow Never Dies*. Truly a cunning linguist.

SECRET IDENTITIES

One of the fun bits of being a secret agent, of course, is that you get to dress up as other people. Bond's done his fair share of this, during the course of his various adventures – so much so that one wonders how he keeps track of who he is on any particular day. Are there times when he walks into M's office, and M says 'Sit down, 007', and Bond says, 'Who?'

There are three broad categories of alternative identities Bond has adopted over the years – people who don't exist, people who do exist and code names. The following is a list of Bond's identities with no correspondence in the real world:

Joe Bain; General James A. Banker (a US military officer); James Bates; Sergei Batovrin; John Bergin; James Betteridge; James Boldman (the name on Bond's alternative passport); Mohammed J. Bond; Wing Commander Jeremy Boone; Jack Boyd; John Bryce (occasionally an ornithologist); John Bunyan; James Busby; Mr Fisher (Managing Director of Empire Chemicals); Jim Goldfarb; Mr Haynes; Mark Hazard (many different versions); John Hunter; Brother James; Mr James; Sergeant James; Mr Jones; James Macbeth (ex-Marine, SAS and mercenary); Charles Morton (a manufacturer's representative from Leeds); Seamus O'Seven; Professor Joseph Penbrunner; Derek Pentecost

(an expert in genetics); David Somerset; Robert Sterling
(a marine biologist); James St John Smythe; James
Stock (of the London *Financial Times*); Taro Todoroki
(a Japanese fisherman); Mr Van Warren; Frank
Westmacott; Pieter Zwart.

Bond has also had cause to pretend to be real people –
either with or without their knowledge. This is a more or less
complete list:

Peter Argentbright (an agent of the Chinese); Sir Hilary
Bray (a reclusive baronet); Mike Channing (another
agent); Mike Farrar (a Canadian test pilot); Peter Franks
(a diamond smuggler); Guy (a video cameraman); Klaus
Hergersheimer (a radiation safety technician); James
Pickard (a London solicitor); Francisco Scaramanga (an
assassin); Colonel Luis Toro (a Cuban military officer).

And, for the sake of completeness, here are the various code
names used by Bond through the years, either relating to a
particular mission or as general designators used to refer to
him:

Peter Abelard (a code name for Peter Argentbright,
whom he is impersonating); Block; Custodian;
Gamesman; Grapefruit (no, really); Grey Fox; Harvester
One; Jacko B (for use only in Ireland); Peter Piper
(another code name for Peter Argentbright); Predator
(his standard designator); Seahawk; Vanya (someone
else's code name he adopts); White Knight.

File 009:
Bibliography

[CD ROM]	*The Ultimate Dossier: James Bond 007*	Eidos, 1997
[LASERDISK]	*Goldfinger* [supplementary material]	MGM/UA Home Video, 1997
	Thunderball [supplementary material]	MGM/UA Home Video, 1997
	GoldenEye [supplementary material]	MGM/UA Home Video, 1997
[TELEVISION]	*Whicker's World*	BBC 1, 25 Mar. 1967
	Breakfast Time – Louis Jordan interview	BBC 1, 1 Jun. 1983
	Wogan – Mark Greenstreet interview	BBC 1, 2 Jul. 1986
	Film '87 – Timothy Dalton interview	BBC 1, 2 Jun. 1987
	Hollywood UK – Johanna Harwood interview	BBC 1, 3 Oct. 1993
	– Wolf Mankiewicz interview	
	– Ken Hughes interview	
	Pebble Mill at One – Lois Maxwell interview	BBC 1, 13 Dec. 1994
[RADIO]	*Desert Island Discs* – Ian Fleming interview	BBC Radio 4, Jun. 1963

[BOOKS & MAGAZINES]

[Various]	[Various]	*007 Magazine* numbers 15, 17, 27, 28
[Uncredited]	*Playboy* interview: Sean Connery	*Playboy*, Nov. 1965
[Uncredited]	Irvin Kershner interview	*Starburst*, Feb. 1984
[Uncredited]	Interview with Michael G. Wilson	*Starburst*, Apr. 1988
Amis, Kingsley	*The James Bond Dossier*	Jonathan Cape, 1965
Andrew, Christopher	*Secret Service*	William Heinemann, 1985
Andrew, Christopher & Gordievsky, Oleg	*KGB: The Inside Story*	Hodder & Stoughton, 1990
Archer, Simon & Nicholls, Stan	*Gerry Anderson the Authorised Biography*	Legend, 1996
Barnes, Alan & Hearn, Marcus	*Kiss Kiss Bang Bang!*	Batsford, 1997
Bennett, John & Woollacott, Janet	*Bond and Beyond*	Macmillan, 1987

BIBLIOGRAPHY

Numerous books have been written about James Bond over the years, and it's tempting to just rely on their research. Tempting, and misleading.

To avoid mistakes, we have attempted, wherever possible, to go back to the original sources for the facts listed in this book — the various novels, films, scripts and comics which have their own individual entries in the text. Where that was not possible, we have attempted to cross-reference between the works listed below, and thus sort out the truth from the fiction.

Treglown, Jeremy (Ed.)   *Roald Dahl*   Faber & Faber, 1994

James Bond Will Return . . .